Media, Communication
and Development

Media, Communication and Development

THREE APPROACHES

Linje Manyozo

SAGE www.sagepublications.com
Los Angeles • London • New Delhi • Singapore • Washington DC

First published in 2012 by

 SAGE Publications India Pvt Ltd
B1/I-1 Mohan Cooperative Industrial Area
Mathura Road, New Delhi 110 044, India
www.sagepub.in

SAGE Publications Inc
2455 Teller Road
Thousand Oaks, California 91320, USA

SAGE Publications Ltd
1 Oliver's Yard, 55 City Road
London EC1Y 1SP, United Kingdom

SAGE Publications Asia-Pacific Pte Ltd
33 Pekin Street
#02-01 Far East Square
Singapore 048763

Published by Vivek Mehra for SAGE Publications India Pvt Ltd. Phototypeset in 10/12 Palatino Linotype by Diligent Typesetter, Delhi and printed at G.H. Prints Pvt Ltd, New Delhi.

Library of Congress Cataloging-in-Publication Data Available

ISBN: 978-81-321-0905-1 (PB)

The SAGE Team: Shambhu Sahu, Dhurjjati Sarma, Vijay Sah and Rajinder Kaur

To the many development communication practitioners,
students and scholars the world over:
We make the road we walk

Thank you for choosing a SAGE product! If you have any comment, observation or feedback, I would like to personally hear from you. Please write to me at contactceo@sagepub.in

—Vivek Mehra, Managing Director and CEO,
SAGE Publications India Pvt Ltd, New Delhi

Bulk Sales

SAGE India offers special discounts for purchase of books in bulk. We also make available special imprints and excerpts from our books on demand.

For orders and enquiries, write to us at

Marketing Department
SAGE Publications India Pvt Ltd
B1/I-1, Mohan Cooperative Industrial Area
Mathura Road, Post Bag 7
New Delhi 110044, India
E-mail us at marketing@sagepub.in

Get to know more about SAGE, be invited to SAGE events, get on our mailing list. Write today to marketing@sagepub.in

This book is also available as an e-book.

Contents

List of Illustrations

TABLES

FIGURES

BOX

List of Abbreviations

ACPO	Acción Cultural Popular
ADCs	Area Development Committees
AIDS	Acquired Immune Deficiency Syndrome
AIR	All India Radio
AMARC	World Association of Community Radio Broadcasters
AMB	African Media Barometer
AMREF	Africa Medical and Research Foundation
APRI	Amazonian Peoples' Resources Initiative
ATI	Access to Information
BBC	British Broadcasting Corporation
BBPs	Best Bet Practices
BDLS	Broadcast-based Distance Learning System
BN	Basic Needs (approach)
BSDC	Bachelor of Science in Development Communication
CAF Latin America	Corporación Andina de Fomento (Latin America)
CARIMAC	Caribbean Institute of Media and Communication
CDC	College of Development Communication
CELAM	Latin American Episcopal Council
CFD&SC School	Communication for Development and Social Change School
CFSC	Communication for Social Change
CGHR	Centre of Governance and Human Rights
CGIAR	Consultative Group on International Agricultural Research

CIAT	International Centre for Tropical Agriculture
CIDA	Canadian International Development Agency
CIFOR	Center for International Forestry Research
CILA	Communication Initiative Latin America
CIH	Community Involvement in Health
CJFE	Canadian Journalists for Free Expression
CTA	Technical Centre for Agricultural and Rural Cooperation
DECs	District Executive Committees
DevCom	Development Communication
DFID	Department for International Development
DRC	Democratic Republic of Congo
DSC	Development Support Communication
DTR	Development through Radio
ECA	Economic Commission for Africa
ECLA	Economic Commission for Latin America
ERI	Enabling Rural Innovation
EU	European Union
FAO	Food and Agriculture Organisation
FRIM	Forestry Research Institute of Malawi
GFMD	Global Forum for Media Development
GIIs	Global Information Infrastructures
GIS	Geographic Information Systems
HCP	Health Communication Partnership
HIV	Human Immunodeficiency Virus
IBRD	International Bank for Reconstruction and Development
ICARDA	International Centre for Agricultural Research in the Dry Areas
ICIT	Information Centre on Instructional Technology
ICSCP	International Commission for the Study of Communication Problems
ICT	Information and Communication Technology
IDRC	International Development Research Centre
IFEX	International Freedom of Expression Exchange
IKCS	Indigenous Knowledge Communication Systems
ILET	Latin American Institute for Transnational Studies
IMF	International Monetary Fund
IPDC	International Programme for the Development of Communication

IPGs	International Public Goods
JHU-CCP	Johns Hopkins University-Centre for Communication Programs
KCP Project	Katine Community Partnerships Project
KDP	Kecamatan Community Development
KMD	Knowledge Management and Dissemination
LSE	London School of Economics and Political Science
MCD	Media, Communication and Development
MCP	Malawi Congress Party
MCRPV	Makhanlal Chaturvedi Rashtriya Patrakarita Vishwavidyalaya
MDDA	Media Development and Diversity Agency
MDGs	Millennium Development Goals
MISA	Media Institute of Southern Africa
MNICC	Mindanao News and Information Cooperative Center
MPS	Master of Professional Studies
MRGC Project	Malawi Rural Growth Centre Project
MS	Master of Science
MSC	Most Significant Change
NCD Policy	National Communication for Development Policy
NGO	Non-governmental Organisation
NHS-NICE	National Health Services-National Institute for Health and Clinical Excellence
NRCP	National Rural Centre Programme
NWICO	New World Information and Communication Order
OSCE	Organisation for Security and Co-operation in Europe
PAR	Participatory Action Research
PCI	Population Communication International
PCT	Primary Care Trust
PDC	Participatory Development Communication
PFA	Press Foundation for Asia
PHC	Primary Health Care
PhD	Doctor of Philosophy
PRCA	Participatory Rural Communication Appraisal
PRSP	Poverty Reduction Strategy Paper
RTD	Radio Tanzania Dar es Salaam

SADC-CCD	Southern Africa Development Community-Centre of Communication for Development
SAHRC	South African Human Rights Commission
SIDA	Swedish International Development Cooperation Agency
SITE	Satellite Instructional Television Experiment
STIs	Sexually Transmitted Infections
TCAT	Tara Community Action Team
TFD	Theatre for Development
TIPOs	Technological, Institutional and Policy Options
TISS	Tata Institute of Social Sciences
UNAIDS	Joint United Nations Programme on HIV/AIDS
UNCSTD	United Nations Commission on Science and Technology for Development
UNDP	United Nations Development Programme
UNDEF	United Nations Democracy Fund
UNESCO	United Nations Educational, Scientific and Cultural Organisation
UNFPA	United Nations Population Fund
UNICEF	United Nations Children's Fund
UNIFEM	United Nations Development Fund for Women
UPLB	University of Philippines at Los Baños
USAID	United States Agency for International Development
VAPs	Village Action Plans
VDCs	Village Development Committees
WHO	World Health Organisation
WST	World Service Trust

Foreword

Some readers may disagree with the premises and conclusions leading to the development communication approaches that the book expounds, but no one can deny the scholarship that went into its writing. The author traverses more than half a century of thought on the subject and then offers his own interpretation of the variegated, often disjointed, discussion of it around the globe.

Linje Manyozo begins by naming and describing six schools that have grown around the worldwide effort to better the lives in what used to be called the Third World and is now euphemistically labelled the developing world. These he calls the Bretton Woods school, the Latin American school, the Indian school, the African school, the Los Baños school and the communication for development and social change school. He then reclassifies them into three approaches that he deems more appropriate for the still nascent field: the media for development approach, the media development approach and the participatory or community engagement approach. In all three, the means of interaction between and among the players is central. While the first two approaches are more media-oriented, the third relies more on interpersonal communication.

The author dwells at length on the nature of each approach, citing examples in the global south and the global north while acknowledging and describing the interfaces between them as well. He does not think the division into north and south is entirely geographic, however, since some economies in the north now show retrogressive traits associated with the south. He highlights initiatives that have evolved outside Western development theories in Africa, Asia and Latin America during the postcolonial struggle of these regions with poverty, inequality and marginalisation. He concludes that no one theory or model can explain the entire field since the approaches grew out of differing social, economic and political circumstances.

In the final chapter, Manyozo reconfigures his approaches in terms of Robin Mansell's typology of participation, power and policy. Meant to engage policymakers, practitioners, and academics, the three Ps refer to the continuing negotiation for the transfer to communities of the power to make the decisions on their own development and the institutionalisation of that process in practice and in theory. The author contends that unless the political economy of a society has been so transformed, then no real development has taken place.

This book is meant to bring order into what the author sees as a largely unorganised field of study and practice. He does this through his alternate typologies and also by bringing forward the experience and contributions of the global south which he says are nearly absent in the literature. He maintains that the theory and practice focusing on media, communication and development are just as much a product of the global south as they are of the global north in spite of what existing literature suggests. In fact Manyozo sees the southern story as more valid because it comes from those who have lived it. The journey towards development is best recounted by citizens of the global south who have personally gone on the trek. In the postscript he repeats his main thesis: the real experts are the internal experts, not those who come from outside.

The book is not one's idea of a light read, being dense with concepts and packed with examples from the developed and developing worlds. Staying with it is well worth the effort, however, since it probably is the first of its kind in the novel slant and treatment given to the subject matter. It certainly is must reading for all of us students interested in the how's and the why's of the relationship between communication as process and medium and the intricacies of human development.

Nora C. Quebral
Professor Emeritus,
College of Development Communication
University of the Philippines, Los Baños

Preface

I have written this book primarily for everyone interested in development communication. To the students, teachers, policymakers and practitioners the world over, this book has been written for two reasons: First, it is a continuation of a conversation with the pioneer of the field, Nora Quebral, whose seminal book, *Development Communication* (1988) still remains a Magna Carta on the topic. The book has been written to revisit Quebral's perspectives on this field, as she remains one of the few people who have used their teaching experience to write on this topic. Second, the book is an attempt to answer the questions from students whom I have taught development communication over the years. When faced with questions such as, 'what is the difference between development communication and media development' or what is the distinction between media for development and participatory communication' —I could not find single texts that put everything into a coherent perspective. Book after book, article after article, I found that scholarship on the topic of development communication (or communication for development, or communication for social change, or as we describe it here at the London School of Economics, Media, Communication and Development) was full of complex theoretical trajectories that could not speak to each other. What made it difficult still was the fact that much of the well-known published and widely available scholarship and research emerges from the West, yet a rich body of development communication tradition and practice emerged and took root in the global south.

For the first time since the field emerged, a book discusses the multiple stories and experiences that formulated the various schools of thought within which development communication emerged. It is out of the interrogation of these schools that this study develops the three approaches, which are theoretical trajectories in themselves—helping many a student, a teacher and a practitioner to understand this heterogeneous field of study. This text is therefore, an attempt, not to tell a single story, but multiple narratives of the field—an attempt to reconnect the field with scholars, scholarship and experiences from the global south. It is disappointing to note that even when it is well established that Nora Quebral and the goblet of scholars at the then College of Agriculture pioneered this field in the 1960s, their work is almost absent if not deliberately overlooked in most Western training programmes. I therefore make no apologies for the dominant Western authors who I have not included here.

As such, the book is written for everybody with an interest in the field—to help them understand where the field is coming from, the conundrums it faces and the opportunities that await it. The chapters and sections of it come from lectures and seminars I have organised (or been invited to deliver and facilitate) in Malawi, South Africa, Uganda, England, Sweden and Denmark. Some of you will recognise the conversations we had, or the questions you raised. Do enjoy reading it, much as I enjoyed writing it. I am sure you will continue writing this book as you learn, teach and do development communication through interrogating the ideas presented here. Writing, as the art of the soul, does not stop even after a book is published—it continues in the conversations and discussions such writing elicits. I am very much hopeful this will be the case with this work.

Linje Manyozo
Department of Media and Communications
London School of Economics and Political Science
April 2012

Acknowledgements

This book is an endeavour comprising a series of encounters and experiences. The tea plantations that surrounded our village when I was growing up made me wonder how the people that worked them were so poor and year after year the companies increased their profits. The theatre for development classes at the University of Malawi introduced me to the world of development communication. I am heavily indebted to Chris Kamlongera for this experience, and for expanding my understanding for indigenous knowledge communication, and years later, participatory rural communication appraisal. The radio for development experiences at The Story Workshop made me rethink notions of community consultation. My work at the Centre for Culture and Media Studies under Keyan Tomaselli exposed me to both cultural critiques and postcolonial theory especially in relation to indigenous notions of development.

Even though I managed to introduce an undergraduate degree in development communication at the University of Malawi, it is the London School of Economics and Political Science that has provided me with the social laboratory to test my ideas and experiences in the field. I am grateful to the most wonderful colleagues and leadership who have entrusted me with the Directorship of the MSc Programme in Media, Communication and Development. This book therefore is born out of the questions that students here at the LSE and wherever I teach in Africa and Europe continue to ask about development communication. I was frustrated, just like they have been, to notice that we could not find a single text that could answer even the simplest of questions, for example, what's the difference between media for development and media development?

This book is not an end to all books in development communication. It is a continuation of conversations with the pioneers and current explorers of the field such as Nora Quebral, Felix Librero, Goran Hedebro, Louis Ramiro Beltran, Everett Rogers, Jan Servaes or Thomas Thufte. This book is just but a small nut in a complex network of theories and concepts. The language has been simplified while remaining theoretically critical, to enable the book to speak alongside those outside the academy. It is obvious that individuals, just like their creative works, are products of a gamut of collective experiences. This book was born on the peasant farms in Malawi and has travelled around Africa and has been nurtured in the social exclusion of South East London.

I am greatly indebted to my son, Biny'amin Manyozo, who despite having a dad who 'is always reading all these big books' brings us the best in me, and teaches me again and again, that in relating to other people, we should always remember to respect their dignity and humanity.

1

Media, Communication and Development
Schools of Thought and Approaches

THE PROBLEM

The book and this chapter in particular introduce and explain the three dominant approaches that inform the theory and practice of development communication or communication for development or, as defined in this book, *media, communication and development*. Building on political economy frameworks, the book rejects the homogeneity that characterises the debates on and about the field; instead, the discussion emphasises the difference between structure and process, and proposes that the three approaches be: *media for development, media development* and *participatory/community communication*. These three approaches have emerged separately from each other, and despite the often-tenuous relationship among them, they continue to coexist, especially in projects and initiatives designed and implemented by governments and development organisations. The chapter is also a critique against the dominant binary thinking in the field, which positions diffusionist and participatory approaches as being antagonistic towards each other. The discussion itself suggests the importance of moving away from such binary thinking and instead focuses on establishing how the three proposed approaches are connected by participation, policy and power. The chapter thus aims at demonstrating that the three approaches should not be seen as entirely independent of each other.

Specifically, this chapter seeks to go beyond the usual scholarly rhetoric of tracing the origins and growth of the field of media, communication and development (MCD) to the dominant (oftentimes Western) development theories. The discussions and the perspectives in this book attempt to rescue the experiences of frontline development officers, development journalists, agriculture extensionists, theatre for development troupe members and educational broadcasters from Colombia, Philippines, India, Ghana, Malawi and other places in the global south, who, in their efforts to establish creative and educational ways of communicating development content to their immediate communities and societies, ended up contributing to the emergence of the field we now call MCD. As such, the book and this chapter in particular trace the roots of development communication, not just to the Philippines (where Nora Quebral invented the term development communication and also pioneered the world's first ever development communication degree programme) but also to other parts of the global south, where social communicators were responding to the growing poverty and inequality, and were asking themselves whether media and communication had any role to play in eradicating poverty, marginalisation and improving livelihoods.

This chapter, therefore, brings up two fresh perspectives as an attempt to rescue the discourse in the field from being drowned in what Mansell (1982) terms as 'superficial revisionism'. First, the discussion argues that Western development theory is not wholly responsible for the origins of the field but that different schools of thought shaped its emergence and growth. Second, the chapter re-inserts postcolonial theory within the discourse, considering that in its different geographical origins, the field itself emerged as a postcolonial response that examined the need for 'another' kind of communication that was needed to meet challenges of rural poverty, underdevelopment, inequality and global imperialism. In their various attempts the world over, the different pioneers of the field sought to place media and communication at the centre of authentic efforts to create a much more equal and open society, to borrow Freire's (1996) words.

DEFINING MEDIA, COMMUNICATION AND DEVELOPMENT: PROBLEMS AND APPROACHES

Concurring with Quebral (1988), who contends that in discussing development communication, we are dealing with a relationship of concepts in which development is a stronger notion, this book argues that to think and rethink the field, development must be defined. Which development are we going to communicate about or communicate for? Is it the development that is imagined, conceived, dreamed and fantasised in the boardrooms of capital cities, expensive hotels, fancy workshops, seminars or conferences? Or the development that most subalterns want to eat, touch and feel in their hearts? For this book, therefore, development is not being conceptualised as described in literature or theories propagated by 'development' experts, nor is it the development that is expressed in tales and narratives. Development is a conflict or a site of it. It is a conflict over resources and of course, over power. From a Marxist perspective, development is a class conflict: it is about the flow and contestation of power between antagonistic classes. It is thus a site of conflict over resources and power between classes that drink tea and those who grow that tea. But importantly, for Marx (1852/1937) and Escobar (1995), development is a conflict over representation and even over the instruments and discourses of that representation. To define development policy, a discourse must be thought of and constructed (Escobar, 1995). For Marx, the classes that grow tea do not have sufficient 'mutual intercourse', reliable communication networks, 'social relationships' nor 'intercourse with society'. Failing to do so prohibits them from "entering into manifold relations with each other", and this disempowers them from "representing themselves" and must, therefore, "be represented" by the "executive power which subordinates society" (Marx, 1852/1937). In the end, it is this class that drinks tea or what Marx (1852/1937) describes as the subordinating power that constructs the discourse of representation on behalf of the subordinate classes. The whole history of development in general is littered with this unequal relationship and has often ended up with 'bullshit' approaches to development.

Propounded by the American philosopher, Frankfurt (1988), the theory of 'bullshit' provides a scientific methodology for understanding deceptive misrepresentation that is 'short of lying', is very 'pretentious', deliberately misrepresents one's own thoughts and feelings and is also false. In this case, the classes that drink tea (perhaps in collaboration with certain power elites from those who grow tea) engage in the production, representation, circulation and implementation of development 'bullshit' that is framed within realities that they are often ignorant about (Frankfurt, 1988). When the new government took power in 2004 in Malawi, the international development imperialists 'advised' the African government against providing subsidised fertiliser as part of poverty reduction growth strategies pursued by these international institutions. Against that advice, the Malawi government provided cheap fertiliser to subsistence farmers and this resulted to increased maize production, the ending of perennial food shortages and the increased opportunities for exporting the yields to other countries. Thus, the Malawi government acted against the 'development bullshit' perpetuated and propagated by the World Bank and International Monetary Fund (IMF) — development strategies that were based on the realities on the ground (Malawians cannot afford unsubsidised fertiliser, increasing pressure on diminishing land resources and obscene perennial food insecurity) rather than the development policies fantasised off-site. This book, therefore, argues that development is not a known fact, it is not given, nor it is common sense. Rather, development is a problem that must be investigated using the social resources of both reason and experience. As such, understanding and articulating development is a collaborative effort that involves what Kant, in the *Critique of Pure Reason*, describes as a transcendental enquiry — in this case, transcendental is that "realm through which experience becomes possible although it does not itself arise from experience" (Adorno, 1959/2001: 21).

So the question of communication for development (or as we tend to define it here at the London School of Economics and Political Science) is not as straightforward as it is imagined in a great deal of definitions and scholarship. It is not just about the communication of development, but also about the contestation of this very notion of development. How does media and communication figure in this contestation of development? Communication for development should, therefore, not ideally perpetuate the 'bullshit' development paradigms and policies that promote inequality and thus advance poverty and underdevelopment. As such, communication for development is basically about three strategies: from the perspective of Marxist historians such as Edward Thompson (1963), communication for development is, first and foremost, a struggle to rescue the development discourse from the perspective of the underclasses by building their consciousness and knowledge of development. Second, from a postcolonial theoretical perspective, communication for development engages in a Gramscian war of position against the orientalist, technologically deterministic, fatalistic and modernist discourses of development that are authored off-site. Third, from Marxist perspectives, communication for development is in itself an exercise in advocacy that works towards the transformation of the political economy of development itself in order to allow a greater number of people achieve what Quebral (2002) describes as greater socio-economic equality and individual potential. So, where does the term *media, communication and development* feature in this discourse?

The term *media, communication and development* has evolved from the concepts of development communication or communication for development (also known by various other concepts such as development support communication or, more recently, communication for development and social change). The concepts and definitions have varied with time and place since Quebral coined and defined the term development communication in the late 1960s. Kumar (1994: 77) observes the confusion and "lack of agreement on the concept" whilst Colle (2003: 1) laments the "different perceptions of defining characteristics" that characterise the field. Likewise, Librero (in Manyozo, 2012) points out the "different concepts that are just flying around". Such confusion exists largely because scholars attempt to fix and locate development communication definitions within prevailing dominant development and mass communication theories and practices. It could be the fact that instead of contribution towards theory building in the field, scholars and practitioners alike have tended to focus on developing prescriptive and descriptive methodologies and strategies.

The first definition of development communication was offered in the late 1960s/early 1970s by Quebral (1975, 1988, 2002, 2011), who defined the term/concept as the "art and science of human communication applied to speedy transformation of a country and a mass of its people from poverty to a dynamic state of economic growth" so as to achieve greater social equality. Quebral's emphasis on 'art' was because of the need for creative and interpretive approaches required to create interesting, informative and educational content on development within the non-formal education framework; whilst the science aspect referred to the theory-informed foundations of the field. What Quebral was proposing, therefore, even in these early days, was a theoretical framework for explaining the new field of study. Unfortunately for the field, and partially due to the failure of Western media and development departments to expand development communication degree training and research programmes, a network of development organisations and institutions have 'taken' over the training and research agenda. The consequence is that theory building has suffered. As a result, even the few scholars and academic programmes that attempt to rescue the scientific engagement in the field (such as Cadiz, 1991, 1994; Hemer and Tufte, 2005; Librero, 2004; Mansell and Wehn, 1998; Melkote and Steeves, 2001; McPhail, 2009; Quebral, 1988, 2002; Rogers, 1993; Servaes, 2008) have found it challenging as the subject is always footnoted in national and international media/communication research conversations.

Many years later, Wilkins and Mody (2001) would define development communication as a process of strategic intervention towards social change, initiated by institutions and communities. Likewise, the Rockefeller Foundation introduces and discusses an integrated model of communication for social change as "an interactive process where community dialogue and collective action work together to produce social change in a community" so as to improve the health and welfare of communities (Figueroa et al., 2005: 5). Whereas the trend has been to trace the emergence and growth of the field within American development theory, Huesca (2003) traces it within the Latin American challenge of the modernisation theory and the region's insistence on a dialogic praxis of communication, the empowerment of individuals and ownership of communication processes. Similarly, Colle (2003) traces the origins of development communication through seven 'threads and patterns'. These are: United Nations Development Programme (UNDP) and Erskine Childers, extension, community participation, population and health communication, social marketing, institutional building and the Information and Communication Technology (ICT) threads (Childers and Vajrathon, 1975). The term 'thread' itself is probably borrowed from Erskine Childers who, in writing to the Information Centre on Instructional Technology (ICIT) Report of October 1976, was arguing for development support communication (DSC) as a "discipline in development planning and implementation, in which more adequate account is taken of human behavioural factors in the design of development projects and their objectives". Colle then locates the UNDP's DSC service, co-founded by Childers himself, as the 'earliest' pioneer in development communication (Childers, 1976; Childers and Vajrathon, 1975).

Since the 1990s, organisations, practitioners and scholars have attempted to harmonise the various concepts of development communication by laying emphasis on coining a term that reflects its importance in both developing and developed societies. The term 'development' is seen as reducing issues of empowerment to livelihoods only and also restricted to programmes in the global south, thus ignoring social change issues such as human rights and similar other issues in the global north. Numerous international conferences and congresses have, as a result, preferred the term 'communication for social change', since it is seen to embrace issues of empowerment, active citizenship and social change (Figueroa et al., 2005).[1]

The Rockefeller Foundation, for instance, argues that its communication for social change model is built on the 'broad literature on development communication'; yet it is largely Western or drawn from North and Latin American researchers such as Freire, Beltrán,

---

[1]Notable among the international conferences organised to clarify the relationship between communication and development have been: the Rockefeller Foundation–funded Communication and Social Change Conferences, held in Bellagio, Italy, in 1997 and 2002; the Entertainment Education Conferences for Social Change organised by the Johns Hopkins University Centre for Communication Programs and hosted by different Universities and organisations since 2000; the 2003 Communication for social change conferences organised by the Universidad de Norte, Communication Initiative in Latin America, South Asian Partnership Canada and Canadian International Development Agency; the July 2006 Communication, Globalisation and Cultural Identities Conference at Brisbane, Australia; the World Congress on Communication for Development held in Italy in 2006, which demonstrated that communication is an essential instrument and process for achieving sustainable development (Communication Initiative, FAO and World Bank, 2007).

Díaz Bordenave, Calvelo, Shirley White, Prieto Castillo, Everett Rogers, Mata, Simpson, Servaes, Portales and Kincaid (Figueroa et al., 2005). No reference is made to African or South East Asian scholars and practitioners, not even to Quebral who has been acknowledged by the Clearing House on Development Communication as the originator of the term development communication (Bessette and Rajasunderam, 1996; Librero, 2004, 2009; Manyozo, 2006, 2012). Surprisingly, after his death, an American communication scholar Rogers (1962, 1993) was anointed as the 'father of development communication' and 'pioneer in the field of communication for development' (Adhikarya, 2004; Manyozo, 2012).

The marginalisation of contributions of developing world scholars to the development communication debate has been due to lack of accessible publishing opportunities for developing world scholars (with the exception of Southbound and SAGE India of course). It has also been due to the inability of Western publishers and scholars to value non-Western and non-English research. One consequence is that it "always appears that everything originated from the United States" (Librero, 2005, 2009; Ramiro Beltrán, 2004; Gumucio, 2004). It is not surprising, therefore, that though the University of Philippines at Los Baños (UPLB) introduced the world's first ever development communication degree-level training by 1974, when writing for the October 1976 ICIT Report, Childers (1976: 5) observed that "as far as I know, there is no academic or technical training institution that fully provides all the essentials (of development communication training) in an integrated program". It was ironic, however, that Childers' colleague, John Woods, the then Director of the UNDP/United Nations Children's Education Fund (UNICEF) Development Support Communication Service in Bangkok, had already officially acknowledged to Quebral in a letter on 4 February 1975 that UPLB's development communication offerings were the first of their kind in any university in the world (Manyozo, 2012; Quebral, 1988).

Acknowledging the many changes her own concept has undergone during the "years of jostling with reality", Quebral (2002: 16) redefines development communication as "the art and science of human communication linked to a society's planned transformation, from a state of poverty to one of dynamic socio-economic growth, that makes for greater equity and the larger unfolding of individual potential". There are three crucial aspects of Quebral's revised concept of communication for development that have become widely accepted in theory and practice. The first is that communication for development focuses on human beings and that media technologies are just instruments for advancing this communication agenda (Quebral, 1988, 2002; Lennie and Tacchi, 2011). Second is that participation is a fundamental component of both development and communication for development, which allows for the articulation and incorporation of multiple voices and interests in the design, implementation and evaluation of development policy (Quebral, 1988, 2002; Lennie and Tacchi, 2011; Servaes, 2008). Last, communication for development strategies should be driven by coherent theory and clear methods in order to strengthen the external validity.[2]

The major change in Quebral's definition is planned change and of course, a recognition that such change cannot be speeded up, as it depends on other social–economic and political factors. In line with Freire's critical pedagogy, Quebral's insights and the Rockefeller Foundation's communication for social change perspective, I have attempted to define development communication as a group of method-driven and theory-based employment of media and communication to influence and transform the political economy of development in ways that allow individuals, communities and societies to determine the direction and benefit of development interventions (Manyozo, 2012). The emphasis on political economy here is crucial. No matter how participatory or

---

[2] Writing to me in a 2008 email to provide feedback to a draft of a proposal for the establishment of a communication for development of honours and master's degrees programmes at the University of Fort Hare (where I was teaching), Quebral observed:

> I myself use the non-formal education framework which, strictly speaking, agricultural extension is also. Devcom, to me, is systematic education with objectives, methodologies and outcomes but which happens outside the formal school system. It does not promote only one course of action for everyone but instead offers an array of choices from which the users of communication select what is right for them, given their needs and circumstances. Devcom must help equip the users, however, with the capability to choose and the information and knowledge base from which to choose. This is the approach that integrated pest management (IPM) now uses and that other sectors are adopting. For people to dialogue, they must have both a knowledge base and the capability to choose. That is why our undergraduate curriculum has a technical course component which introduces students to the discipline of learning subject matter that they can communicate.

bottom-up development communication approaches can be, as long as the dominant political economy framework of development (that promotes inequality and underdevelopment) remains in place, there will be no sustainable positive change in society. Quebral's pioneering thoughts on development communication seem to suggest that the discourse was not just about informing or educating people to adopt new attitudes, knowledge, practices or technologies. It implied the unpacking and uprooting of the root causes of structural inequality, marginalisation, disempowerment that prevent individuals and societies from making radical changes to improve lives and welfare.

The argument is that even the notion and model of development itself has to be contested. The role of media and communication, in this case, is to offer a platform where people can contest both political and economic power to enable them to transform specific development systems to their benefit. As discussed in the 'Postscript' to this book, the central idea in development communication, therefore, is to contest the external and imperial development theories, as to whether they are relevant in much of the global south. The notion of the global south needs qualification here. It no longer refers to a geographical category of countries sharing similar socio-economic attributes. The global south is no longer out there, but here, that is, even within the north. Rising unemployment, immigration or the banking crises are producing a large underclass of the 'global south' in the Western world.[3]

Even some development scholars are already questioning the Western development epistemologies that do not take into consideration the local socio-economic institutions and realities. Yunus (2007) proposes the decentralisation of economic power through the establishment of self-managed enterprises, which should be owned and managed by the people. Similarly, Yunus (2007) believes that the free enterprise model has increased poverty, disease, pollution and inequality. Without rejecting capitalism, Yunus (2007), through the microcredit banking model, makes

---

[3]Writing in another email, Quebral observed back in 2008: "As for the charge that devcom is relevant only to developing societies because it mainly addresses poverty, it might be pointed out that developed countries have their ghettoes and backwoods as well where the principles and methodologies of devcom would be relevant."

a case for a humanitarian model of development known as social business. Despite the controversy surrounding his ousting from the Grameen Bank (that he founded), Yunus has been largely concerned with developing a humanitarian form of capitalism that produces profit for local people. Instead of enriching individuals, Yunus' capitalism invests the profits back into community ventures. Likewise, Sen (1999) introduces the notion of development as freedom, in which he proposes development models that meet non-economic goals such as happiness, satisfaction, well-being and spirituality.

Within development communication, therefore, the concept of development is not self-evident. It is not just about communicating or mediating the very concepts and models of development that, as Yunus (2007) and Sen (1999) have observed, increase poverty, inequality and underdevelopment. The ownership, management and social benefits of the development models are a huge concern, hence the need to bring in political economy perspectives. Development, therefore, is a *contested space*. Sachs (1992) and Escobar (1995) have traced how the neo-imperialist discourses of and within development emerged within American domestic and foreign policies. Sachs (1992) specifically argues that the discourse of development constructed the global south as homogenous, linked together through their underdevelopment and backwardness, which could only be eradicated by projecting a model of Anglo-American society. In fact, for Lerner (1958: 38), "what the West is, in this sense, the Middle East seeks to become". In this case, development was not the end itself but rather a means for achieving Western modernity.

Such inevitability of the Western model of development (and modernity) was already under serious question when, in the 1960s, development communication emerged as a postcolonial discourse and practice that aimed to rescue non-Western epistemologies and theories in global development discourses. Even today, development communication is characterised by diverse methodological and theoretical trajectories, but is primarily about recovering development discourse from neo-imperialist assumptions that the rest of the world seeks to become like the West, as Lerner (1958) alleged. The aim is to empower people to achieve ownership and management of development models and interventions that strengthen their communities and societies, improve livelihoods, create jobs, as well as increase social justice and equality (Freire, 1972, 1996; Melkote and Steeves, 2001; Quebral, 2002; Servaes, 2008).

APPROACHES TO MEDIA, COMMUNICATION AND DEVELOPMENT

This book argues that a critical reading of Lerner (1958), Rogers (1962), United Nations Educational, Scientific and Cultural Organisation (UNESCO) (1980) and, more importantly, Quebral (1988) shows that the pioneering scholarship in the field did not refer to the homogeneity of development communication as we understand it today. Such literature referred to one or two components of the approaches that are being proposed in this book. It was Quebral (1975, 2011) who would attempt to define the field for the first time. Yet when she produced what many in the field consider to be a Magna Carta (*Development Communication*, 1988), Quebral clearly made distinctions between the different elements that I have identified as approaches. While Lerner (1958), Rogers (1962), UNESCO (1980) and Quebral (1988) might not have named them as approaches, they did provide the structural and functional characteristics upon which the proposed approaches in this book have been built. Since the 1980s, field practice has demonstrated the clear distinctions between and among these approaches. From the analysis of these different field practices, it has become clear that different theoretical and methodological approaches emerged within different social-economic and political contexts. It is because of these different approaches and the way they antagonistically interact with each other that this book prefers to use the term *media, communication and development* and not *development communication* (or *communication for development*). To come up with these approaches, the book developed a methodological matrix that comprises key concepts, history and origins, key theories and theorists, functional objectives, levels of participation and key policymakers.

I would then use this framework of analysis to re-read the past and current scholarship in the field, from which I would eventually propound the three main approaches that define and characterise the field of development communication today. It is this typology of the three approaches that demonstrates that the concepts of development communication, communication for development or communication for development and social change do not necessarily refer to a homogenous field of study. The debate is no longer about communication and development, but media, development and democracy as well. Consequently, the term *media, communication and development* is much more pertinent as it captures the different but interrelated dominant strands and approaches that characterise the field. These strands and approaches demonstrate that the field is not as homogenous as previously conceived but rather comprises elements that are loosely connected to each other, and these elements share certain similarities at certain points to the extent that it is difficult to distinguish them from each other. What distinguishes them, however, are the theoretical and conceptual categories employed to unpack them.

Increasing scholarship is beginning to reject the homogeneity of the field whilst acknowledging the existence of different approaches (FAO, 2005). The 9th United Nations Roundtable on Communication for Development spelt out 13 approaches. These approaches were: (*a*) extension/diffusion of innovations; (*b*) network development and documentation; (*c*) the ICTs for development; (*d*) social marketing; (*e*) edutainment; (*f*) health communication; (*g*) social mobilisation; (*h*) information, education and communication; (*i*) institution building; (*j*) knowledge, attitudes and practices; (*k*) development support communication; (*l*) Human Immunodeficiency Virus (HIV)/Acquired Immune Deficiency Syndrome (AIDS) community approach; and (*m*) community participation. Recent round-table meetings trimmed these approaches because of a number of factors: the explosion of ICTs, the widening gap between the rich and the poor, the increasing role of the private sector in development, globalisation and changing identities and notions of the nation state (FAO, 2005; Lennie and Tacchi, 2011).

Recently, however, the common approach to communication for development has settled on four main 'approaches, namely: (*a*) behaviour change communication; (*b*) communication for social change; (*c*) communication for advocacy; and (*d*) an enabling media and communication environment (Lennie and Tacchi, 2011). Important about this latest categorisation is that it is no longer communication-centric like the other approaches before it, but it recognises the question of media structures, institutions and policies as a separate communication for development agenda—something that Lerner (1958), Schramm (1964) and UNESCO (1980) raised hitherto. The first three approaches, however, are all about communication, whether using media or other interpersonal communication mechanisms. Such communication approaches are located within either the diffusionist or participatory communication strategies (Lennie and Tacchi, 2011; Servaes, 2008). This book, however, observes that discussions of approaches within the field must address the differences in the structural and institutional organisation, the methodological instruments employed in developing and implementing strategies—instead of focusing on the medium. In essence, to discuss the different approaches towards communication for development requires a careful understanding of the political economy driving such strategies.

From a political economy of communication perspective, it can be observed that the first acknowledgement of the different approaches towards doing development communication appears in the work of Lerner (1958), Rogers (1962) and Schramm (1964). Whereas Lerner and Schramm discuss the expansion of Western media technology in the global south, Rogers focuses on using such media to circulate content that will speed up the periods of adoption and diffusion of new knowledge and technology. Hence, while Lerner and Schramm think about the media structure and system, Rogers discusses communicating development content through media. The similarity for Lerner, Schramm and Rogers is that for them, development is a given and known phenomenon. As if building on Lerner's, Schramm's and Rogers's conceptualisations of communication for development, in the 1970s, the International Commission for the Study of Communication Problems (UNESCO, 1980) would similarly distinguish the 'building of media systems and structures' (development of community press in rural areas and small towns, strong national news agencies or comprehensive national radio networks) from the concept and practice of 'communication between men' as being crucial to bringing people in the development process. So among Lerner (1958), Schramm (1964), Rogers (1962) and UNESCO (1980) lie the foundations of the three major approaches that this book propounds.

The first approach emphasises the development and expansion of usually Western media systems and structures (Lerner, Schramm and UNESCO). The second approach revolves around the generation and circulation of development content from international public goods (IPG) institutes through media in order to increase the adoption of best-bet practices (Rogers). And the third approach emphasises the consolidation of 'communication between men' that enables the rescuing of subaltern voices in development policy formulation and implementation (UNESCO). Likewise, Quebral (1988) did manage to distinguish between what she termed 'human communication' and the development of mass media that are part of a distance learning system and that must not be used for propaganda. More recently, Arnold (2010) rejects the homogeneity of the field of development communication, by spelling out the difference between concepts of communication for development and media development, in relation to structure and process, arguing:

> Media development starts from the assumption that the media have an important role in the state as they hold those in power accountable and provide citizens with information that they need to actively participate in the political sphere. Only an independent and free media system can achieve this. Therefore, media development targets the capacity of journalists and other media actors to fulfil their democratic function, the sustainability of independent media, and the legal environment that guarantees media freedom and independence. So it's about capacity, sustainability, and legislation. Media development takes a systemic perspective, treating media as a sector. [On the other hand] Communication for development is about process. Many development projects in health and education use communication tools to get their messages across, hoping to raise awareness about issues and, eventually, to change norms and behaviours. [...] To do communication for development successfully, a deep understanding of opinion formation and behaviour change is necessary.

In the above quotation, Arnold clearly distinguishes between the 'structure' of the media and the 'process' of communication. The concepts of *media development* and *media for development* that she introduces were earlier introduced by Deane (2008), who distinguished them in relation to their functional objectives. Deane

(2008) defines media development as the establishment of a "media that serves the public good, which holds governments to account, which is plural and acts in the interest of all citizens". This is exactly what Arnold (2010) highlights when she describes media development in relation to the building and strengthening of institutional, financial and social capacity. On the other hand, Deane conceives media for development as the media that "serves a set of social objectives which development organizations share", thus, he is referring to a "media in the context of a certain kind of development outcome" (Deane, 2008).

Deane's conceptualisation and definition of media for development seem to be reflected in one part of Arnold's (2010) notion of *communication for development* as a process and strategy of developing informational and educational content on development issues. The aim is to "raise awareness about issues and, eventually, to change norms and behaviours" (Arnold, 2010). What is similar in the definitions by both Deane and Arnold is the fact that media and communication tools are deliberately used to communicate development issues: that media are employed to market and sell behaviours within corporational (and even capitalist), donor-driven contexts. What these scholars (Lerner, Rogers, Arnold and Deane) seem to agree upon, however, is that in these two approaches (media development and media for development), the media are at the centre of the initiatives. The corollary to their agreement is that they both footnote the question of communication as participation, especially without the implication of media. This is the strategic communication that does not rely on media instruments, is very participatory and oftentimes, designed and implemented at the community level, not to market and sell behaviours. This will be introduced as the third approach.

This book, therefore, draws on Lerner's and Schramm's concept of developing media systems, Rogers' notion of communicating development content, Arnold's and Deane's categorisations of media development and media for development as well as UNESCO's (1980) concept of 'communication between men' (with or without the media), in order to propose three approaches of *media for development, media development* and *participatory communication* (Manyozo, 2012). These three approaches have implications for the naming of the field, in that the first two approaches centre on media (technology and content) whilst the third one centres on participation and community. As such the field cannot just be termed communication for development nor development communication, but rather media, communication and development—in recognition of the differing roles of media and communication in these processes and structures.

The first approach, the *media for development* approach, encompasses centralised processes of reporting and communicating development, in which the mass media formulate the central strategy in public communication, campaigns and advocacy on and *about* development issues. The objective is, as Rogers (1962, 1993) contended, to communicate development in ways that educate audiences and influence positive behaviour changes. Media for development sees the media (print, electronic and new media) as the fundamental strategies that drive the process of communicating development, largely based on the thinking emerging from development journalism, social psychology or behavioural change communication. A very good example is the entertainment–education approach, in which music, drama and folk media are employed to educate communities and societies about social problems and motivate them to do something about them. The P-process, developed by the Health Communication Partnership (2003), is a model of strategic communication that has been employed in health and population communications as a framework for using media and communication to mobilise and educate mass publics on pertinent health challenges. A similar model of health communication has been developed by the Soul City, a Health and Development Communication Institute in South Africa, and combines multimedia communication strategies with other public engagement initiatives. From a political economy of communication perspective (Graham, 2005; Mansell, 2004), in the media for development approach, the media and communication experts are at the centre of the whole process, and together with subject matter specialists and funding agencies, they control the process of research, message development and production of development content that is scaled out and scaled up using relevant media.

The second approach, the *media development* approach, is not just restricted to developing world contexts, and involves supporting and building the capacity of media policies, structures and ownership as a way of strengthening good governance and fragile or transitional democracies. Media development programmes and projects are premised on the concept of 'free flow of information' (as enshrined in Article 19), which is informed by the thinking emerging from Continental European and North American political science (liberal democratic political theory), libertarian and utilitarian philosophy (John Stuart Mill), public sphere (Habermas), modernity (Weber) and modernisation (Rostow). The neoclassical assumption is that since free media have apparently contributed to stronger democratic societies in the West (have they really?), they will similarly strengthen transitional and nascent developing world democracies (Arnold, 2010; Deane, 2008; Lerner, 1958, 1971; Mansell, 1982; Schramm, 1964; UNESCO, 1980, 2008). As such, media development projects encompass the promotion of media independence and pluralism, the development of community media, radio and television organisations, the modernisation of national and regional news agencies and the training of media professionals (UNESCO, 1980, 2008).

The third approach, the *participatory and community communication* approach draws on UNESCO's (1980) notion of dialogical 'communication between men' to refer to community-based engagement approaches through which development stakeholders employ participatory communication in order to author development from below. The approach builds on participatory action research strategies from which community communication emerges to facilitate the implication of indigenous knowledge systems in deliberative development dialogue (Bessette, 2004; Tufte and Mefalopulos, 2009). The theoretical foundations for this approach come from rural sociology, community health development, rural development, agricultural extension and/or Participatory Action Research (PAR). The objective is to initiate a 'cyclical' approach of looking, thinking (reflecting) and acting in ways that engage development stakeholders in collective planning and decision-making in order to influence local development and social change (Bacon, Brown and Mendez, 2005; Tufte and Mefalopulos, 2009). In this approach, participatory dialogue and communication become the glue that mediates deliberative development by providing an avenue for consultative, collaborative and collegial decision-making (Bacon, Brown and Mendez, 2005; Bessette, 2004; Tufte and Mefalopulos, 2009). The approach is rooted in local social capital and networks (Putnam, 2000), social infrastructure (such as stories, proverbs, morality) with minimal or no mediation by the media in order to allow informed and participatory and inclusive decision-making in relation to the formulation of the development agenda (Kivikuru, 1994, 2005; Tufte and Mefalopulos, 2009). Table 1.1 presents the three approaches.

Table 1.1: A Typology of Three Methodological and Theoretical Approaches within Communication for Development

Attribute/ Principle	The Three Approaches		
	Media for Development	Media Development	Participatory and Community Communication
Key concepts	• Entertainment–education • Behavioural change Communication • Modelling • Para-social interaction	• Media and political pluralism • Media power • Freedom of speech • Media freedom • Censorship • Intellectual property rights • Media policy, law & regulation • Internet governance • Global information infrastructures • Community radio • Information societies • Rights and citizenship	• Agriculture extension • Rural communication • Community engagement • Community-based natural resource management • Participatory action research (PAR) • Indigenous knowledge
Origins/ History	• Modernisation theory • Economic development	• International Commission for the Study of Communication Problems (ICSCP)	• Indigenous knowledge systems • Agricultural Communication • Postcolonial theory
Major theories	• Social change • Social marketing • Health and population communication • Educommunication • Rural educational broadcasting • Farmcasting	• Liberal democratic political theory • Political economy • Democracy	• Participatory action learning • Collaborative decision-making • Community engagement • Participatory democracy and decentralisation • Community health development

(Table 1.1 Contd.)

(Table 1.1 Contd.)

Key theorists	• Daniel Lerner, • Wilbur Schramm • Everett Rogers • Nora Quebral • Felix Librero • Alexander Flor • Jan Servaes • Arvind Singhal • Wilbur Schramm • Louis Ramiro Beltran • Juan Diaz Bordenave	Among others: • Robin Mansell • Nora Quebral • James Deane • Monroe Price • Jan Servaes • Clemencia Rodriguez • Alfred Opobur • Karl Nordenstreng • Michael Meadows	Among others: • Nora Quebral, Paulo Freire, Jan Servaes, Ulamaija Kivikuru, Alfonso Gumucio, Clemencia Rodriguez, Keyan Tomaselli, Celeste Cadiz, Chris Kamlongera, Ricardo Ramirez, Silvia Balit, Guy Bessette, Bella Mody, Helen Hambly, Rico Lie, Alfonso Gumucio, Thomas Thufte, Teresa Stuart
Functional objectives	• Using media to promote and sell positive attitudes and behaviours	• Development of media [infra] structures, policies and capacities to promote good governance	• Engagement among development stakeholders within decentralised decision-making processes
Levels of participation	• Footnote participation (during pretesting of communication interventions)	• Externally driven processes (Co-optation and therapy)	• Citizen and delegated power
Key policymakers	• Johns Hopkins University Centre for Communication Programs • Health Communication Partnership Soul City, RSA • Farm Radio International • Frontline SMS	• Annenberg School for Communication • Lifeline Energy BBC World Service Trust • African Media Development Initiative • IPDC, UNESCO • Global Forum for Media Development (GFMD) • World Association of Community Radio Broadcasters (AMARC)	• University of the Philippines • IDRC • FAO • SADC-CCD • Communication for Social Change (CFSC) Consortium

Source: Manyozo, 2012.

MEDIATING THE THREE APPROACHES: ICT FOR DEVELOPMENT

The emergence of the internet and social and new media has blurred the boundaries between and among the three approaches, hence they must not be considered mutually exclusive. At the level of media development, ICT for development implies providing the technological infrastructure (transmitters, network, servers), affordable access and literacy to enable the use of the technology within development contexts or for development objectives. At this level, questions of regulation/policy come into play, and so too do questions about the economic capabilities that such technology affords people. If we are talking about e-banking opportunities, do people have enough incomes to enable them open bank accounts or conduct banking business via internet or SMS? Other examples of media development approaches in ICT for development include the participatory development of technologies such as the geographic information systems (GIS), video, radio or open source software (as in MapKibera, Ushahidi or OpenStreetMap initiatives), in which "individuals contribute to the creation of a shared resource for their own benefit, but also to make the world a better place and, in some cases, also to make money" (Berdou, 2011: n.p.).

At the level of media for development, ICT for development implies the generation and use of content via internet, mobile phones or computers within development contexts. A good example is the e-banking, e-governance or e-agricultural marketing and extension opportunities made available to developing countries and societies. At this level, attention is paid to how ICTs are transforming and radicalising the production, sharing and consumption of development content.

At the level of participatory communication, the ICT for development debate challenges us to think of the participatory methodologies employed in bringing communities of practice together in solving development challenges, or how technology enables the participative strengthening of social capital and knowledge infrastructure within development contexts. Focus is, therefore, as demonstrated in the Ushahidi project during the

Haitian earthquake crisis, on how "improved communication are seen to flow as result of investments in infrastructure and policies geared to enable access" (Berdou, 2011, n.p.). Thus, within one ICT for development project, all the three approaches can be seen to come into play, in processes that are difficult to distinguish from each other. In this case, then, in thinking about the field itself, what is important is to demonstrate how the major development thinking has influenced the way the three theoretical trajectories are conceived and implemented. Table 1.2 elucidates this point:

In Table 1.2, the three approaches (also themselves theoretical trajectories) of media for development, media development and participatory communication have been and continue to be influenced by dominant thinking in development. As Mansell (1982) observes, these paradigms (especially modernisation and dependency/structuralist) have not passed away—they have undergone superficial revisionism, to an extent, even the participatory/multiplicity paradigm itself continues to demonstrate some attributes of these other theories. Mansell's 'superficial revisionism' is expounded on by Quebral (1988: 55) who argues that in development communication, "paradigms do not pass, they just accommodate to one another".

The challenge in teaching the field is that it is important to demonstrate to students, as Mansell (1982) and Quebral (1988) point out, how, in the practical application of the theories and concepts in development communication, the major development theories continue to be reinvigorated. Modernisation thinking might have been critically analysed and deconstructed in the 1970s, but we still have each of the approaches being, at different levels and certain times, influenced by modernisation thinking. It is for this reason that the last row in Table 1.2 draws on Mansell's (1982) critique of Rogers' (1976) declaration that modernisation had 'passed away', to show the conflicting reality. The indicators, informed by what Mansell (1982) describes as 'superficial revisionism', demonstrate that dominant development paradigms still hold sway in development communication thinking, probably because all this 'new' thinking in development and development communication has failed to unsettle the dominant political economy paradigms of development itself.

Table 1.2: The Three Approaches in Relation to Development Theory

Development Thinking	The Three MCD Approaches		
	Media for Development	Media Development	Participatory/ Community Communication
Modernisation	• Top-down Traditional approaches to Entertainment–education (no audience consultation)	• Top-down, externally driven and funded, institutional, technologically deterministic • Focuses on scaling up/out Western-like media systems, structures & professional values	• Top-down systems and approaches • Institutionalised, instrumentalist initiatives
Dependency/ Structuralism (postcolonial critiques to modernisation)	• Still top-down But now beginning to capture limited audience voices & perspectives through formative research, pretesting	• Still top-down, externally driven/ funded, but beginning to consult public in media policy formulation, emergence of public broadcasting (global south)	• Therapeutic participation • Minimal consultation within system/institutional approaches
Multiplicity paradigm (another development)	• Combining top-down approaches with stakeholder/ community engagement, as in *Soul City*	• Combined top-down with bottom-up • Democratisation of communication (community media) • Emergence of ICT for development which improves access and participation	• Delegated power • Consolidation of researcher–subjects partnership through PAR • Local ownership and control of communication/ engagement initiatives
Mansell's (1982) indicators of 'superficial revisionism'	• Western-driven and funded initiatives • Cost–benefit approach • Media-centric and technologically deterministic initiatives fail to unsettle dominant political economy of development	• Global Information Infrastructures (GIIs) still Western-driven/controlled • NIIs driven by market interests (and not poverty reduction) • ICT increasing digital divide • Not paying attention to economic divide debate	• Lack social, financial, institutional and ideological sustainability • Too context-specific • Decontextualised from global debates on power • Become depoliticised once project funding comes in as they become sectoral-specific

Source: Author.

SCHOOLS OF THOUGHTS IN MEDIA, COMMUNICATION AND DEVELOPMENT

As a result of different approaches towards challenging development theories and models, different models of development communication have emerged within specific cultural, geographical and ideological contexts. Concurring with Ansu-Kyeremeh's (1994) and Amin's (1989) rejections of postcolonial *euro-centralisation* of knowledge, I have elsewhere suggested that development communication be discussed in plural and divided into six schools (Manyozo, 2006). The concept of *euro-centralisation* is drawn from Samir Amin's (1989: vii) notion of eurocentrism, which describes a culturalist phenomenon and a systematic distortion that "claims that imitation of the Western model by all peoples is the only solution to the challenges of our time". These six schools of thought in development communication comprise: Bretton Woods, Latin American, Indian, African, Los Baños and the Communication for Development and Social Change schools. These categorisations are based on planned, systematic and strategic communication strategies; coherent method; attachment to academic, training and research institutions; and sources of project funding.

The Bretton Woods School: Emphasis on Media for Development and Media Development

Origins of the Bretton Woods School can be formally located within the post–Second World War Marshall Plan economic strategies and the subsequent establishment of the World Bank and the IMF in 1944 (Manyozo, 2006; Melkote and Steeves, 2001; Kumar, 1994; Servaes, 2008). The New Hampshire conference, alongside Harry Truman's inauguration speech of 1949, would mark the beginning of Western-driven systematic and strategic employment of centralised development in much of the global south (Sachs, 1992). The school's modernist development communication paradigm has often propagated the dominant view of development promoted by Western institutions and governments—the production and planting of development in indigenous and uncivilised societies (Lerner, 1958; Melkote and Steeves, 2001; Quebral, 1988; Rogers, 1962; Servaes, 2008; Schramm, 1964). The Bretton Woods School's financial and academic institutions have, over the years, comprised, among others, UNESCO, FAO, Rockefeller Foundation, Department for International Development (DFID), Ford Foundation and universities like Michigan State, Texas, Cornell, Ohio, Wisconsin, Leeds, Columbia, Iowa, Southern California or New Mexico. Among the school's major publications have been the *Development Communication Report*, which used to be published by the United States Agency for International Development (USAID)–funded Clearing House on Development Communication (between the 1970s and 1980s), under the Academy for Educational Development; *Mazi: Newsletter on Communication for Social Change* published by the Communication for Social Change (CFSC) Consortium (funded by the Rockefeller Foundation); journals and book series published by SAGE, Hampton, ZED Books or other Bretton Woods University presses.

At least before the consolidation of the multiplicity paradigm in the 1980s, researchers working within the Bretton Woods School used to emphasise the communication of modernist and orientalist development that had been propounded in economically deterministic scholarship such as Walt Rostow's *The Process of Economic Growth* (1950), Daniel Lerner's *The Passing of Traditional Society* (1958), Everett Rogers' *Diffusion of Innovations* (1962), Wilbur Schramm's *Mass Media and National Development* (1964). For this school, it was not development that was a problem. What was needed was to find creative and more participatory ways of communicating this very development that had been exposed for promoting gross structural and social inequalities by the Latin American postcolonist critiques (Ascroft and Masilela, 1994; Diaz Bordenave, 1977; Hedebro, 1982; Kumar, 1994). What makes this school modernist is not the fact that it initially advocated and supported the modernisation approaches. What makes this school modernist is the fact that its communication approaches are located within the dominant development paradigms. From the *media for development* perspectives, the school's approaches continue to emphasise the power of media, as "knowledge derived from appropriate, useful and well-tested information" is a product of careful "capturing and translating" of development research into appropriate and usable formats for the end users (World Bank, 1990: 1). Even when overwhelming evidence suggests the failure of modernisation development paradigms in eradicating poverty and underdevelopment, the Bretton Woods School has continued to promote superficial revisionism of theories, concepts and approaches (Escobar, 1995; Mansell, 1982). Amin (1984: 204) observes that the 'objective failure' of the modernisation model in the 1970s gradually motivated developing countries to "embark upon a new strategy with the aim of consolidating" their political and economic independence. Communication thinking (as in development communication) has always been shaped by dominant development theory (Quebral, 1988). Resulting from the dependency/structuralist criticism of modernisation, communication scholars also critiqued the modernisation communication approaches, which opened a way for a rethink of concepts of culture, communication and participation. But even this so-called rethink and revision of dominant communication perspectives that would result in Rogers (1976) declaring the passing away of the dominant paradigm would still lie within the framework of the dominant development paradigms (Mansell, 1982). For Mansell, there has been nothing radical and transformative about it, insofar as the political economy of development remained intact.

As the Manyozo (2012) study observes, there were two major developments that contributed to the emergence of this school. First were the early farm radio experiments in the US in the early 1900s, which were marked by the University of Wisconsin using the earliest ham radio inventions to broadcast weather reports on a daily basis (Hilliard and Keith, 2001). Such micro-power radios provided important agricultural information to regional and remote communities about weather, soil and air, market reports, flood warnings and other information affecting farming communities. These experiments were strengthened by the involvement of major public and national broadcasters who later embarked on farm radio programming for rural and farm areas, and were later joined by the US Department of Agriculture

(Hilliard, 2003). Second were the development communication experiments in Canada, which comprised of farm radio forums (in the late 1930s) and the Fogo Process participatory video and film experiments, in which the screening of locally generated videos on rural poverty provided a space where local people were conscientised about local development and then challenged to improve their livelihoods (Manyozo, 2012; Williamson, 1991).

Today, the Bretton Woods School's strongest supporter, the World Bank, conceptualises development communication as an "integration of strategic communication in development projects" that is based on a clear understanding of indigenous contexts. Seemingly paraphrasing Quebral's 1970s definition, Jayaweera conceptualises development communication as a communication aspect of a country's development plan (Jayaweera, 1987; Quebral and Gomez, 1976). The realisation has been, even during the emergence of the dominant development paradigm, that communication involving community participation formulates a very important facet in the promotion of sustainable social change and development (Bessette and Rajasunderam, 1996; Cadiz, 1991; Servaes, 2008). It is obvious from these definitions that development is considered a known phenomenon, not a problematic that has to be explored, rethought and revisited. After the launch of the development and reconstruction project in 1944, the application of Western media and communication theories and approaches to the modernisation of the global south became imperative (Lerner, 1958; Melkote and Steeves, 2001; Rogers, 1962, 1976, 1993; Sachs, 1992; Servaes, 2008; Schramm, 1964). Such approaches received impetus from the scholarship being generated within the communication effects paradigm, which conceptualised mass media as all powerful, direct and uniform (Mansell, 2011; Melkote and Steeves, 2001; Schramm, 1964). These Western mass communication theorists had themselves been attempting to demonstrate the direct and powerful impact of media messages on societies and individuals. Communication researchers would build on mathematical or sociological models of linear communication to show how media messages could influence behaviours or public opinions. Their focus was on the effects of media propaganda on public action and opinion. It follows, then, that the design, implementation and management of development communication experiments in the global south had modernisation objectives (Melkote and Steeves, 2001; Quebral, 2011). As a consequence, the farm and educational radio projects in India, South East Asia, Africa and Latin America were based on these diffusionist models of knowledge management and dissemination.

Such scientific approaches were characterised by studying media effects under laboratory-like conditions, in which the basic methodological approach was manipulating independent and dependent variables, where one sample was used as a control. By the 1970s, however, the emergence of the cultural studies school of thought challenged the mass communication effects approach by positing that there is a space for negotiation between active audiences and media texts.

So by the time Lerner (1958), Rogers (1962) and Schramm (1964) published their major works on using media and communication to scale up/out social change, the US and World Bank were beginning to scale up/out their model of development to the rest of the world. The combination of the two dominant perspectives (development and communication) would prove powerful as Western institutions and governments embarked on intensifying the use of media and communication within the development contexts of the global south. This was the foundation of the Bretton Woods School of development communication. Meanwhile, however, other approaches were being tested the world over, either independently of or influenced by this school.

Latin American School: Emphasis on Media for Development and Participatory Communication

The emergence, growth and expansion of the Latin American School was built not on Western development theory, but rather on postcoloniality (as a rejection of a specific historical experience of colonial and neocolonial subjugation), religious Catholicism (especially liberation theology) and adult literacy. Manyozo

(2006, 2012) argues that Latin America may have introduced the earliest experiments in development communication. Emerging largely independent of Western development theory and influences, the Latin American School can be partially traced to 1947 in Colombia, when Radio Sutatenza was established by a Roman Catholic priest, Jose Joachim Salcedo. Radio Sutatenza pioneered and perfected the concept and practice of *las escuelas radiofonicas* (or radio schools), promoted by the country's Acción Cultural Popular (ACPO). The ACPO itself was formed in an attempt to broaden and diversify the Catholic Church's distant education initiatives (Diaz Bordenave, 1977; Gumucio, 2001). It was an independent organisation whose cultural division was responsible for structured and unstructured adult educational initiatives, largely comprising a radio network through which the institute offered training lasting between six months and three years (Diaz Bordenave, 1977; Gumucio, 2001).

The Sutatenza rural development education experiment would later receive funding from UNESCO and the Colombian government in order to scale up and scale out its programmes. It can even be argued that this specific approach, combined with Freirean concepts of conscientisation and trancendentality, would formulate the theoretical backbone of the *educommunication* movement and approach within the formal education system in Brazil, Latin America and the world. For Diaz Bordenave (1977), Gumucio (2001) and Manyozo (2012), Sutatenza's approach was rooted in the liberation philosophy of the Catholic Church, which emphasises total independence from ideological and material institutions and structures of oppression. Such a theology was clarified when the Second Vatican Council was organised.

The Second Vatican Council (1962–1965), held in Latin America, released a number of documents and declarations in relation to liberation theology that also specifically detailed the role of media and communication as instruments of empowerment and poverty eradication. For instance, the Declaration of *Gravissimum Educationis*, Declaration on Christian Education (Second Vatican Council, 1965a), included a section on 'The Meaning of the Universal Right to an Education'. The use of educational technology, as was the case with the Sutatenza radio schools, was encouraged as a reliable critical pedagogical pathway for developing social, political and cultural citizenship. The declaration encouraged educational communication approaches to develop the physical, moral and intellectual capabilities of the students with the aim to help them pursue 'true freedom', and thus enable them to become "actively involved in various community organizations, open to discourse with others and willing to do their best to promote the common good" (Second Vatican Council, 1965a: Section 1).

What is important in this extract is the notion of 'pursuing true freedom', which would become a defining message of this Second Vatican Council. Pursuing 'true freedom' extended to the institutions and experiences lying outside the formal institutions of instruction, in which the pursuit of freedom was to become the goal of individuals and their societies. One can sense a salient reference to Immanuel Kant's *Critique of Pure Reason*, who, years earlier, had argued for the harnessing and development of practical rationality as an educational strategy towards discovering and attaining truth and freedom. In line with Kant, the declaration of *Gravissimum Educationis* was specifically arguing that the pursuit of truth (and freedom, of course) had to be carried out freely and independently through "the aid of teaching or instruction, communication and dialogue", the aim being to assist everyone to discover this truth (Second Vatican Council, 1965a). What is this truth that the Second Vatican Council was talking about? In another document released by the Council, the *Gaudium et Spes* (Second Vatican Council, 1965b), a 'Pastoral Constitution of the Church in the Modern World', it was observed that there is need to explore the "anxious questions about the current trend of the world, about the place and role of man in the universe, about the meaning of its individual and collective strivings, and about the ultimate destiny of reality and of humanity" (Section 3). To facilitate and aid this exploration and "scrutinizing the signs of the times and of interpreting them in the light of the Gospel" (Section 4), it is imperative to have independent and free media and communication systems.

Likewise, the Decree on the Media of Social Communications, *Inter Mirifica* (Second Vatican Council, 1963), recognises the role and power of 'new avenues of communicating', to "reach and influence, not only individuals, but the very masses and the whole of human society, and thus can rightly be called the media of social communication". This specific Decree provides guidelines not only on how the 'media of social communication' can promote citizenship, good governance and humanity, but also the utilitarian values and principles of such media. The Decree even places responsibilities with producers, publishers and broadcasters as well as audiences, observing that:

> The Church recognizes that these media [of social communication], if properly utilized, can be of great service to mankind, since they greatly contribute to men's entertainment and instruction as well as to the spread and support of the Kingdom of God. [...] It is, therefore, an inherent right of the Church to have at its disposal and to employ any of these media insofar as they are necessary or useful for the instruction of Christians and all its efforts for the welfare of souls [...] to instruct and guide the faithful so that they, [...] May further the salvation and perfection of themselves and of the entire human family. [...] For the proper use of these media, it is most necessary that all who employ them be acquainted with the norms of morality and conscientiously put them into practice in this area. They must look, then, to the nature of what is communicated, given the special character of each of these media. [...] In society men have a right to information, in accord with the circumstances in each case, about matters concerning individuals or the community. The proper exercise of this right demands, however, that the news itself that is communicated should always be true and complete, within the bounds of justice and charity. In addition, the manner in which the news is communicated should be proper and decent. (Second Vatican Council, 1963: Chapter 1)

It is important to note that when the Council refers to man, it oftentimes refers to the collective individual, the subaltern, the oppressed and marginalised constituents, those that require the truth and the pursuit of it to gain freedom. What is important in this excerpt is that the Council was probably aware of the Article 19 on the Freedom of Expression within the Universal Declaration of Human Rights. It, however, raises questions about the neutrality of information that Article 19 assumes or takes for granted. For the Catholic Church and the Council in particular, such freedom of expression should be driven by truth and freedom, justice and charity. What it implies here is that information should serve the purposes of both informing and liberating, that is, it "should further the salvation and perfection" of humankind (Second Vatican Council, 1963). It is important to highlight these because when the Second Vatican Council was in progress, the US was increasing its political, economic and military presence in the Latin American region. It would be within this historical context that the 1968 General Secretariat of the Latin American Episcopal Council (CELAM) meeting in Colombia attempted to contextualise the ideals and objectives of the Second Vatican Council to the region (Rodriguez, 2003). Neocolonialism and imperialism were identified as two key causes and sources of socio-economic underdevelopment, especially for the many classes of subalterns (Rodriguez, 2003). The CELAM bishops would acknowledge in the Medellin Declarations of the need for the Church to pay attention to the increasing public discontent with the oppressive information, social, economic and political order (Rodriguez, 2003).

The postcolonial question would be clearly articulated in other Second Vatican Council Pastoral Instructions such as the *Communio et Progressio* (Second Vatican Council, 1971) that detailed the question of social communication. As was decreed in the *Inter Mirifica* of 1963, the *Communio et Progressio* seems to have drawn on two earlier Declarations—the 1957 *Miranda Prorsus* and the *Gaudium et Spes*—in order to advance the notion of 'seeing the media as gifts of God'. This implied that social communication has the challenge of "deepening social consciousness", thereby helping human beings to "know themselves better and to understand one another more easily" (Second Vatican Council, 1971: Chapter 1). Thus there was a utilitarian perspective, in which the media's impact could only be determined by the extent to which they liberated the consciousness of men, deepened man's relationship with the Church and, importantly, contributed to the common good. The *Communio et Progressio* (Second Vatican Council, 1971) provided three key aspects about the media's role in society.

First, this Pastoral Instruction conceived the media as a Habermasean public sphere, a "public forum where every man may exchange ideas" and this exchange involves the "confrontation of different opinions" (Second Vatican Council, 1971, Chapter 1: 24). Under the section 'The work of the media in human society', the *Communio et Progressio* observes that "the modern media of social communication offer men of today a great round table" where they can "participate in a world-wide exchange in search of brotherhood and cooperation" (Chapter 1: 19). The emphasis on 'every man' is significant here because the Church was aware of the increasing knowledge monopolies through various challenges such as the commercialisation of news, the competition for audience markets, the concentration of media ownership in conglomerates and corporations and increasing entertainment programming that lacks any educational value (Second Vatican Council, 1971). Second, the Pastoral Instruction advanced the pre-Castellsian notion of a 'networked society' since the "swift advances of the means of social communication tear down the barriers that time and space have erected between men" (Chapter 1: 20). Third, is the recognition of the role that media plays in development, as such, "communications media can be seen as powerful instruments for progress" (Second Vatican Council, 1963, Chapter 1: 21). One way of contributing to this progress, unlike the modernisation approaches of the Bretton Woods School, is to have a media that 'deepens and enriches contemporary culture' by promoting the 'traditional folk arts of countries where stories, plays, song and dance still express an ancient national inheritance' (Second Vatican Council, 1971, Chapter 3: 50–51). By the 1970s and 1980s, the Catholic Church would begin introducing communication projects around the world. This encompassed newspapers, and by 1983, the Radio Maria initiative was born, and by the 1990s, the initiative was scaled out to the rest of the world.

For Radio Sutatenza, the radio-based educational campaign for adults was an attempt, indeed, to meet the Church's goals of social communication, even if the Second Vatican Council came long after the station was established. Likewise, the emergence of the miners' radio stations network in Bolivia in 1949 also marked a key moment in the region's approach towards media, communication and development, with much emphasis on political economy questions. Between 1949 and 1970, the network of the miners' radio stations increased from one to 26. Unlike the *Sutatenza* model of privately owned community broadcaster, the miners' stations were owned by a civil society institution, the union of miners, which Gumucio (2001: 44) describes as very "powerful and politically advanced". Such stations were alternative media of social communication in all the three forms of alternative media advanced by Carpentier, Lie and Servaes (2003) and Bailey, Cammaerts and Carpentier (2007). Such stations were alternative to the mainstream (in technology and coverage); they were alternative in that they served a particular community of miners (who had a different ideological perspective to the rest of the country), and the stations were also alternative in that they functioned as a civil society institution and space. The political economy of such stations, therefore, was organised around the union of miners. The closure of many tin mines in the country in the 1980s and 1990s, due to the fluctuation of tin prices on the international market, eventually weakened the miners' unions and consequently resulted in the close of the various stations (Gumucio, 2001).

By the 1970s, the Latin American School was strengthened further by the adult literacy work of Paulo Freire in Brazil; the Economic Commission for Latin America's (ECLA) scathing critique against the inequalities inherent in the capitalist approaches towards modernisation and the entertainment–education approach of Miguel Sabido in television. The works of Freire and the *dependistas* at ECLA was built on a long tradition of Marxist postcolonial critiques against capitalist modernisation in the region that denounced foreign capital and the growing influence of imperialist powers on the continent. The concepts of development and modernisation as articulated in Western scholarship were placed under serious scrutiny, especially after the failed World Bank mission to Colombia in 1949 as well as the Western support for military coups. For Freire (1972, 1996), critical dialogue has to be the foundation of formal and non-formal education, in order to produce students who would question their own position and status of subalternity, and in the process, begin to *speak and unspeak* their world—that is, to participate in the reconstruction of a better society. Alongside the more radical approaches towards development were the entertainment–education approaches in public television, which built on social marketing models in order to sell behaviours and products. To support research and intellectual dialogues, the Latin America School publishes journals such as *Signo & Pensamiento*, published by the Department of Communication at the Pontificia Universidad Javerian in Colombia. Whilst these developments were taking place on the Americas, another approach to development communication was taking root in India.

The Indian School: Emphasis on Media for Development and Media Development

The origins of the Indian School of development communication can be traced to three sources. These were: (*a*) the rich traditions of folk media and indigenous knowledge communications that go as far as back before the arrival of the earliest explorers and missionaries; (*b*) the entertainment–education experiments (for example, the television soap *Hum Log* (We People) that was broadcast from 1984) whose strategic communication approaches were borrowed from the pioneering Latin American campaigns; and (*c*) the early 1900s development and science journalism experiments, when 'rural radio listening communities' were formed in the Bhiwandi region in Hyderabad in order to listen to rural broadcasts in the indigenous Marathi, Gujarati and Kannada languages (Khan, 1995; Kumar, 1981; Manyozo, 2012). In the Hyderabad State, the growth of an indigenous language press was meant to disseminate information, promote language and literature and develop an informative and healthy atmosphere, as a means of "moulding public opinion in constructive directions" (Khan, 1995: 27). These rural newspapers, however, provided different ideological coverage, with some supporting the political dynasty and others opposing it (Khan, 1995). By the 1950s and 1960s, the Indian School would begin to specialise in development broadcasting and educational ICT experiments with much significance being placed on using educational programming to "convert people with bad behaviour" as well as initiate social change within the country (Velacherry, 1993: 127).

What makes the Indian School stand out as a school is the fact that over the years its institutes and organisations have been able to develop coherent theory to explain its own praxes. A huge body of theoretical work has been explored in farm and rural development journalism, educational communication and ICT for development. Some of these initiatives were provided with logistical and financial support by Western governments and organisations. In fact, the initial theoretical capital within which some of these projects were conceptualised were very Eurocentric and Western-centric—to an extent. Over the years, however, the Indian School has been able to locate and define its own theoretical and methodological approaches within research institutions such as the Tata Institute of Social Sciences (TISS). For example, the production of the entertainment–education television *Hum Log* was carried out with the active collaboration of India's national television authority (Doordarshan) with Mexico's *Televisa*, of course, with the involvement of the Population Communications International (Singhal and Rogers, 1999). The television programme *Hum Log* thus enabled India to experiment with the knowledge generated in the global south and adapt that to suit the country's development needs, by focusing on family planning, gender equality and social harmony (Singhal and Rogers, 1999).

Alongside the development communication school in the Philippines, the Indian School was theoretically coherent and methodologically sound, even though much funding and logistical support initially came from the Bretton Woods School. As in the Philippines, Indonesia and Sri Lanka, the school also relied on academic institutions to experiment in development communication. Notable among the academic centres were the University of Poona, the Centre for the Study of Developing Societies, the Christian Institute for the Study of Religion and Society and the University of Kerala. There were also other institutes and colleges affiliated to the Delhi University that have, over the years, contributed to the growth of development communication. Yet, the political economy of these experiments favoured the government, private enterprises and donor organisations (Thomas, 2001, 2010). It is partially for this reason that development communication was associated with government propaganda (Quebral, 1988; Shafer, 1996).

At the policy level, by the 1960s, the question of people's participation in broadcasting preoccupied Indian politicians and communication and development scholars. Thomas (2001, 2010) provides a political economy perspective of broadcasting in India, especially after independence. He argues that the post-independent

Indian government gave a strong commitment to state intervention in the public and private sector, and that included the media,
especially broadcasting (Thomas, 2001, 2010). Committees were
set up to examine how to restructure the broadcasting industry.
These committees comprised the Chanda Committee of 1966,
Verghese Committee of 1978, Joshi Committee of 1985 and the
Sen Gupta Committee of 1990, all of which eventually resulted in
the Prasar Bharati Act of 1990 that was based on the recommendations of the Verghese Committee (Kumar, 1981). Among other
recommendations of the Verghese Committee was a section on local broadcasting, which highlighted the need for establishing local radio stations within various districts, to provide educational
broadcasting for both formal and non-formal instruction (Kumar,
1981). This committee underscored that decentralised and participative development from below suggests the need for decentralised messages through local radio and television (Agrawal, 1981;
Kumar, 1981; Thomas, 2010).

One characteristic of these other schools of development communication is their rhizomatic behaviour (Bailey, Cammaerts
and Carpentier, 2007; Carpentier, Lie and Servaes, 2003), that
is, their ability to work and extract funding from the Bretton
Woods School if and when necessary. For example, in the 1950s
and in collaboration with the Bretton Woods School institution
of UNESCO, India introduced a carefully designed network of
rural radio forums, known as the *Charcha Mandals* (Rural Radio
Listeners' Forum), first implemented in Pune (Kumar, 1981). Masani (1976) and Melkote and Steeves (2001) argue that such radio
forums provided the 'top-down component' of important rural
development information, especially on agriculture, which was
transformed into horizontal communication through participatory discussions. The Bretton Woods School would dominate the
conceptualisation, implementation and evaluation of the project
through the TISS and UNESCO (Rogers, Braun and Vermilion,
1977). By 1959, the Indian government introduced the rural radio
forum project on a national scale. These forums became a national
programme incorporated in the country's development plans,
with an objective of establishing 15,000 radio forums by March
1966 (Rogers, Braun and Vermilion, 1977).

By 1975, the Indian government introduced two rural television projects—the Satellite Instructional Television Experiment

(SITE), which would be followed up by the Kheda Communication Project (Agrawal, 1981; Kumar, 1981; Melkote and Steeves, 2001). The SITE expired in 1976 and the Kheda Communication Project's cycle ended in the mid-1980s (Agrawal, 1981; Kumar, 1981; Thomas, 2010). Under the SITE and Kheda Project initiatives, India embarked on both rural television and television for development programmes, with the assistance of a Bretton Woods School institution, American Satellite ATS-6, under which 'community television sets were installed in village schools and the programmes were received directly' from locally installed satellite receivers (Agrawal, 1981; Kumar, 1981; Thomas, 2010). The design and implementation of these projects was carried out with the collaboration of two government institutions, the Doordarshan (the Indian Public Service Television Broadcaster) and the Indian Space Research Organisation (Agrawal, 1981). The projects survived on community involvement in the research and production of programming, as such content was based on local themes such as dowry, widow remarriage, women's empowerment or early marriages (Kumar, 1981).

As I have earlier argued (Manyozo, 2012), within the Indian School, the systematic, theory-based and method-informed experiments in development communication eventually emerged in the 1960s with the establishment of the Press Foundation for Asia (PFA). The foundation, based in Manila would, through its flagship publication, the *Depthnews* (development, economic and population themes news) pioneer the first experiments in development journalism (Loo, 2009). Development journalism has been conceptualised as the strategic reporting of development issues in line with national development goals (Jamias, 1991; Loo, 2009; Quebral and Gomez, 1976). For India, development journalism has been implemented as rural journalism, considering that the subcontinent, then as well as now, remains largely rural, poor, illiterate and underdeveloped (Verghese, 2009).

When the PFA was established in 1968, George Verghese, the then editor of the *Hindustan Times* introduced and began regularly publishing a column about village life, known as 'Our Village *Chhatera'*, based upon a village located about 25 miles from Delhi (Verghese, 1976, 2009). Verghese (1976: 3) himself observes that this development journalism experiment enabled the *Hindustan Times* newspaper to 'win the affection of a village community and encouraged it to grow'. The newspaper's reporters became extension workers, change agents and public relations officers and were able to 'play the role of catalysts, planting new ideas in the minds of the villagers and articulating their aspiration' (Verghese, 1976, 2009).

Over the years, India's development communication experiments and institutions have been scaled out. As arguably the largest democracy, India also boasts of the largest country offices in development communication being run by Western agencies. Degree-level training institutions have emerged and become consolidated, such as the Indian Institute of Mass Communication, Chaudhary Charan Singh Haryana Agricultural University or the Makhanlal Chaturvedi Rashtriya Patrakarita Vishwavidyalaya (MCRPV) University.[4] Interesting also about India's development communication is that they have been implemented within a well-defined government policy, a case in point being the First Five Year Plan of 1951, soon after India's Independence. The Plan observed that a widespread understanding of development priorities enables citizens to embrace a country's vision of the future (Raghawan and Gopalakrishnan, 1979). It highlighted the development of appropriate communications to be used in approaching people, with a focus on providing development research to the people in "every home, in simple language and symbols of the people, and expressed in terms of their common needs and problems" (Raghawan and Gopalakrishnan, 1979: 3).

Despite such clear policy guiding the implementation of communication projects with developmental objectives, India has lagged behind in offering communities an opportunity to control and own rural radios. One challenge facing India's development communication has been the widening unequal social relations, resulting from the political economy of media and communication that favour the elites and those who own the means of production (Loo, 2009; Thomas, 2001). This has been the case because of the efforts to centralise media and communication, marked

---

[4]The MCRPV University is not necessarily a development communication–oriented institute. The Indian Institute of Mass Communication (in New Delhi) did start as a development communication institution. In fact, Wilbur Schramm was initially consulted to design the syllabus that was originally targeted at information personnel within the Indian civil service.

by the intervention of the state and the public sector (Thomas, 2001). Such intervention has been marked by liberalisation of the economy, deregulation of the telecommunication industry and the easing of cross-media ownership as well as convergence and concentration (Thomas, 2001).

The African School: Emphasis on Participatory Communication

The African School of development communication emerged a little earlier or around the 1960s, largely out of the postcolonial and communist movements, which provided a springboard from which African scholars began to rethink concepts of culture, communication and development (Kamlongera, 1988, 2005; Manyozo, 2012). During the period of its emergence and growth, the school comprised of two faculties, folk media and rural radio (Manyozo, 2012). Its growth should be directly connected to the independence and negritude movements, especially in Francophone Africa. Negritude is both a concept and a practice. It is a concept in postcolonial theory that refers to a movement of largely French-speaking African and Caribbean black intellectuals who have used the ideological platform of 'black pride' or 'black is beautiful' to speak back against colonial oppression of indigenous African values, identities and knowledge. Negritude has also been a strategic practice of black liberation theology, in which social movements (such as the Nation of Islam, the Black Panthers or Rastafarians) have become forms of organised social consciousness that reject the political, social and moral domination of the West, whilst emphasising the pride and consciousness of being black (Manyozo, 2012).

A major proponent of the negritude movement, Leopold Sedar Senghor, used his poems to idealise the intellectual strength and renaissance at play within indigenous and traditional Africa, though he totally rejected the concept of 'racial purity'. Other negritudists such as the Senegalese Egyptologist, Cheikh Anta Diop or Walter Rodney (1972) vehemently denounced the West for destroying the cultures and economies of Africa and the Caribbean through slave trade, colonisation and supporting illegal armed conflicts that destabilise the continents. Alongside the negritudist movement, postcolonial thought and practice also evolved in the 1950s during the liberation wars against colonial governments. In *The Wretched of the Earth*, Fanon (1960) draws on the moral, political and material violence of French colonialism in Algeria to propose a radical approach towards decolonisation for the whole continent. It is a theme that also appears in his other book, *A Dying Colonialism* (1965), in which he discusses the nature of colonial relationship as well as forms of resistance that the 'wretched' can engage in.

For theorists emerging after independence (such as Ngugi wa Thiong'o), postcolonial critique would focus on criticising the newly independent governments and the phony nature of independence. Wa Thiong'o takes on corruption, nepotism, tribalism and violence as key criticisms against the new colonisers, the undemocratic governments that succeeded the European colonisers. Among many modern thinkers, postcolonial theory has become a tool for destabilising the centre in relation to questions of power in everyday lives. For example, Mbembe (2001) examines the questions of the banality of power, how everyday practices and behaviours either consolidate or challenge established power structures and processes.

For Africa, three institutions have played a huge part in the growth and expansion of the theory and practice of communication for development. First, the early missionaries who came to the continent on a modernisation mission understood the importance of theatre as a tool for civilising the African other (Kamlongera, 2005). Second, the universities in post-independent Africa adapted the indigenous practice of travelling troupes into the concept of travelling theatres and started advancing the notion of 'taking theatre to the people' (Kamlongera, 1988, 2005). Such travelling theatre plays started off by taking European plays to local community halls, but later on began to create educational indigenous language plays on popular themes. Third are the non-governmental organisations (NGOs) whose emergence as subsidiary service providers have allowed them to use theatre, music and dance for mobilising and empowering communities to become active participants in the development process. Communication for development, as it is practised using theatre, dance and music, still retains these attributes.

Theatre for development is a term describing a group of methodologies which strategically and consciously employ song, drama and dance as modes of sensitising and empowering communities to improve their status quo (Kamlongera, 1988, 2005; Mda, 1993). The objective is to strengthen initiatives towards development and social change through the employment of performance as a communication process rather than one oriented towards communicating development content (Kamlongera, 1988, 2005; Mda, 1993). In theatre for development, therefore, theatre becomes a discourse and a forum through which local people critically analyse development issues, linking effects to causes, thereby attaining mental liberation or conscientisation in the Freirean praxis. University travelling theatres have, since the 1980s, moved away from performing English plays in the Shakespearean tradition and started developing indigenous language plays which carry social educational messages on popular issues of alcoholism, adultery, witchcraft or agriculture (Kamlongera, 1988, 2005; Mda, 1993). The plays draw from oral cultures, including music and religious symbolism, and building on these, the troupes perform traditional social functions of providing community education.

Alongside the theatre for development movement has been the rural and community radio sector. Ilboudo (2003) traces the development of rural and community radio on the continent, from indigenous language programming on development through farm radio forums, rural stations linked to public broadcasters and then finally to independent rural and community stations. In francophone West Africa, the development or rural radio involved huge state intervention (of course, with financial and technical assistance from foreign governments and development organisations), whilst in anglophone Sub-Saharan Africa, the development of the sector has been led by the civil society sector (Ilboudo, 2003). Today, however, there seems to be a convergence of the different communication for development trajectories. Theatre for development and other participatory action research strategies are being increasingly employed by networks of development NGOs and community broadcasters in order to increase audience participation in message and content generation to support various development projects. The expansion of the ICT sector has also enabled radio stations to become increasingly connected to the knowledge society, which helps programme producers to use internet and other ICT-based knowledge resources to improve their reach in terms of meeting audience needs.

Los Baños School: Emphasis on the Three Approaches

The origins of theory-based and method-informed 'development-oriented communication practice' can be traced to two sources. First were the land grant universities in North America, where most UPLB professors would be sent for graduate studies. Second was the College of Agriculture at the University of Philippines, where academics intensified the efforts to extend the results of agricultural sciences research to the farmers and other end users of the new knowledge and technology (Jamias, 1975, 1991; Librero, 1985, 2009; Quebral, 1988, 2002). Like the case of other schools, the Los Baños School received logistical and financial support from the Bretton Woods School. But over time, it recreated itself into an autonomous institution and eventually managed to develop its own theories and methodologies.[5] The development of communication strategies such as the broadcast-based distance

---

[5]Responding to the announcement that the LSE had awarded Nora Quebral an honorary doctorate in honour of her pioneering contributions to the field of development, Professor James Brewbaker, a close associate of Nora's for five decades, through an email sent to me on 11 July 2011, observed:

You know of course that I was with the Cornell team that came to Los Baños in 1952 (I arrived the year Nora did in 1953). But back at Cornell, I'll never forget Al Johnson, Extension Specialist in my department at Cornell. This was a department of "Plant Breeding and Biometry" that prided itself on quality basic research. Al Johnson always sat in the very front row at every weekly department seminar (we were required to participate). He was a very large man with a penetrating voice. Almost every seminar he'd rise and ask, in effect, "what in hell is this all about? how will it help New York's farmers?" i.e., bring us quickly back to the importance of applied research and demonstration. So the Cornell professors who came during that 30 years to Los Baños brought with them the Al Johnson concern that an agriculture college "serve the farmer". Nora was quick to understand that in application to the developing tropical worlds, those applications had to include not just the farmer but the entire family (and especially women), not just food but health, not just the farm but the village, etc. And Nora's incredible interest in and caution with words made a huge difference in articulating these challenges.

learning system, rural educational broadcasting or folkmedia for development demonstrate that the Los Baños School eventually became independent theoretically, and this was manifested, as has been discussed later in this chapter, with the establishment of the world's first ever development communication degree in the Philippines. Development communication, therefore, grew in response to some of the most pressing problems of development and underdevelopment (Flor, 1995, 2004). This type of development communication started out as communication for rural development, since, as citizens of developing countries, there is need to pull resources together in order to fulfil goals and dreams of the majority of citizens (Manyozo, 2012). Without trumpeting Los Baños as a 'School', Quebral is well informed of other development communication experiments going on the world over, and thus discusses 'development communication, in the Los Baños style', that is, development communication as interpreted at Los Baños (Librero, 2009; Manyozo, 2006, 2012; Quebral, 1988, 2002).

Also known as the College of Development Communication, the Los Baños School details its historical development from the time it started as the Office of Extension and Publications of the College of Agriculture in 1954, under which some staff members began to carry out research into how communication could be used to address problems of rural development (Librero, 2009). Quebral (1988) reminisces about the contribution of 'a little nudge' from Cornell University and a 'visiting extension Professor from Tennessee' and the subsequent establishment of a unit, which ended up being the Extension and Publications Office. In 1960, the first development communication courses were introduced in the Agriculture curriculum after which, in 1962, the College of Agriculture elevated the Extension and Publications Office into a Department of Information and Communication. In 1968, this Department was renamed the Department of Agricultural Communication. In 1974, the Department changed its name to the Department of Development Communication. Between 1987 and 1998, the department was elevated into an institute and then later a college, a process of transformation that involved 'progressive decisions, some of which were rational and some not' (Quebral, 1988, 2002). Among the pioneering group were Quebral (1975, 2002), Librero (1985, 2004, 2009), Jamias (1975, 1991) and Quebral and Gomez (1976), who were the first to use the term development communication. The current Los Baños School contends that development communication 'cannot really change people', but can only 'help them change themselves, at their own enlightened pace' and that 'there is no speedy transformation of societies', as development is a protracted and long process (Quebral, 1988, 2002; Freire and Horton, 1990).

I have argued (Manyozo, 2006 and 2012) that working alongside the Los Baños School were institutions such as the University of Philippines' College of Mass Communication, the Philippine Press Institute, the Press Foundation for Asia, the Asian Institute of Journalism and Communication, the Asian Institute for Development Communication, Asian Mass Communication Research and Information Centre, UNESCO/UNDP's Development Communication Support Service, the International Rice Research Institute, the Universities in Singapore, Indonesia and Malaysia and the Manila-based Communication Foundation for Asia. The school has been responsible for publishing groundbreaking development communication research, manuals and journals, the most notable being the *DevCom Quarterly, Journal of Development Communication* and *Asian Journal of Communication.*

Two important developments occurred in the 1960s. First was the introduction of a development communication Master's programme within the mainstream agricultural programme. By 1974, Quebral introduced a full-fledged undergraduate degree programme in development communication, and by doing so, the College of Development Communication (CDC) became the first institution to offer such a degree programme in the world (Quebral, 1975; Manyozo, 2006). Second was the establishment of a rural radio station at the university, which was 'conceived as an experimental rural radio station', for serving as an agricultural extension tool and assisting the school in conducting rural broadcasting research relating to the effective dissemination of agricultural information (Librero, 1985, 2009).

As of today, the Los Baños School has been joined by many schools in Europe, Africa and the Americas. Added to this is the growing list of international development bodies like the World Bank, International Development Research Centre (IDRC), United Nations FAO, UNESCO and many others that appreciate development communication. The school continues to "stand out as a pioneer in development communication teaching and the most productive in development communication education" in the world (Cadiz, 1991: v; Quebral, 2002). The school is now a full college on its own, and its curricula offer training in development broadcasting, educational communication, science communication and development journalism. The school offers four degrees: Bachelor of Science in Development Communication (BSDC), Master of Professional Studies (MPS) (distance mode under the UP Open University), Master of Science (MS) and the Doctor of Philosophy (PhD) (Librero, 2009; Manyozo, 2006). For the Bachelor of Science, the school seeks to help students acquire a broad-based understanding of the arts and sciences that define and locate development communication in ways that will help them empower people to deal with challenges of underdevelopment. By engaging in and completing the programme, the school's students will holistically exercise leadership in development communication by applying the knowledge and principles learnt in class towards solving real-life development challenges (Manyozo, 2006).

Though students in the masters programme in development communication will also acquire strong foundation in both theory and practice, the programmes are geared towards communication practitioners who are working in government and other research and development institutions, community media sector, colleges and universities (Manyozo, 2006). For the doctorate programme, the school's objective is to empower candidates to experience a deep and comprehensive understanding of the theories and principles of devcom from research, through programme planning, policymaking, implementation and evaluation. Like the pioneering 1974 curriculum, the current curriculum is broad-based. As Quebral (2002: 15–16) observes:

> A curriculum is not a random patchwork of courses. It is a representation of a worldview that the curriculum developers think their intended learners should have. [...] Reciprocity of thought is the very essence of communication, and its practice is central to genuine human development. [...] Because in the academic scheme, development communication is classed as a branch of communication, we teach our students that communication derives from sociology, psychology, linguistics and other social sciences and we try to steer them to study those basics. [...] Development communicators would not be true to a principle of their profession were they to insulate themselves and others from give-and-take with other minds. Development communication would not stay development

communication for long if it were cut off from ideas coming from various sources and disciplines—and by which it is nourished. [...] The field was never meant to stay in place. It is expected to branch out, to reinvent itself from time to time, even to lead the way as we grow in wisdom. [...]

In development broadcasting, the school's college trains students to purposively and strategically design and test techniques in using radio and television as educational mediums (Librero, 2009; Manyozo, 2006). Courses in this department include development writing, broadcast-speech and performance of community, writing and programme planning for community radio, radio drama and documentary, broadcast-based distance-learning systems and telecommunications (Librero, 2009; Manyozo, 2006). In science communication, the college trains students in using science for development, with focus on the content, product and process of science (Librero, 2009; Manyozo, 2006). Courses in the department include scientific reporting, telecommunication, scientific and technical information processing, scientific and technical publications editing and knowledge management. For educational communication, which Cadiz (1991: 22) identifies as a "major field in development communication", the college provides training in the audiovisual component of development communication. The focus is on exposing students to methodologies in "innovating, piloting, testing, refining and assessing mediated and non-mediated approaches in inducing and enhancing leaning among disadvantaged groups, who make up a substantial segment of populations in Third World countries". The courses in the department include writing for educational communication media, basic photography, broadcast-based distance learning systems, visual design and techniques, visual aids planning, production and video production. Emphasis is thus on collaborative, interactive and participative production of communication materials and participatory management of the communication programmes themselves.

Quebral (1988), however, notes some factors that impede successful design and implementation of development communication interventions, as being: the undervaluing of notions of rural, agriculture and indigenous media programmes and people; lack of unified policy frameworks on communication and information technology and their role in development; the rising commercialism in both public and community media; misunderstanding over what development communication entails, resulting to equating the practice with public relations, especially by administrators; inadequate training opportunities; and misconceptions about development communicators as constituting producers of educational materials only.

Importantly, the school acknowledges and supports the growth of other development communication training institutions in the world (Librero, 2009; Manyozo, 2007). Some are offering few specialist degrees in development communication, while others are offering the same under general media, communication, public health or international development degree programmes. Probably taking a swipe at the patenting hysteria in the West, where corporations are seeking ownership of biological and scientific discoveries, Quebral (2002) unselfishly argues that the school does not own the intellectual property rights to development communication as a field of study or teaching. This unselfishness is manifested in the willingness of the old guard of Los Baños in helping other training institutions in the region to establish their own postgraduate development communication programmes "seen from your own background", a case in point being Librero and Gomez, who have helped the Department of Agricultural Extension and Communication, Kasetsart University in Thailand, to establish a full-fledged development communication degree programme (Librero, 2009; Manyozo, 2007). Kasetsart's development communication courses like broadcasting for development, writing for development, management of communication systems, scientific information management for development, and so on do indeed reflect the influence of Los Baños, more so considering the agricultural origins of both development communication and the Los Baños development communication model (Librero, 2009; Manyozo, 2006).

The Communication for Development and Social Change School

The Communication for Development and Social Change School comprises institutional collaboration involving research and development organisations from the five schools of thought, as well as between the north and south. It must be observed that this collaboration has not been smooth, as there seems to be some disagreement over concepts of social change, communication process, training and methodological approaches. As a result, there are broadly two saliently tenuous approaches towards studying or teaching development communication: the development theory approach and the communication theory approach, since "we are talking about processes that go hand in hand" (Quebral, 1988: 7). The development theory approach has involved researchers and practitioners locating the origins, definitions and practices within dominant development paradigms as having formulated the springboard for the emergence of development communication. Quebral (1988: 8) argues that development communication is "coloured" more by how we define development, which is "the stronger principle in the tandem" to the extent that, when the definition of development changes, the "definition of development communication also changes". The development theory approach, on the one hand, offers parallel comparisons between the evolution of development communication in relation to development theory. Research and training programmes working within this approach have often located their initiatives in agricultural extension, rural development, rural sociology, community health development or indigenous knowledge systems. This is the approach that has dominated the research and training programmes in much of Africa and Asia.

The communication theory approach on the other hand, involves practitioners and scholars focusing on examining histories of how media and communication experiments impact governance, democracy and livelihoods. Such approaches have usually been built on bodies of work in media effects research, social theory, political economy or liberal democratic political theory. The concept of social change has become key to this, especially in the Americas. The models of training programmes that are being promoted by the Communication for Social Change Consortium reflect this approach. An increasing number of universities in Latin America are adopting this social change training model, whose origins can be attributed to the 'media of social communication' declarations by the Second Vatican Council as well as Goran Hedebro's (1982) book, *Communication and Social Change in*

Developing Nations: A Critical View. Without comparing the two approaches, Servaes (2008) emphasises the centrality of participation in conceptualising development communication. Dismissing the emphasis on diffusion within the two approaches, especially with regard to their reliance on the persuasive power of media, that is, being sender-and-media-centric in nature, Servaes (2008) contends that understanding development communication can only be successful if built on participation theories advocated by UNESCO and Freire, an undertaking that must be accepted as common sense.

With strong financial resources, the Bretton Woods School seems to be dictating the communication agenda again, as it controls access to funding, conferences, workshops and publishing avenues (Ansu-Kyeremeh, 1994). For instance, replacing the *Development Communication Report* has been *Mazi*, a newsletter being published by the Rockefeller Foundation–funded Communication for Social Change Consortium. A new *Global Journal of Communication for Development and Social Change* is being published by Hampton Press, and its production is being coordinated by Jan Servaes, arguably the leading scholar in the field alongside Quebral, Thufte, Cadiz, Gumucio, Rodriguez and Tomaselli.

As a theory, practice and field of study, development communication has reoriented itself to focus on social challenges of the first world as well as issues like child prostitution, art forms, human rights and culture, because by being "seamless in nature", human development entails economic, social, political and cultural independence (Quebral, 1988: 22). Rockefeller Foundation researchers and practitioners have started 'asserting' the relevance of development communication 'in the context of developed countries' and as such, a 'new and longer label', communication for social change, is being proposed (Cadiz, 1991, 1994). For others, the term communication for development and social change is more appealing (Servaes, 2003, 2008).

The collaboration of different schools has produced interesting results with regards to testing theory against practice. The *Isang Bagsak* network has involved community-based natural resource management initiatives by Latin American, South East Asian, African and Canadian institutions. Bessette (2004) observes that *Isang Bagsak* is a research and development initiative that empowers development partners to employ participatory development communication (PDC) tools and approaches in order to promote community-based natural resource management. The PDC is a communication tool with which to facilitate community involvement in local development (Bessette, 2004). The implication of Bessette's assertion is that communication systems and approaches should be 'indigenised', a process that involves the deliberate implication and inclusion of indigenous communication systems into the mainstream communication systems so as to create holistic communication initiatives (Ansu-Kyeremeh, 1994). In terms of rural radio and development, major contributions of the Communication for Development and Social Change (CFD&SC) School have been to clarify the concept of rural radio in relation to development journalism and rural radio forum, which were largely restricted to either rural or agricultural communications by all these schools.

AFTERTHOUGHTS

Today, development communication has become what Jamias (1975) terms the "in" word for many development and communication organisations, institutions and researchers. From its humble beginnings as a series of empowerment practices in South East Asia and Latin America, then a course, and later a series of comprehensive strategically media and communication interventions, the theory and practice of media, communication and development has become an integral part of development planning and implementation. It must also be emphasised that the emergence and consolidation of MCD as an academic field of study could be attributed to the pioneering work of the Los Baños School, under the guidance of Nora Quebral and her colleagues at the College of Development Communication. Quebral's thoughts formulated the foundation glue that erected the Los Baños School, and though she has never blown her trumpets, she and the Los Baños School are the manifesto of development communication itself. As a series of practices that augment development planning and implementation, MCD's foundations can also be traced in the work of the Second Vatican Council, Radio Sutatenza, Las Radios Mineras, the Farm Radio Forums of

Canada, the ham radio experiments in the US, the development journalism experiments in the Indian subcontinent and the theatre for development exercises in Africa.

This foregoing chapter has attempted to meticulously trace the different schools of thought in which MCD evolved and grew. The chapter has proposed and described the six schools, namely, the Bretton Woods, Latin America, India, Africa, Los Baños and the Communication for Development and Social Change Schools. This analysis of the field in terms of different schools is very important in two ways. First, it enables us to demonstrate that various development communications evolved outside dominant Western development theories. Later on, for much of the developing world, the growth of MCD was a postcolonial attempt to reject Western development epistemologies and programmes that only increased rural poverty, underdevelopment and social exclusion. Second, it has also provided a springboard for showing that within these various schools, the three dominant approaches to the study of MCD can be generated. These three approaches, as has been raised in the chapter, are: media for development, media development and participatory/community communication, otherwise known as community engagement. These three approaches are informed by different theoretical trajectories and serve different purposes.

This chapter, therefore, makes important observations. It argues that the different approaches that characterise the study and practice of the field of MCD makes it very impractical to develop a single theory or model that may attempt to explain the heterogeneous field. The communication for social change model (Figueroa et al., 2005), for example, aims to elucidate a community-based approach towards collaborative decision-making. This makes it a useful tool for the participatory and community communication approach, much more than the media development or the media for development approaches. The same applies to the media for development models (such as the P-Process or Soul City social change), which would offer little to the media development or community engagement approaches. The chapter, therefore, argues that, much as the field has been defined and redefined since it was conceived in the 1950s/1960s, there is not a single theory that has been developed to explain one problem statement—as the three approaches are in constant tension against each other and are loosely held together by the concepts of three Ps: Participation, Power and Policy. Participation refers to the constant negotiation between those that have power and those that do not in order to enable all stakeholders to contribute to decision-making regarding programme planning and implementation. Power refers to the capacity to influence decisions and results and is thus a necessary concept in understanding empowerment. Policy refers to the constant interaction of reflection, theory and practice, and within MCD, refers to the levels of involvement of experts and stakeholders and their ability to inform the strategy. The next three chapters seek to demonstrate how these three approaches differ from and interact with each other.

2

The Media for Development Approach
Emphasis on Content

THE PROBLEM

The chapter presents and critically analyses the first approach towards the study of media, communication and development—the media for development trajectory—which describes the strategic employment of media and communication as facilities for informing, educating and sensitising people about development and pertinent social issues. The discussion interrogates the process of doing media for development, especially in relation to the challenges of developing content that satisfies the diverse needs of multiple stakeholders without promoting the single story. This chapter builds on case studies of development and civic journalism from both developing and developed countries, in which the mass media, especially newspapers, radio, internet and television have been used as instruments and spaces for communicating about and in development.

Debates over the role of media in reporting development has largely been framed within the development journalism approach. During a series of training workshops organised in the Philippines in the 1960s, Chalkley (1972) used the term 'development journalist' to refer to reporters working in specialised areas of development that required them to provide, interpret and promote facts and also to provide conclusions for their readers and audiences. In fact, Jamias (1991), Loo (2009), Manyozo (2012) and Verghese (1976, 2009) argue that development journalism is a theory and practice that argues for an alternative approach towards reporting development issues in ways that capture and engage with data, facts and audiences proactively. This form of journalism can be traced back to South East Asia and the Indian subcontinent in the 1950s, when newspaper editors began to raise questions about the lack of critical, effective and accessible coverage of development news in the national press. Since then, the term and practice became synonymous with rapid rural development (including agrarian revolution) as a means of modernisation. Over the years, another strand of development journalism has evolved, whose objective has been to bring 'suffering out there' to Western audiences, a praxis that Chouliaraki (2006) terms 'humanitarian communication'.

As a result, we have two binary perspectives in development reporting or journalism: the organic or bottom-up development journalism, and the external top-down development reporting strands. These strands are not entirely exclusive. There are moments, especially during media development initiatives, when the two strands dissolve and metamorphose into each other. For example, the Soul City model of social communication was developed organically as a health and development communication model for South Africa. Yet due to the sociocultural connections in the Southern African region, the multimedia communication campaigns were taken to other countries in the region, a development that might seem an external top-down form of development journalism. From the mid-2000, however, Soul City would help the establishment of national health and development communication partners in the region (media development), whose responsibility was to adapt the South African Soul City campaign content and approaches to apply to specific national contexts. This was the origin of national Soul City partners such as *Pakachere* in Malawi or *Nweti* in Mozambique.

THE POLITICAL ECONOMY OF DEVELOPMENT JOURNALISM: THREE MAJOR STRANDS

One major question that political economy of communication approaches attempt to answer is with regards to ownership and control of media and communication structures and institutions. In development journalism, discussions of ownership and control are oftentimes framed within debates on funding, journalistic practices and capacities, which Vargas (1995: 5) defines as "the daily routines of people producing and transmitting messages as well as institutional ideologies and constraints that frame these routines". This chapter provides a matrix for understanding the media for development approach from a development journalism perspective. In this matrix, three key strands are proposed based on the journalistic strategies and the political economy within which these strategies are construed. As elucidated in Table 2.1, the three journalistic strands are: (*a*) factual news and content; (*b*) creative and educational journalism; and (*c*) indigenous knowledge communications. In terms of the political economy of these journalistic strategies, the matrix presents three major trajectories, namely: (*a*) the top-down/external perspective; (*b*) the 'co-optation' perspective; and (*c*) the bottom-up/organic perspectives. This chapter will, therefore, provide an empirically informed critical analysis of these three development journalistic strategies.

Table 2.1: Various Strands in Development Journalism

	Journalistic Approaches	Political Economy Indicators	Examples
1	**Factual news/ Content**	Top-down/External donor funding	• Project Chhatera • Project Katine • Humanitarian Communication & Campaigns • PositiveNews.org.uk • Radio School (*La Escuela Radiofonica*)
2	**Creative and educational reporting**	Shared/Co-opted	• Entertainment–education • Theatre for Development • Development Through Radio (DTR) • Radio Listening Clubs
3	**Indigenous communications**	Bottom-up/Organic	• Indigenous performances (*Gulewamkulu* in Malawi, *Gelede* in Togo or *Egwugwu* in Nigeria)

Source: Author.

In this typology, the *factual news/content* trajectory refers to, from a political economy perspective, a top-down approach towards the research, production and circulation of news content from experts and subject-matter specialists who research, produce and publish/share development reports with massified audiences. The political economy of this strand refers to corporate finance, emphasis on ICTs and new media, concerns with representation (of others), journalism and mass communication theories. The *creative and educational reporting* aspect refers to processes and structures in which communication and subject-matter specialists limitedly consult target groups and audiences in generating and producing development information. These are initiatives that require shared responsibility from both the institutions and communities that are involved, but the 'delegated authority' (Arnstein, 1969) rests with funding agencies, communication and subject-matter specialists and producers. In terms of *indigenous knowledge communications*, emphasis is on organised organic efforts by local groups and communities to generate educational communications that speak to local/specific contexts.

THE THREE DEVELOPMENT JOURNALISM STRANDS IN PRACTICE

Strand 1: The Factual News/Content Trajectory

This strand of development journalism refers to either externally or internally generated communications in which journalists, subject matter specialists and policymakers develop and circulate development content so as to raise public awareness regarding development challenges and opportunities existing in a particular community or society. At the centre of these factual reportages is media technology, especially ICTs, new media and mobile communications. The trend and strategy towards factual news reporting in and about development traditionally involve research, data collection, synthesis, story-writing by professional journalists and editors and mass circulation (through newspapers, radio, internet, television). There are two strategies that define this strand.

The first involves local reporters writing about their own society or community, with minimal outside influence. This is how the whole debate about development journalism emerged in the 1960s in the Philippines, India and South East Asia. The second strategy involves external and transnational/international media or development organisations attempting to write on and about development concerns in other places, especially the global south. In this specific approach, transnational/international media focus on humanitarian crises sometimes result in the spectacularisation of the suffering of others (Chouliaraki, 2006).

Internal Development Reporting: Local and Community Journalism

At the centre of this strand is the production and circulation of local development news. The concern is not just with development issues and content but also with framing and representation—the articulation of development challenges from the perspective of those that live them, a perspective that Thompson (1963) described as history from below. In the introduction to *The Making of the English Working Class*, Thompson attempts to recover not just history as a fact but rather the experiences of history (of those that lived through certain times and spaces). Recovering such experiences enables us to understand what it meant to live through "these times of acute social disturbance" (Thompson, 1963: 13). Development journalism aims to re-articulate the experiences and reactions to living through the 'social disturbances' of poverty, social exclusion and underdevelopment. As a practice, therefore, internal development journalism emerged as a postcolonial discourse that aimed to liberate the art and performance of reporting from the 'telling it as it is' approach to one in which the development content also captured the historical material conditions characterising class experiences and consciousness.

The theoretical springboard for the emergence and consolidation of this development from below reporting approach comes from combined efforts of rural and community journalists as well as frontline development officers from India, the Philippines, South East Asia and of course, Colombia. Manyozo (2012) observes that in the late 1940s, emerged the very first experiments in rural development reporting in Colombia, when a small community radio broadcaster, *Radio Sutatenza*, introduced the radio school as an instrument of educating the rural peasants on literacy and development issues. This broadcast-based distance learning model would be adapted by the University of Phillipines' College of Agriculture, when its campus-based community broadcaster, Radio DZLB introduced the first rural educational broadcasting experiments in South East Asia (Flor, 1995, 2004; Librero, 2004, 2009). In India, the 1950s had seen the introduction of radio forum experiments, and probably building on the established culture of rural reporting in this country by the network of well-established indigenous language media network, the then editor of the *Hindustan Times*, George Verghese (1976, 2009) would, in the late 1960s, introduce a rural development reporting experiment that came to be known as Project Chhatera. The actual contribution towards the putting together of a coherent theory and a scientific approach for explaining the reporting of development would finally come from three key institutions, the Philippine Press Institute, the Press Foundation for Asia and the College of Agriculture at UPLB (Librero, 2009).

Although the first manual on development journalism was produced and published in the 1970s (Chalkley, 1972), it was only until the 1980s and 1990s that coherent theoretical frameworks on development journalism were spelt out in two key publications. The first was Felix Librero's (1985) *Rural Educational Broadcasting*, which built on the long tradition of the UPLB in agricultural communication strategies that had been borrowed from land grant universities such as Wisconsin and Michigan (where most UPLB College of Agriculture staff were sent for their PhDs) and also from Latin America (especially the radio school models). The second was Juan Jamias' (1991) *Writing for Development* that provided a theory of development journalism informed by the empirical reality of the Philippines. It must be highlighted that the thinking around the praxis of development journalism was largely framed within development communication debates that Nora Quebral had already started since the 1960s. For Librero (1985, 2009), Jamias (1975, 1991) and Quebral (1988, 2002), development journalism is the strategic and deliberate production, packaging and circulation of development reports as a way of contribution towards meeting goals of national development policies. In fact,

Jamias (1991:1) defines development journalism as the "purposeful sharing of information to bring about desirable change". For Jamias (1991), Verghese (1976, 2009), Loo (2009) and Librero (1985), the development journalist ceases to be an observer and a documenter, and becomes rather a key and active participant in the development process. Development reporting as a strategy of doing media for development is common among public, commercial and community broadcasters in the global south, not necessarily because there is no such other reality to sell their audiences but because the journalists themselves feel an obligation to recover the experiences of dealing with development problems. Such an overarching objective is captured well by the Philippine-based online news, *MindaNews*, whose motto is 'This is OUR Mindanao!', and aims to provide a relatively fair and ethnographic representation of a region that is plagued by a military rebellion against the state. Box 2.1 shows the history-from-below approach in *MindaNews*' mission statement:

Box 2.1: *MindaNews* Mission Statement

Mindanao News and Information Cooperative Center (MNICC)

VISION

Mindanao News and Information Cooperative Center (MNICC) is the leading provider of accurate, timely and comprehensive news and information on Mindanao and its peoples, serving economically, politically and culturally empowered communities.

MISSION

Professionally and responsibly cover Mindanao events, peoples and issues to inform, educate, inspire and influence communities.

(Box 2.1 Contd.)

(Box 2.1 Contd.)

WHO ARE WE?

We are a cooperative composed of independent, professional journalists who believe and practice people empowerment through media. We also believe that Mindanao is not all bad news and that our responsibility as journalists and information providers is to ensure a mixed balance of reports beyond the usual fare published in national newspapers or aired on radio and TV.

STATEMENT OF VALUES

Social responsibility is the priority in our undertakings as a cooperative. This involves integrity, honesty, conscious search for the truth, sensitivity and respect for faiths and cultures, promotion of peace amidst pluralism, environmental advocacy and dovetailing our services to the needs of the peoples of Mindanao, particularly the marginalised sectors. Viable and sustainable enterprise will enable us to undertake the above.

Source: http://mindanews.com/main/about/ (accessed on 12 April 2012).

The *MindaNews* vision statement captures Thompson's (1963) history from below approach in three ways. First, it attempts to 'rescue' the experiences of this small island by demonstrating that 'Mindanao is not all bad news' as is portrayed in the national media. As such, the content is aimed at policymakers, decision-makers and the public to help them understand the Mindanao region and its peoples much better. Second, this online news source aims to 'inspire and influence' Mindanao communities—to show them that amidst the military conflict, local people can do something towards improving living conditions. For this reason, development journalism is alternative in its critical perspective, riding against the whirlwind of the sensationalism of corporate media institutions that are not necessarily interested in objective representation or community empowerment. Third is the deliberate attempt to represent the 'marginalised', the very subaltern whose ability and capacity to speak is being questioned by Spivak (1988). Supporting this principle of objective representation of the subaltern are four objectives that motivate the conceptualisation of development journalism: the need to bring development news to the front page and therefore, to the awareness of policymakers; the need to provide scientifically and economically complex policy and research documents in ways that average readers and listeners would understand; the need to support the governments in their development initiatives; and the imperative need by editors to undermine corporate media ownership which focuses on sensationalist news in order to increase sales whilst undermining professional ethics.

Bringing Development News to the Front Page: One of the development concerns in the global south today is the tension between the first and third economies that exist side by side within nation states, especially those that are struggling to cope with rapid economic growth, such as China, India, Brazil or South Africa (Pejout, 2010). Referring to these two coexisting economies, the former editor of the *Hindustan Times,* George Verghese (2009), observes that within the global south, there is a huge economic and emotional gap between town and country. One consequence of this gap is that with increasing corporate ownership of mass media, newspapers or electronic media focus on the consumers, most of who live within the bracket of the first economy (Zuma, 2010). City journalists and their consumers are oftentimes ignorant of the other world, its issues and inhabitants (Verghese, 2009). And so, too, the urban-based government official, policymaker and decision-maker. It was for this reason that in 1969, the *Hindustan Times* launched a development journalism initiative known as Our Village Chhatera. The aim was to represent the experiences and development efforts of the small community of Chhatera and other villages with similar socio-economic attributes in order to provide the urban readers with a window to the reality of rural poverty and underdevelopment (Verghese, 1976, 2009).

Familiarity with the content and characters enabled and encouraged Chhatera villagers to contribute by voicing their everyday problems. The villagers were keen for 'Our Village' to feature their development priorities in education, health, communication, sanitation and agriculture (Verghese, 1976, 2009). The input from the communities allowed the column to become 'a change-agent and publicity input in development', linking villagers to service providers (Verghese, 1976, 2009). The column developed to include coverage of the village's immediate neighbours, Majra and Barota villages (Verghese, 1976). Transformatively, the project developed a 'faithful readership', empowered villagers, galvanised administration and service agencies into improving service provision, stimulated economic investment and development, whilst city journalists who worked on the Chhatera project acquired a better understanding of their profession, the 'other' country and its citizens (Verghese, 1976, 2009). As if acknowledging Chhatera's positive impact on the journalists themselves, an established rural development journalist, Sainath (2009), observes that development journalism is very educative and sensitising, since working through people's lives enables the reporters to deepen and sharpen their perspectives.

The Need to Provide Relevant Scientific and Economic Reporting: One of the earliest forms of development journalism was economic reporting, which combined strands of financial and business reporting from the West and community journalism in the south (Chalkley, 1972; Jamias, 1991). The aim then was to unpack policy language and development research that was (and often is) presented in the most inaccessible languages and presentation format, especially to the majority of poor and marginalised communities. Such a concern would culminate in a strand of development journalism that is now known as science reporting (Jamias, 1991; Librero, 2009). When Quebral led the University of the Philippines to establish the world's first ever degree programme in development communication, four areas of expertise were introduced, namely, development broadcasting, educational communication, development journalism and, importantly, science communication (Librero, 2009; Manyozo, 2006). In *science communication*, the university trains students in 'using science for development', with a focus on 'the content, product and process of science' (Librero, 2009).

As a subject, *science communication* aims to produce graduates who can use various creative skills in order to translate complex scientific data relating to development into forms and formats that everyone can understand. As if concurring with the UPLB, journalist Rowley, who presided over the annual Developing Asia Journalism Awards, observed that "good journalism can make people aware of the human dimensions of development in a way that official reports can rarely do" (Mettam, 2005: viii, in Loo, 2009: 18). He encourages development journalists to unpack the complex and inaccessible official jargon and "restore" the human dimension in ways that enable people to understand the depth of development situations and not just through figures and statistics (Mettam, 2005: viii, in Loo, 2009: 18).

The Need to Support the Governments in their Development Initiatives: This objective requires journalists to function as development workers to help developing countries achieve rapid social and economic development. It is for this reason that most Western scholars misconstrued development journalism as an ideological state apparatus through which governments exerted control over the media (Loo, 2009; Maslog, 1999; Quebral, 1988). It must be understood that after the 1960s, when a lot of countries became independent in Africa, Asia and South East Asia, the new governments inherited colonial infrastructure and telecommunication networks that were weak, underdeveloped and in most cases non-existent. In countries such as the Democratic Republic of Zaire, Sudan, Nepal, Chad, Nigeria and India, the mass media were the only reliable means through which the governments could communicate with their citizens. It was also the only means through which the government could clarify its development policies to the populace. Since the print media have often been published in colonial languages, the majority of populations do not read them and cannot even afford them.

It is for this reason that in the newly independent states, radio became the most affordable, effective and extensive form of mass communication that could mediate development discourses between the power holders and citizens. The farm and rural radio initiatives in India, Ghana, Philippines, Nigeria, Malawi, Benin and Togo were meant to provide the much-needed agricultural information to the farming constituents residing in rural and remote areas. Such initiatives would be augmented by the radio listening clubs, through which the community-based agriculture extension officers helped learners with practical demonstrations. The emergence of the rural and community radio movement would also consolidate the government-to-citizen communication. Development journalism was, at this level, an instrument of nation building and focused on assisting the newly independent governments in providing basic information about agriculture, health and other development issues (Quebral and Gomez, 1976; Librero, 2009). It connected farmers to markets, communities to service providers, informed communities of new health or agricultural practices. It was not meant to be critical, largely because during the cold war, most of the newly independent countries transformed into dictatorships that did not tolerate criticism of government policies. Development journalism was about providing what Hilliard (2003) defines as 'life-saving' information.

The Editorial Need to Undermine Corporate Media Ownership: Ideally, development reporters should not just tell the story but rather become involved in a class struggle by becoming "more subversive, undermining the established order" (Sainath, 2009: 37). As an instrument of class struggle, development journalism engages its reporters to become active participants in the processes of empowerment and social change, hence the term 'emancipatory journalism' (Gunaratne, 1996; Melkote and Steeves, 2001). In relation to this specific objective, the US would, in the 1980s, pioneer another interventionist model of journalism known as civic/public journalism, whose objective was to build local citizenship and strengthen community participation in public polity (Shafer, 1996). These class struggles cannot be achieved by mainstream media, whose ownership and control is increasingly coming into the hands of corporate institutions. Verghese (2009) and Sainath (2009) criticise what they think are the 'structural flows' of the conventional and mainstream media when it comes to reporting development issues. Such structural flows originate in the increasing ownership of the media by corporate institutions that create competition for markets and thereby giving rise to consumerism, in which journalists are interested in increasing audience readership, listenership or viewership.

In this ownership conundrum, the social responsibility of journalists to audiences and communities ceases to exist. By abdicating this responsibility, journalists begin to perpetuate the *Weltanschau-ung* of shareholders and all those who own the media institutions. Sainath (2009: 36), however, sees development journalism as a "child" of political struggles for liberation, which "came into being by questioning, challenging, exposing, investigating the human condition and asking why the poor, exploited and oppressed were exploited and oppressed". In practice, development journalism thus involves "analytical interpretation, subtle investigation, constructive criticism and sincere association with the grassroots rather than with the elite" (Gunaratne, 1996: 6). An example of corporate interests overriding development interests is provided by Sainath (2009), who cites two incidents that took place in 2006 in India, in Vidharbha region, where over 400 farmers committed suicide, but this event was poorly covered by the conventional media, few of who sent reporters to investigate. This was in sharp contrast to the 500 journalists they would send to cover a popular fashion event, which for Sainath (2009: 37) demonstrated a clear "disconnect between mass media and mass reality".

Development journalism emerged over the years as a bottom-up, pluralistic, community-oriented form of news production, as a practice in print media and broadcasting newsrooms and as a theory in academia (in Malaysia, Philippines, India) that lay within the "triangular interaction of news, communication and community" (Gunaratne, 1996: 8). Emphasising this bottom-up or history from below approach, Sainath, a rural affairs editor at *The Hindu*, demonstrates the 'essence' of constructing development representations from the perspective of those that live through the challenges. He argues that one's perspective is located within their class consciousness and experience, noting that "if you have not been in the hut that has no electric power, not a single bulb, how will you understand why the children in that home can never do well in studies" (Loo, 2009: 14).

The External Development Reporting: International Media and the Global South

This strand of development journalism is largely driven by external and transnational media institutions, depends on external funding, targets external or global audiences, and in most cases is profit-oriented. Unlike the organic bottom-up strand, where content is meant to inform and educate local people and policymakers, the international development journalism strand aims to *expose* the specific development problems (especially humanitarian crises) to the outside world. In the production of such reportage, there is often little or no consultation with national stakeholders by the journalists or personnel. In the end, as much as journalists, foreign correspondents and other media practitioners attempt to research, produce and disseminate realistic portrayals of subjects, events and crises, their representations are oftentimes questioned, contested and criticised as entrenching the subjugation, colonial displacement and dehumanisation of the global south through "visual metaphors" and other significatory regimes (Chouliaraki, 2006; Said, 1978; Tomaselli, 2006). The questions that are often brought up are: what moral authority do Western and international journalists have in telling the stories and experiences of others? To what extent do unequal power relations between the Western observers (with the funding and media space to tell their story) and the subaltern subjects (observed) impact on the way stories on and about the global south are told and retold? Can the global south tell its own stories realistically? Or, can the underclass represent itself?

Concerns with such critical questions has oftentimes resulted to discursive conflicts between, on one hand, the international and transnational media organisations (who are more interested in exercising their right to freedom of expression) and, on the other, national governments, over questions of representation, the right and authority to represent and the motivation for representation. A good example is the recent debate between a group representing Bosnian women war victims who were raped during the 1990s war and Angelina Jolie who has been producing a film about their experiences. The question raised by the victim group has revolved around the moral eligibility of Jolie to tell their story, a narrative of the actual reality (as imagined and imaged by Jolie). The notion of 'actual reality' is problematic again because other women who were raped think Jolie's film is going to *expose* their plight to the world.

Along the same lines, in South Africa, in 2011, another debate has raged over the production of a movie about Winnie Madikizela-Mandela, an apartheid struggle icon (Smith, 2011). Though the movie is being directed by a South African, Darrell Roodt, the controversy emerges because a black American Jennifer Hudson was cast to play the South African icon, but also because Madikizela-Mandela herself feels she was not consulted regarding her own representation. In an interview with CNN, Madikizela-Mandela observed: "I was not consulted. I am still alive, and I think that it is a total disrespect to come to South Africa, make a movie about my struggle" (Smith, 2011). Even though in this case, it was not a known international or transnational media institution that is framing Madikizela-Mandela, the whole political economy of this filmic representation has been executed with the international audience in mind, hence the casting of Jennifer Hudson, an Oscar winner. By apparently discarding the voice of Madikizela-Mandela herself, the filmic representation is less concerned with the questions of voice raised, by those being represented, an approach that has been popular in colonial and modernist ethnographic documentaries by Western culture industries.

Thus, the question we can draw from this debate is, can Angelina Jolie, a white woman, a rich woman, a very privileged woman, an American woman (whose country is being accused of rising Islamophobia), tell the story of Bosnian women, Bosnian women who were raped, Bosnian women who are Muslims? Such questions become generic in cases where international media organisations are implicated: can Western and international media tell the development story in the global south fairly and perhaps faithfully? 'Faithfully' here is important because it alludes to motivation and intentions. In the new 2003 preface to his book, *Orientalism*, Said (1978) distinguishes between the careful and empathetic study and analysis of issues and people in the global south from orientalism that reflects colonial arrogance, carelessness and feelings of superiority. What is Angelina Jolie's intention in telling the story of Bosnian Muslim rape victims? Why would not she tell the story of American women who continue to be raped? Why do international media report on development issues in the global south?

As if he could prophetically foresee the emergence of these ethical questions in the representation of the self and the 'other', Marx (1852/1937) observed that the subaltern groups who are not interconnected in a political struggle do not constitute a class, and in that case, "they cannot represent themselves, they must be represented". What Marx (1852/1937) was addressing here is the difference between *speech* as a linguistic act of narrating and *representation* as a political act of witnessing. Can the subaltern speak (Spivak, 1988)? Yes, they can and they do. The Bosnian war victims continue to speak, but perhaps no one hears them, because their speech has oftentimes remained local. The same applies to the women victims raped in the conflicts in the Democratic Republic of Congo (DRC) or in the war zones of Afghanistan, whose voices remain muted and confined to their respective locales.

What Angelina Jolie provides in this case is a historicised and problematised witness, not necessarily as a speech on behalf of these women but rather a political act of representation that links the global struggles and experiences of women who have been raped during war. Such women oftentimes are not identified within structures and processes of international and national justice as victims of war, and are thus not compensated, nor provided with adequate and relevant medical care (for those that contract sexually transmitted infections [STIs] or are traumatised by children born from rapists). Nevertheless, such Jolie-sque role played by international media should be structured within adequate research and stakeholder consultation to increase the moral legitimacy of such acts of representation. An example of international/transnational media's reportage of development that involved partial research and consultation in subject communities in the global south is *The Guardian Media*'s development journalism experiment in Uganda.

The Guardian's *Katine Development Reporting Project*: "It starts with a village": Writing on Charlie Beckett's blog (http://www.charliebeckett.org), the former Christian Aid's Head of Media, John Davidson (2009) propounded the concept of "Media *about* Development" as a coherent strategy for putting the development agenda and content "into the mainstream UK media". The implication of international media in development issues is not motivated by the need to empower or just inform. Rather, the debate has been framed within notions of modernity and good governance through *exposure*. In this case, exposure has become an instrument for achieving modernity by *exposing* the global south (the developing world) to the strategies that the developed North undertook in order to develop. Development reporting in this case becomes a strategy for comparison—comparing the global south to the global north—and using the north as a benchmark of what the south should ideally become. In fact, Lerner (1958: 38) observed that the Western economic growth–oriented development model is "virtually an inevitable baseline" for development planning and implementation in the global south. In this case, the West becomes a comparative indicator, a development code for comparing development and governance issues between the south and the north. The involvement of international (especially Western) media in reporting development and the global south brings up questions on authority, especially in relation to motivation. Are these reports trying to show us that the West is still the best model for development and good governance?

The question of *exposure* first emerges in the case study by the *Hindustan Times* in the 1960s, when George Verghese (1976: 3) of the *Hindustan Times* launched Project Chhatera in order to "open a little urban window on rural India". This exposure was meant for Indian audiences and of course, Indian primary and secondary stakeholders. This experiment was organically developed and was not funded by corporate institutions. The motivation was to bring development to the front page, in a way to try to wash dirty linen in front of the local public. Many years later, in London, Alan Rusbridger, the editor of *The Guardian* would alongside the Barclays Bank, Farm-Africa and AMREF, similarly launch the three-year Katine Community Partnerships (KCP) Project in October 2007, which would metamorphose into the Bill Gates–funded initiative, 'Development' (Rusbridger, 2007). Whilst the KCP project involved consolidating and expanding the already ongoing development initiatives that two development organisations were already carrying out in the Ugandan rural African village, *The Guardian's* involvement allowed development journalism to be incorporated as an important component of the KCP project. The objective was to use it to monitor the development projects which were implemented on the ground and also to raise funds from an empathetic British public on community development projects, having been moved by Chouliaraki's (2006) 'pity'. As such, *The Guardian's* role constituted observation, reporting and, for Chouliaraki (2006), 'witnessing' the development in Katine.

This development journalism project would become known as the '*Katine: It Starts with a Village*' (hereafter Katine) Project.

The financial support was obtained from Barclays Bank, and *The Guardian* itself; the logistical support came from two local development organisations that have experience in working with communities in Northern Uganda, Farm-Africa and the African Medical and Research Foundation (AMREF). At its launch, the Katine Project was considered a strategy for building a 'relationship with the people in and around' Katine village (Rusbridger, 2007). This development journalism project was primarily addressed to *The Guardian* readership as observed by Rusbridger (2007: 'Introduction') himself:

> We want with your assistance, to try to improve their (Katine villagers) prospects in a lasting way. The success of a previous appeal to *Guardian* readers, which asked for long-term financial commitment to support HIV/Aids clinics in Africa, caused us to think more deeply about development aid. Could we help finance a project that would attempt to address a range of issues? Could we involve local people to ensure sustainable progress? Can we advise a model that, if successful, could be replicated or even scaled up? [...] Our job is to report on the progress (and setbacks) of the project in the *Guardian*, the *Observer* and *Guardian Weekly*, as well as on a dedicated section of our website, Guardian Unlimited. Our coverage will take you inside the lives of those who live in Katine, week in, week out. [...] The rest is up to you. Barclays will match your pledges, pound for pound, up to £1.5m over the next three years.

The 'We' in this quotation refers to the project management team comprising *The Guardian*, Farm Radio, AMREF and Farm-Africa. And the 'You' here refers to the English-speaking and middle-class readers of *The Guardian*, who, due to increased reporting of 'distant suffering' (Chouliaraki, 2006) in 'other' places, are becoming more sympathetic to humanitarian causes. During the POLIS[1] dialogues organised at the London School of Economics between 2008 and 2010, questions were being raised regarding the role of Ugandan media in reporting development in, around

---

[1]The name POLIS is derived from the ancient city-states and, as used by the London School of Economics, refers to the space where journalism engages with society. The POLIS itself observes that it is 'the place where journalists and the wider world can examine and discuss the media and its impact on society'. Cf. http://www2.lse.ac.uk/media@lse/POLIS/about.aspx (accessed 12 April 2012).

and beyond Katine. It was pointed out by Richard Kavuma, the *Observer* journalist reporting on the ground for *The Guardian*, supported by AMREF and Farm-Africa representatives, that there are many areas like Katine in Uganda which are even more accessible than Katine itself. These areas receive some coverage in the print and electronic media, but not on the front page as *The Guardian* was doing. This was/is because Katine news, like all other development news, does not sell papers as much as politics. So, primarily, *The Guardian*'s development journalism project was intended to be a fundraising initiative. It was also meant to be an educational diary of how the £2.5m funding was being spent on improving Katine livelihoods, education, health, water and governance; how development operates; and how the lives of villagers themselves were being affected by the development initiatives (Ford, 2007). The Katine communication process involved five key components: the Research and Reporting Team (comprising Ugandan journalist Richard Kavuma working for the Kampala-based *Weekly Observer; The Guardian* and *Observer* journalists); the Moderator (Rick Davies who independently monitored the implementation of projects in the community); the Fundraising Section (allowed readers to make donations or raise money for the Katine Project); the Documentation Team (which supported the journalists reports but also captured audio and video texts in order to enable readers take a virtual tour of Katine); and the Audience Interaction Initiative (that comprised the Katine Chronicles Blog that allowed audience feedback to the Katine site or Project) (Ford, 2007).

The content of Katine reports revolved around informing, educating, monitoring implementation of development projects and mobilising resources. The reports themselves comprised auto-ethnographic and reflexive accounts that allow the subaltern voices to be heard. Actually, Rubsridger (2007) talks about exploring "inside the lives of those who live in Katine". Such kind of approach, pioneered in subject-generated documentaries in anthropology in the 1950s, enables a construction of history from below (Thompson, 1963) by capturing the subjectivity, the experience and the consciousness of those who live through the development problems. The reports themselves have been supported by photographic texts that are, at the depiction level, seemingly empowering, unlike the condescending representations that have

become a hallmark of orientalist representations of 'the other' —
dirty looking, hungry and unhappy faces or suffering women and
children.

Katine reports on the one hand, have attempted to balance the
need to tell the truth about the reality of the abject material conditions in a place neglected by even the central Ugandan government,
and on the other, to tell empowering stories that depict and represent Africans as very strong individuals who are working hard
to improve their lives; that despite their poverty, they are happy,
family-oriented, love sports and are working hard to improve their
lot. The screen print (Figure 2.1) shows the Katine online page.

Figure 2.1: *The Guardian* **Katine Project**

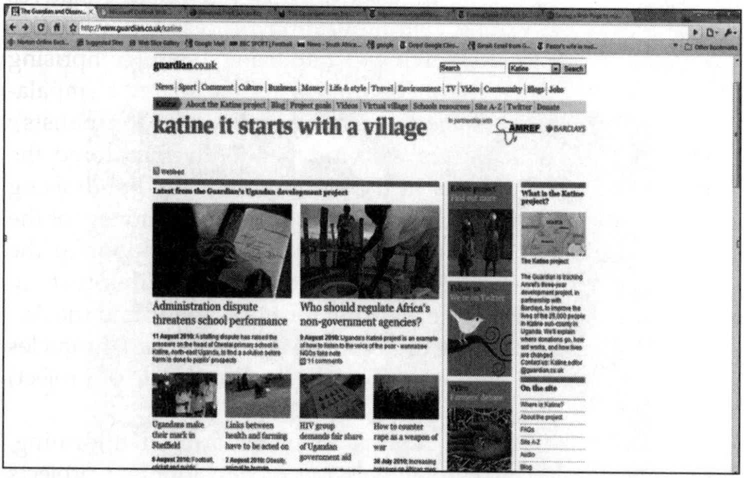

Source: www.guardian.co.uk/katine (accessed on 12 April 2012).

The Guardian has also attempted to demonstrate that it is possible to report a people's experiences and their struggle with modernity without subscribing to orientalist significatory regimes
that create spectacles of both the other as subjects as well as their
suffering (Chouliaraki, 2006; Ford, 2007; Rusbridger, 2007). The
articles identify subjects by their names, their individuality, their
hopes and aspirations for the future, the past that haunts them and
their dreams for the community. The subject-generated reporting

is evident in the story published on 14 May 2008, in which *The Guardian* discusses the issues of traditional birth attendants in relation to maternal and child mortality very sensitively, by focusing on the efforts of those who are doing something about the problem of lack of proper health service provision by the government, an endemic feature of African governments, especially in Uganda (See Figure 2.2).

Figure 2.2: A Typical *Guardian* Development Report on Katine

Midwife training delivers safer childbirth

A local health worker explains how the Katine project is helping improve survival rates for mothers and newborn children

Josephine Achen, known as Sister Josephine, is 60 years old and was featured in the original Guardian Katine supplement. She was born in Ochuloi village in Katine sub-county and became a traditional birth attendant (TBA) after she delivered her own baby at home by herself. She is highly respected in the community and supports and trains many other TBAs in Katine.

"Yoga" (Hello!) she says excitedly, as she extends her hand to us. "You should have told me you were coming, I would

(Figure 2.2 Contd.)

(Figure 2.2 Contd.)

have dressed up!" Josephine is proud of her work and clearly has a new-found confidence in her skills and experience.

"I got training about 11 years ago," she tells us. "I was trained to sensitise mothers on family planning, and on referrals in case of complications. So many mothers came to us after that."

Skilled and motivated midwives are a vital health resource in Uganda, where the maternal mortality rate is very high and more than one in 10 children die before their fifth birthday. But as Sister Josephine told us: "We had been promised refresher training but that never happened."

Amref recently ran a week-long training course for TBAs in Katine. Josephine participated in the course and clearly enjoyed the experience. "I learned so much! We were trained on hygiene practices — for example, if a mother is bleeding, that we should wear gloves to prevent HIV transmission. We got training on how to deliver babies using locally available resources, then how to weigh the baby and record their weight."

The course also taught midwives how to recognise pregnancy danger signs, and when to refer a mother to a local health centre. Just last month Josephine recognised a mother who was having difficulty giving birth, and referred her to the main hospital in Soroti. "I saw the uterus was really small and she was unable to push the child. I heard they had to operate on her in the end and both mother and baby are alive now."

The new training also offered information on how pregnant women can protect themselves against diseases like malaria. As Josephine explained, "I now always advise mothers to get mosquito nets for themselves during pregnancy and for their babies after delivery. I tell them to ask their husbands to get them." She went on to discuss other ways in which the Katine project is making a difference to local people's lives.

"One of the changes I have seen is that a number of communities around here have clean water now, so less people seem to be getting ill with diseases. Village health teams have

(Figure 2.2 Contd.)

(Figure 2.2 Contd.)

> been visiting us, training us on the importance of having and
> using a pit latrine at home, and good hygiene and sanitation.
> It means we are avoiding getting diseases like diarrhoea."
>   When asked what she would like to say to all the people
> who have donated to the project, she responds: "Tell them"
> (and here she speaks excitedly in English) "Sister Josephine
> is greeting you all, thank you!"

Source: http://www.guardian.co.uk/katine/2008/may/14/life?INTCMP=SRCH (accessed on 12 April 2012).

At the same time, the articles also demonstrate the depth of despair, the corruption in the community, the criticisms against local NGOs who are conducting training workshops to teach cassava growing to people who know more about growing the crop than any of the workshop facilitators. The articles themselves are also diaries of stories and anecdotes of Katine inhabitants told in styles that capture the past, the present and the future as seen from the eyes of those who live through those experiences (Thompson, 1963).

Questions have been raised about the Katine Project both on the implementation of development on the ground and in the manner in which *The Guardian* has reported development.[2] To what extent

---

[2]I have been privileged to attend some public sessions in which the Katine Community Project has been discussed. In 2008, POLIS, the journalism and society think tank based in the LSE's Department of Media and Communications organised a small discussion session on the project that brought together AMREF, Farm-Africa, *The Guardian* and Barclays representatives. In 2009, another discussion session was organised by POLIS in the Old Theatre, which saw key *Guardian* people working on the project, Eliza Anyangwe and Elizabeth Ford present the project to staff and students taking development-related subjects. In 2010, I took my development communication class to visit *The Guardian* Media offices where Liz Ford and Eliza Anyangwe also presented a talk on the project. Towards the end of 2010, another POLIS dialogue brought in Elizabeth Ford to the New Theatre, where I was a respondent to her Katine presentation. Importantly, *The Guardian* would organise in late 2010 a huge event where I was on the panel that 'looked back' on what Katine had achieved in its three-year span. Meanwhile, I have had numerous opportunities of interacting with the Katine journalist, Richard Kavuma (who has been studying in London after the project) on his experiences on the project.

are Ugandan local media reporting on Katine and other development projects? How can *Guardian* journalists be critical of the work
of Farm-Africa and AMREF if they are 'embedded' in the work of
the same organisations that sponsor their field trips to this village? To what extent do Katine villagers challenge *The Guardian,*
AMREF, Barclays and FARM-AFRICA discourses about development implementation in the community and the development
reports themselves? Do Katine villagers, especially the majority,
who cannot read and write English, access the reports about their
own lives and communities? Are the *Guardian*–Barclays–AMREF–
FARM-AFRICA initiatives promoting dependency instead of radical transformation of communities? These questions are important considering that apart from very few community members
who participated in live online discussions with *Guardian* journalists on what was going on in Katine, it should be pointed out that
no community members were invited to *The Guardian* premises to
participate in a public assessment of the project in late 2010.

Emerging from these Katine experiences, the Bill Gates Foundation has funded another development reporting initiative, Global
Development (http://www.guardian.co.uk/global-development),
in which the focus is on using *The Guardian* newspaper as a facility
for tracking global efforts at meeting the Millennium Development
Goals (MDGs). These eight goals encompass: eradicating extreme
poverty and hunger; achieving universal primary education; promoting gender equality and empowering women; reducing child
mortality rate; improving maternal health; combating HIV and
AIDS, malaria and other diseases; ensuring environmental sustainability; and developing a global partnership for development.
Supplementing the Global Development work of *The Guardian* are
the various development practitioners and researchers who have
experienced and observed the implementation of specific projects.
Apart from being available on *The Guardian* online site, Global Development can also be accessed through Facebook and followed
through Twitter. The project also has its own network of institutions that produce development material, some of whose content
is republished on *The Guardian.*

The organisations in this network include: the Centre for Global
Development (http://www.cgdev.org/); the Institute of Development Studies (http://www.ids.ac.uk/); the Inter Press Service (http://
www.ips.org/); the humanitarian news and analysis service, IRIN

Global (http://www.irinnews.org/); Panos London (http://www.panos.org.uk/); Women News Network (http://womennewsnetwork.net/); and the sustainable development news service of the AllAfrica.com (http://allafrica.com/sustainable/). Unlike the Katine Project, in which a local Ugandan journalist, Richard Kavuma, was based at the specific project site of Katine, where he observed and wrote his development reports, the Global Development Project has London-based journalists tracking the work of governments, institutions and NGOs as they design and implement various development projects. Most of the articles are no longer ethnographic nor the history from below analyses of development in process, but rather factual reports, opinion pieces and analyses by non-participant and expert observers.

The NGOs as Development News Organisations: Perhaps in response to the rising humanitarian crises that often overwhelm traditional transnational/Western media when it comes to unpacking their sheer complexity, there has been a steady increase in the role played by international development organisations working on the ground in the global south, who have become key media players, especially in conflict areas. In places such as Zimbabwe, Central African Republic, Democratic Republic of Congo or Somalia, international media correspondents often lack access due to many reasons: lack of proper accommodation, impassable roads, lack of knowledge of the remotest areas or fear of violence (Chambers, 1981). Davidson (2009) raised two important facts that augment Chambers' (1981) observations. He advances two key arguments: first is that journalists and media practitioners lack space for professional reflexivity, as they live in a "media bubble that is short-term, deadline-driven and have never taken the time to engage with the wider debate about what we do" (Davidson, 2009: n.p.). Second, he contends that the conventional development policy "acknowledges the increasing importance of international NGOs in news gathering" (Davidson, 2009: n.p.). There are two crucial implications regarding these two observations. The first implication regards the contention that mainstream journalists (working for local and international media) focus on meeting the mercantile demands of news media and do not necessarily have the time (and of course, the resources) to carry out in-depth and reflexive investigations into how their practice and professional values impact on development reporting. Chambers (1981) introduced the notion of 'rural development tourism', referring to the failure of major development institutions to establish the facts surrounding development dilemmas, largely because 'real' poverty and development are hidden behind officialdom, the impassable road networks, language barriers and public relations performances put up by local and central government officials. The second implication, more relevant to this specific discussion, is that international NGOs are beginning to play a critical role in news gathering and development reporting as part of their advocacy initiatives. This is largely due to the fact that international news correspondents do not have the time, the resources and the patience to observe and document development stories in the remotest parts of the global south (Chambers, 1981; Loo, 2009). The NGOs in question benefit from the presence of front-line officers working on the ground (allowing them the experience of Peirce's semiotic *firstness*), their relatively objective knowledge of local people and development issues at play (including knowledge of local language) and their understanding of local politics, all of which place them in a privileged position to report on the experience in question.

The NGOs are also increasingly becoming involved in reporting on and about the global south as a way of bringing to the fore human rights abuses and other forms of crises in order to motivate global pity and action urgently (Chouliaraki, 2010). Chouliaraki (2010) argues that distant events and crises are mediated to Western audiences through television, by allowing these audiences to experience pity for certain Western-related events whilst leaving others outside the West's remit of emotion and action. For Chouliaraki, pity therefore, becomes a commodity. As a consequence, even though television news contribute to global efforts to alleviate such suffering (examples in the case of Tsunami), more often than not, Western news reproduce Eurocentric hierarchies of place and human life. Similarly, Mamdani (2007) points out the representations regarding humanitarian crises such as the Darfur Conflict/Genocide, by Western/international media and NGOs, have covert imperial and ideological motivations. He argues that compared to almost similar political conflicts elsewhere (such as Iraq) that have seen Western media institutions and human rights organisations calling for a withdrawal of foreign troops, the conflict in Darfur has seen overwhelming support for military intervention. This is largely due to what Mamdani (2007) terms the consequences of the politics of 'naming', which is determined by who does the naming, who is being named and the implications of such naming. In the case of Darfur, the regime of 'naming' has seen the emergence of international campaigns to 'Save Darfur' that suffer from de-politicisation, naturalisation and demonisation of the conflicts and its key protagonists (Mamdani, 2007). The implication of such humanitarian communication is not to elicit public pity but rather global/public anger and of course, humanitarian intervention. For Mamdani (2007), the root causes of the Darfur conflict have to be understood in terms of power contestation among local elites as well as over recourses; therefore, humanitarian intervention would never address these root causes.

Likewise, Suzman (2002/2003) discusses the politics of naming in relation to the tension between the Botswana government and its attempts to develop and modernise Central Kalahari Bushmen communities. The tension has seen the Botswana government at loggerheads with Western/international human rights institutions over the issue of the first peoples of the Kalahari, especially with regards to the 'development' of these indigenous populations and their subsequent integration into modern society (Suzman, 2002/2003). The modernist perspective of the Botswana government is based on the assumption that the traditional lifestyles of such indigenous populations are responsible for their underdevelopment and poverty (Suzman, 2002/2003). The traditionalist perspective of these NGOs and international media is that Bushmen communities want to remain traditional—as hunter-gatherers who just want to be left alone.

So, where do we locate the compromise equilibrium when it comes to representing, naming and framing the global south? Building on the concepts of citizens' media and citizen journalism, Beckett (2008) introduces the notion of networked journalism, a practice that calls for the collaboration of professional communicators (journalists and advocacy organisations) and citizens (amateurs) in producing news. For Beckett (2008), traditional journalism has been faced by increasing lack of public trust. A good example has emerged in the political/social conflicts in the

Arab world, starting with the popular uprisings in Iran, followed by Tunisia, Egypt, Algeria, Libya, Bahrain, Yemen, Jordan and Morocco—in which the traditionally dominant news channels have been superseded by citizen voices in articulating what has been going on. In other cases, traditional news channels such as Al Jazeera have ceased being objective and non-participant reporters by becoming active advocates of the revolutions, by siding with and representing events from the perspective of those who have risen up against political dictatorships.

Strand 2: Creative and Educational Reporting

The creative and educational journalism strand refers to organised strategies of using entertaining popular art forms and genres (such as music, comic strips, theatre or drama) in educating the public about development issues. From political economy perspectives, this strand involves subject-matter specialists (in the specific sectoral development), experts in popular art form and journalists who work together to produce entertaining educational content. They do this by drawing on adult education or behaviour change theories so as to influence positive changes in audience knowledge, attitude and practices. Creative and educational reporting also involves partial or minimal consultation of sections of targeted audiences in order to collect background material as well as pretest the development messages and content for relevance. The problem is that such consultations raise fundamental questions on how power relations are conceived in participation, considering the widely established pattern of co-opted notions of participation employed by development and media institutions. This strand comprises of numerous approaches, but the key ones are social communication and theatre for development.

Social Communication

In terms of historical development, this strand can be traced to the development sociology of Lerner (1958, 1971), Schramm (1964) and Rogers (1962). In describing the development aspirations of the Middle East, Lerner (1958) argues that the West is the only and useful blueprint for the creation and expansion of modernity. Similarly, Rogers (1962) describes the communicative mobilisation that leads to acceptance (adoption and diffusion) of new knowledge and technology (innovation) among members of a social group. In development communication, the term 'social communication' can be attributed to the Second Vatican Council (1965a, 1965b) in which the Catholic Church defined media content as that which promotes critical thinking in individuals. Over the years, that aspect of liberation theology has been lost. As it is widely used today, social communication refers to organised efforts by organisations and institutions to use strategic communication approaches to influence positive change in knowledge, attitudes and practices.

The central thesis in social communication is the use of largely Western social marketing models to mobilise and motivate a mass of people towards achieving social, geographic and psychic mobilities within societies. By the 1970s, social psychology would become central in social science experimental research combined with these theoretical trajectories in order to understand how individuals learn and adopt new behaviours. It is by building on these experiments that communication specialists would begin to design and implement social communication projects so as to advance modernity. These approaches would become widely used in agriculture extension, educational communication, adult literacy and health communication. Key to all these models was (and still remains in many ways) the controlled, centralised and strategic generation, management, dissemination and utilisation of new knowledge and technology. A very good example of social communication is the way entertainment–education has been employed in health communication.

Entertainment-education as Social Communication: The employment of entertainment–education in health communication has increased tremendously since the 1970s' discovery of the entertainment-education model within radio and television soap operas in Latin America and the emergence of the theatre for development model in postcolonial Africa and Asia (Singhal and Rogers, 1999). The approach has been consolidated with the establishment of numerous IPGs in North America and Europe specialising in health communication and promotion research, such as the Family Health International, John Hopkins Centre for Communication Programmes, Development Media International, the National Institutes of Health, National Cancer Institute, American Institutes for Research, PCI-Media Impact and so on. Journals such as *Health Communication* and *Studies in Family Planning* have become knowledge centres where Western institutions and their selected southern counterparts provide technical advice towards the design, implementation and evaluation of health communication interventions. This brings up pertinent concerns about cultural imperialism. Cultural imperialism is a strand of postcolonial critique that is concerned with increasing forms of Americanisation, Westernisation and cultural homogenisation, in which Western governments and institutions influence the structure, format and nature of epistemologies, policies and livelihoods in the global south (Fanon, 1960, 1965; Said, 1978). An aspect of self-orientalism and self-inflicted cultural imperialism can be observed in the emergence of southern health communication and promotion organisations established or modelled after Western blueprints.

The geographical location of such IPGs notwithstanding, available evidence points to the preponderance of Western-centric social marketing and social psychology theories and models in global health communication and promotion campaigns (Airhihenbuwa and Obregon, 2000). The dominant 'change' theories still comprise the health belief model, the theory of reasoned action, social learning theory, adoption and diffusion of innovation and technology, theory of planned behaviour, steps to behaviour change, stages of change model and social marketing (Airhihenbuwa and Obregon, 2000). The theories explain how individuals come to learn and consolidate new behaviour and how such an understanding can be used to facilitate the adoption of positive behaviour and practices among new groups and societies. There are four factors that define all these change theories: (*a*) they assume individuality as independent of the community; (*b*) they are rooted in studying observable behaviour; (*c*) they assume that behaviour and social change can be produced and controlled through certain catalysts; and (*d*) they are rooted in Western epistemologies and have tended to ignore or footnote the appreciative enquiry and learning approaches that are indigenous and communitarian. This becomes a convenience for Western evaluators who have to use almost similar evaluation instruments and methodologies (based on these cognitive and rationalistic theories) to develop 'scientific indicators' and evaluate different health communication and promotion programmes in the global south.

The integration of these theories in policy and practice is made possible through strategic communication models such as the P-process or the Soul City model, which, like other southern models, is more or less a localised model of the same P-process. The Health Communication Partnership (HCP) proposed the P-process, which the Johns Hopkins University Centre for Communication Programs (JHU-CCP) defines as a "framework designed to guide communication professionals as they develop a strategic and participatory programme with a measurable impact on the intended audience" (HCP, 2003: 2). The P-Process is most used for the design of health education and communication programmes and comprises five main steps: situation analysis; strategic design; development and testing; implementation and monitoring; and evaluation and replanning (HCP, 2003). The P-Process has usually been applied in entertainment-education, which Singhal and Rogers (1999) define as a process of deliberately designing, producing and implementing media messages in ways that entertain and educate. The aim is to increase knowledge gain among targeted demographic groups, sow favourable attitudes and change overt behaviour in relation to a development issue (Singhal and Rogers, 1999). The institutional industry that promotes this approach consists of government departments, broadcasting institutions, educators and educational institutions, funding and sponsoring organisations (Singhal and Rogers, 1999). A case in point was the Tanzanian health radio drama campaign *Twende na Wakati* (Let's Go With the Times), which ran between 1993 and 1997, or the 1990s Indian radio drama, *Tinka Tinka Sukh* (Happiness Lies in Small Things), or the Peruvian *Bienvenida Salud*, a radio-based campaign against domestic violence in Peru. The next three sections analyse these radio dramas as institutions, as communication processes and as catalysts for behavioural and social change.

Twende na Wakati was a Swahili-language radio drama series that was broadcast on Radio Tanzania Dar es Salaam (RTD) between 1995 and 1999 in Tanzania. It sought to educate, increase awareness and improve health practices in relation to HIV/AIDS prevention, family planning, gender equity, general public health and socio-economic development (Vaughan and Rogers, 2000). As an institution, *Twende na Wakati* radio drama was a collaborative creation of the public broadcaster, RTD; the Ministry of Health; the Ministry of Community Development, Women Affairs and Children; the United Nations Population Fund (UNFPA); the New York-based Population Communications International (PCI) Media Impact and, to an extent, the University of New Mexico and the Population Family Life Education Program (Vaughan and Rogers, 2000). Teams from these organisations were actively involved in all the processes of strategic communication, from developing the concept note, conducting formative research, message development, pretesting, roll-out of communications, monitoring and evaluation and consolidating the communication intervention or planning for other similar communication interventions (Piotrow et al., 1997). The participation of primary stakeholder communities was limited (and is often is) to placation consultation in which delegated institutions seek local information from target audiences that will increase the epistemological legitimacy of the development messages and content. The whole process of formative research, pretesting of communication content and materials and evaluation provided no opportunities for sharing power between the principals (institutions) and subalterns (primary stakeholders).

As a communication process, *Twende na Wakati* was designed as a quasi-experimental survey, in which Dodoma district was 'opportunistically' sampled to function as a comparison/control and hence radio dramas were not broadcast in the district between 1993 and 1995 (Vaughan and Rogers, 2000). It was claimed that the contamination effect, that is, Dodoma residents coming into contact with the radio programme or people who had listened to the programme, was minimised. This raises critical questions about radio listenership. Fanon (1965) describes the important role of memory and narrative in repeating and spreading the clandestine radio reports of the *Voice of Free Algeria* during the Algerian War of Independence. The act of listening to the frequently jammed broadcasts and the repetition of these messages to more people was itself celebrated as an act of participating in the liberation war (Fanon, 1965). This has implications for audience research. There is no demarcation between listeners and non-listeners, since even those who do not directly listen to traditional messages are exposed to the contents through repetition and proceed to repeat the messages as if they were the primary listeners themselves. In the case of Dodoma, mediated interactions probably transformed non-listeners to listeners, thereby raising critical questions about the relevance of the comparison/control sample.

The format of *Twende na Wakati* radio dramas drew heavily on the modernity continuum propounded by Lerner (1958), in which change is unilinear, moving from traditionalism through transitionalism to modernity. In *Twende na Wakati*, like in all entertainment-education dramas, this was achieved through role modelling. Vaughan and Rogers (2000: 86) observe that:

> The characters [...] were designed to provide negative, transitional, and positive role models for HIV prevention behaviours. Negative characters provide models of the consequences of HIV-risky behaviours. For example, the main negative role model in the storyline, Mkwaju (walking stick), is a highly promiscuous truck driver who does not use condoms and who ultimately becomes sick with AIDS. [...] Transitional characters are the key identification characters for the audience and provide self-efficacious models for how to change behaviour for audience members to emulate. Shime, a transitional role model, is a friend of Mkwaju's, who warns him about AIDS and tries unsuccessfully to get him to change his sexual behaviour, as he himself has done. [...] Positive characters act as opinion leaders who provide wise counsel to others. Bina, a nurse (a positive role model), provided accurate counselling to various characters about HIV/AIDS.

Such an approach (traditionalism–transitionalism–modernism) would feed into the evaluation process, during which the largely quantitative assessments would come to a conclusion about certain contestable fundamentals: (*a*) the dramas increased interpersonal communication regarding HIV and AIDS issues within the treatment areas, from 46 per cent in 1994 to 61 per cent in 1995 (Vaughan and Rogers, 2000); and (*b*) the dramas increased adoption of positive behaviours in relation to HIV and AIDS as well as family planning, from 73 per cent in 1994 to 82 per cent in 1995. Such changes in behaviour involved reducing numbers of sexual partners, using condoms or stopping to share razor blades. An important aspect of the evaluation established an improved self-efficacy among audiences regarding their collective belief

in living positively with or preventing HIV and AIDS. A similar institutional communication evaluation approach to health
communication was also implemented in the production of the
television soap opera, *Hum Log* (We People) or the radio drama,
Tinka Tinka Sukh (Happiness Lies in Small Things) in the Indian
subcontinent.

Tinka Tinka Sukh used to be a very popular radio drama serial
comprising 104 episodes in India when it was broadcast on the
27 radio stations affiliated to All India Radio (AIR) in the Hindi-
speaking North India between February 1996 and February 1997,
and it was estimated to have reached over 40 million listeners
(Sood, 2002). Like the Tanzanian *Twende na Wakati* campaign, *Tinka
Tinka Sukh* carried development messages on gender equality,
women's empowerment, dowry-related issues, small family size,
family harmony, environmental conservation, issues facing youth,
community living, substance abuse and HIV and AIDS prevention
(Sood, 2002). As an institution, the production of the radio drama
was made possible by the collaboration of AIR and the PCI Media
Impact (Myers, 2002). Though the input of the American organisation was considered "minimal" (Myers, 2002: 33), its contribution was fundamental, considering the institution's experience
in organising a similar initiative in Tanzania a few years back.
Likewise, the evaluation of the dramas was again a responsibility
of Western institutions, specifically the Universities of Ohio and
New Mexico, where research leaders Arvind Singhal and Everett
Rogers were, respectively, based.

As a communication process, *Tinka Tinka Sukh* was modelled
after so many entertainment–education dramas that place social
change on a linear continuum of modernity conceived by Lerner
(1958) and Schramm (1964). The story is set in a traditional farming
community of Navgaon, "struggling to understand the value of
modern traditions and moving in progressive directions" and this
sets up the scene to examine social change along the Lernerian
model (Singhal and Rogers, 1999: 137). Describing the storyline,
Singhal and Rogers (1999: 137–38) observe:

> Suraj, his father Chaundri, and his mother Chaundhrain, represent
> an ideal family. Whereas Chaundhri and his wife understand the
> role of tradition, progressive ways are growing in importance.
> The couple represents women's causes—anti-dowry, marriage and

divorce, women's empowerment—and the importance of an integrated harmonious community based on co-operation and self sufficiency. [...] This family's virtuous ways earn the loyal support of their poor workers, Jumman and his wife Rukhsana. [...] Chacha, his wife Chachi, and their children Ramlal, Champa, Sundar, Suman and Papu, are the antithesis of the Chaudhris. [...] Chacha believes he is absolved of all parental responsibilities. Chachi is domineering, blindly traditional, and very vocal—the village gossip. [...] The lives of Gareebo, a widow, and her daughters Nandini, Kusum and Lali show the trials of being a woman in a patriarchal society. [...] Tragedy occurs when Poonam is abused by her husband and his parents because her family lacks an adequate dowry. Poonam commits suicide. Sushman [...] finds herself abandoned by her husband, also for dowry. [...] Sushma overcomes her trials and establishes a sewing school, which provides her with economic independence. [...] Ramlal is transformed by the quiet determination of Nandini and realizes his delinquent acts upset the peace of the community.

In evaluating the impact of these dramas, the notion of audience involvement loomed large. For Sood (2002), audience involvement in entertainment–education entails two aspects: affective-referential involvement, and cognitive-critical involvement. Both forms of involvement facilitate an increase in individual and collective self-efficacy and belief as well as interpersonal communication surrounding a development conundrum. The key for Sood (2002) is that involvement refers to both social judgement and participation. Within social marketing, consumer and communication behaviour, audience involvement refers to audience responses, reaction to, conversation on or identification with messages and products (para-social), a development that could unfortunately result in audiences 'participating in participation' itself (Arnstein, 1969). The qualitative and quantitative impact assessment revealed a great degree of individual and collective self-efficacy, increased awareness of development issues and problems, para-social interaction (identification with drama characters) and interpersonal communication regarding issues raised in the dramas (Sood, 2002).

Likewise in Peru, another social communication intervention was designed and implemented as *Bienvenida Salud!* (Welcome to Health!) in the Peruvian Amazon (Davenport Sypher et al., 2002). The origin of the design and implementation of this radio-based health communication project can be traced to the 1990s International Conference on Population and Development in Cairo and the Fourth World Conference on Women in Beijing, both of which emphasised community health development approaches in eradicating social determinants of health. The institutional support came from an American NGO, the Amazonian Peoples' Resources Initiative (APRI), Minga Perú (a community-based health and development organisation), and the United Nations Development Fund for Women (UNIFEM) (Dura, Singhal and Elias, 2008). It should be mentioned that by the time the radio initiative was launched, Minga Perú was already established in 1998 by Eliana Elías and Luis Gonzalez and working towards improving livelihoods of Amazonian populations (Dura, Singhal and Elias, 2008). Minga Peru's central strategy to achieve local development has been through participatory communication, and the name 'Minga' translates 'collaborative community work' (Dura, Singhal and Elias, 2008). The organisation's work is based in the region of Loreto, which suffers from socio-economic marginalisation, extreme poverty, lack of basic and adequate social services and underdevelopment. To combat these challenges, the organisation has taken on a multi-sectoral approach towards development by promoting reproductive health, sexual rights, gender equality, women empowerment (Dura, Singhal and Elias, 2008).

To strengthen its grassroots interventions, Minga Perú also engages in mass media campaigns by producing and broadcasting a radio programme, *Bienvenida Salud*. Alongside this development radio programme are a series of supporting communication processes such as radio listening clubs. The development of this entertainment–education programme has taken local knowledge into consideration, by involving audiences during programme design and also during the whole communication process. Such 'involvement' includes "popular music, contests and raffles, listener letters, recorded testimonials, and news reports from communities" (Davenport Sypher et al., 2002: 196). By doing this, it is expected that *Bienvenida Salud!* will effectively promote community participation and facilitate attitude and behavioural change (Davenport Sypher et al., 2002). In the end, the radio programme becomes part of a larger communication intervention operating at the community level through community-based facilitators (peer promoters) and development workers. As has been the case elsewhere, radio listening clubs reify the reception and legitimacy of radio messages, as is the case in Loreto, where clubs have been formed to listen to and promote the development initiatives promoted in the *Bienvenida Salud!* The network of development workers, therefore, links the entertainment–education radio programme to the actual development interventions on the ground, such as organising and facilitating workshops and technical apprenticeships on reproductive health, safe motherhood, domestic violence and community mobilisation (Davenport Sypher et al., 2002).

The radio programme itself is based on real-life events that come up from community promoters in the communities, through research and also through letters contributed to the programme by listeners. Dura, Singhal and Elias (2008) observe that such contributions are then woven into a short social drama that is spiced with catchy jingles, music, informational spots, testimonials and contests in order to increase the programme's appeal among audiences. The actual drama content is structured in a way that builds up a development challenge and then demonstrates how to deal with it. An episode "might discuss how pregnancy happens, how to prevent it, how to manage an abusive relationship, or what to do when your child has diarrhoea" (Dura, Singhal and Elias, 2008: 9).

The evaluation of *Bienvenida Salud!* has, like most social communication interventions implemented in the global south, been led by or carried out by external institutions. Dura, Singhal and Elias (2008) from the University of Texas (El Paso) carried out a more qualitative assessment of the impact of the radio programme in relation to community development and social change. A more quantitative evaluation was executed by scholars from University of Kansas in collaboration with the Directors of APRI and Minga-Perú (Davenport Sypher et al., 2002). The funding as well came from American institutions, the David and Lucile Packard Foundation, the Global Health Program of the Bill and Melinda Gates Foundation and the University of Kansas.

Theatre for Development as Creative Journalism

The developmental uses of theatre in Africa emerged as theatre and folk media for social mobilisation when Travelling Theatres in Anglophone universities started developing concepts of 'taking theatre to the people', otherwise known as theatre for development (Kamlongera, 1988; Manyozo, 2002; Mda, 1993). Theatre for development has been described as those non-formal educational approaches that draw on popular culture, art and other forms of performances in order to sensitise communities to improve their status quo (Kamlongera, 1988; Manyozo, 2002; Mda, 1993). In theory and practice, theatre for development becomes a discourse that challenges local people to, in Freirean (1996) terms, *speak* and *unspeak* local development conundrums. This book recognises that theatre for development can be discussed both under *media for development* and *participatory communication* approaches. Where the model deals with the development of messages that are packaged in theatre and drama products in order to influence changes in knowledge, attitude and behaviour so as to improve livelihoods, theatre for development falls under the media for development approach, especially under the creative journalism strand. And where theatre for development is employed as an instrument of participatory action research, it falls under the community engagement approach.

In this chapter, theatre for development is being posited as an approach within the creative journalism strand that draws on folk media and other oral and interpersonal forms of communication in order to facilitate behavioural and social change in communities. Kamlongera (2005) observes that the theatre for development paradigm owes its origin to three factors during the colonisation process: (*a*) the colonial attempts to modernise Africans through drama/theatre; (*b*) the recognition by colonialists and missionaries that indigenous knowledges had positive elements that they could incorporate into dramas and plays in order to teach good morals to indigenous peoples; and (*c*) indigenous responses to colonial attempts to develop them through drama. Yet, these colonial perceptions of 'good elements' of indigenous knowledges prevailed even after independence, and became a feature of governmental and non-governmental approaches towards creating developmental theatre. In fact, in 1974, a workshop organised in New Delhi (Valbuena, 1986: 9–10) articulated some 'Principles in Using Folk Media for Development Communication', among which were:

> Folk media should be an integral part of any communication programme for rural development. [...] The utilization of folk media in

communication programmes should be viewed not only from the perspective of socio-economic development but also cultural development. [...] Folklore injects the changes that society undergoes. [...] Not all folk forms can be used for developmental or population communication purposes; thus they should be carefully studied [...] for their possible adaptation in order to carry developmental or population messages. [...] Their utilization should be related to local events, and their function in the local communication strategy should be properly assigned. [...] Collaboration between the folk artists and the media producers is absolutely essential for the successful integration of folk media and mass media communication strategies for developmental purposes.

The evolution of the theatre for development movement after independence in Africa and Asia coincided with dictatorial regimes that had inherited weak social-economic systems. Political ideologies demanded that resources and services patriotically support national development goals, and that included the mobilisation of folk and indigenous media as communication for development (Valbuena, 1986). In the Philippines, folk media resources that were (and continue to be) co-opted in the country's theatre for development models comprised the *Zarzuela* (musical play), *Cancionan* (song and verse argumentation), *Balagtasan* (poetic debate), the *Balitao* (courtship debate), *Bantayonon* (poetic debate) and puppet theatre (Valbuena, 1986). Institutions such as the University of the Philippines and other regional universities have collaborated with various government ministries and departments; development organisations have used theatre to promote development themes in family planning, agrarian reforms, nutrition education and other developmental themes.

Mda (1993) is concerned with the different levels at which Theatre for Development (TFD) can be conceived and practised. Mda lists five TFD methodologies: agitprop, participatory agitprop, simultaneous dramaturgy, forum theatre and comgen theatre. Agitprop involves university students or any other extension workers going into villages, setting up camp, conducting research and then privately analysing collected data, preparing plays and presenting them to villages in pre-packaged form. Mda (1993) admits that with such an approach, there is always little or no conscientisation. Participatory agitprop is an advanced stage of agitprop but selected villagers work with extension workers whom Mda refers to as development agents. Simultaneous dramaturgy and forum theatres require full participation of villagers at all stages during which there is a provision for switching roles—spectators becoming actors temporarily. Comgen theatre is performed by community members without outside influence. Much as it may educate the spectators, this type is mainly for entertainment. From Mda's (1993) definitions, emerge two approaches of theatre for development: the externally driven and organic models.

From a political economy perspective, the *externally driven models* of TFD are characterised by NGO funding in which the agenda setting and delegation of power in these developmental theatre projects rest with the funding agencies and departments. This includes the choice of sites, the length of campaigns, the structure of consultations and the nature of development messages, which in some cases, have to be verified by 'message experts'. For example, Kamlongera (1988) details how, with funding from the Malawi government, the Chancellor College Travelling Theatre employed TFD to sensitise people of Mbalachanda community in northern Malawi on the newly built rural growth centre by the same name. Likewise, Mda (1993) discusses how, with the Morotholi Travelling Theatre, he toured Lesotho, sensitising communities on sanitation, alcoholism and health, among other issues. In Tanzania, Mlama (1971) relates how traditional modes of communication have contributed to sustaining culture and development. While linking popular theatre to TFD, Mlama (1971) argues that TFD is the employment of theatrical expressions at the grassroots level in order to research and analyse development problems—to create critical awareness and potential for action to solve those problems. Just like Kamlongera (1988, 2005), Mlama's conceptualisation and approach is straightforward: outsiders go into the community and stay there for a few days, during which time, they must know the people and their culture and then produce plays around familiar themes—but coupled with development messages.

On the other hand, *organic models* of TFD result from the collective creativity of local people (sometimes with the help of professional directors) in which theatre is employed to critically analyse not just the socio-economic issues but even question the development discourse itself. This is the radical model propagated by Augusto Boal (1979) in his treatise, *Theatre of the Oppressed*. Oftentimes such a model has been used to undermine oppressive political hegemonies.

In apartheid South Africa, playwrights such as Mbongeni Ngema, Robert McLaren and Athol Fugard developed the workshop approach in which student or township actors engaged in intensive and deliberative creative processes in developing highly political plays that shed light on how black people were suffering under the system (Kruger, 1999). Space Theatre in Cape Town or Market Theatre in Johannesburg became sites where such political plays were performed, with some of them ending up being censored or eventually banned. For Kruger (1999), such drama and the resultant performances constituted 'testimonial theatre', one that evolved organically to act as a key witness to the anti-apartheid struggle.

In Kenya, such testimonial theatre emerged in the 1970s, during the height of dictatorship, marked by arbitrary arrests, imprisonment, disappearance and harassment of those who raised moral and political questions against political oppression. For Ngugi wa Thiong'o (1993), testimonial theatre is a postcolonial space and discourse where local people conduct public examinations of their societies. Ngugi reminisces how, as a lecturer at the University of Nairobi in 1982, one old woman from Kamiriithu community urged him to provide the community with 'education for the uneducated'. He teamed up with Ngugi wa Miiri and wrote a script for the people of Kamiriithu, but further discussions and debates involving villagers resulted in the creation of *Maitu Njugira* (Mother, Sing for Me) (Bjorkman, 1989). This project followed in the footsteps of *Ngahiika Ndeenda* (I Will Marry When I Want) (Bjorkman, 1989), which the Kenyan government had banned in 1977. Through *Maitu Njugira* and *Ngahiika Ndeenda*, Ngugi's focus was on the process of creating the performance and the extent to which villagers identified with or participated in the production process. The community reworked the scripted story, adding things that meant much to them, thereby removing unnecessary details and preserving local memories. They recreated the story to suit their conception of the world, from problem identification to implementing proposed solutions. Through the creation process, the villagers were able to educate themselves (Wa Thiong'o, 1993).

Unlike Valbuena (1986), Kamlongera (1988), Mda (1993) and Mlama (1971), who emphasise the centrality of Travelling Theatres in collecting information and perfecting a performance, Ngugi (1993) defines it as one created by and for the people in their own language. Like Kruger's (1999) concept of testimonial theatre, Ngugi's definition reflects Augusto Boal's (1979) concept of community theatre, which he calls 'poetics of the oppressed', thereby giving us three Freirean (1972) concepts of community theatre: theatre as a weapon, as a discourse and as a postcolonial public sphere where local people design realistic development strategies. Community members interpret and reconstruct their lives rather than strangers coming to advise—otherwise, theatre for development would be reduced to a form of cultural imperialism (Manyozo, 2002).

Strand 3: Indigenous Knowledge Communication Systems (IKCS)

The third media for development strand involves the media and communications that are rooted in local and indigenous epistemology, prior to being co-opted by external organisations and institutions. Such indigenous knowledge has always had educational elements that catalyse communities to adopt knowledge and practice that could strengthen communities, lead to bumper harvests, protect women and children, avoid unplanned pregnancies, become good citizens and other positive messages. This section examines these organic media for development approaches as indigenous knowledge communication systems (IKCS). The section expresses concern with the preponderance of modernisation epistemologies and strategies towards media for development in which IKCS are footnoted, sampled and selected from the perspective of Western media for development theories and frameworks.

In mainstream development and media/communication discourses, past and current research on indigenous knowledge has been conceived within the binary axis of *descriptive commodification* on one hand and *analytical perspective* on the other. On the basis of descriptive commodification, indigenous knowledge is homogenised and oftentimes orientalised, and described as the ways of living, thinking and perceiving as practised by indigenous people, who, in classical anthropology and development, refer to very traditional, rural, uncivilised and underdeveloped societies and communities (Finnegan, 1970; Malinowski, 1926; Pottier, 2003; Sillitoe, 2002; Tomaselli, 2006; Warren, 1991). It is sometimes known as traditional or local knowledge, citizen science or primitive epistemology (Sillitoe, 2002). This perspective treats indigenous knowledge as material Weltanschauung, a sort of commodity that comprises a "unique formulation of knowledge coming from a range of sources rooted in local cultures, a dynamic and ever changing pastiche of past tradition and present invention with a view to the future" (Sillitoe, 2002: 113). Likewise, Pottier (2003: 4) describes local knowledge as "people's understanding of the social universe and also their rights". Indigenous knowledge has, therefore, been conceptualised as the way of knowing that a social group generates and accumulates over generations of living in an environment, allowing them explain the essential and existential phenomena.

The second level of conceptualisation is the analytical perspective, in which indigenous knowledge is a postcolonial perspective that aims to carry out two specific tasks: first, it is an attempt to 'move the centre', that is, to reject the generalisation and universalisation of Western experience of history and the subsequent localisation of the heterogeneous 'other' experiences (Wa Thiong'o, 1993). The second task is to enable scholars to understand power — the operations of "structures of domination and control and resistance" (Wa Thiong'o, 1993: 25). As a postcolonial perspective in communication, indigenous knowledge (in plural) provides an opportunity to "rethink communication through new visions and revisions, through new histories and geographies" (Shome and Hedge, 2002: 249). Such knowledge incorporates the heteroglossia of voices, the plurality of traditions and practices, the multi-accentuality of speech and discourses, especially by subalterns. As such, the postcoloniality of indigenous knowledge lies in its ability to 'interrupt' dominant and institutionalised knowledge and its discourses (Shome and Hedge, 2002) and also transformatively work towards recovering 'history from below' (Thompson, 1963) and as a political attempt to decolonise the process of naming the world (Mamdani, 2007; Wa Thiong'o, 1993). This interruption not only targets modernity itself but also the dominant theoretical and methodological approaches, even within the postcolonial approaches towards indigenous knowledge themselves (Shome and Hedge, 2002).

While this discussion recognises the importance of describing and categorising indigenous knowledge in their plurality, it nevertheless attempts to understand the implication of power within their political economy—but to do this, it is important to employ strategic essentialism (Spivak, 1988), even though there is not really a singular and homogenous category of analysis termed indigenous knowledge. Building on Mansell's (2004) approach towards political economy of communication, this discussion identifies the four different mediation processes within which such knowledge operates: (*a*) the content of that knowledge; (*b*) the functions, rules and regulations governing its generation and management; (*c*) the skills required to sustain that knowledge; and (*d*) the power structures and relationships within which it is generated, managed and utilised (Brokensha, Warren and Werner, 1980; Warren, 1991). For Mansell (2004), mediation allows the production and reproduction of symbolic forms of power. To understand this process, it becomes necessary to study the institutions and structures that frame the mediation processes allowing for the brokerage and sustenance of indigenous knowledge—the indigenous knowledge communication systems themselves.

For Warren (1991), indigenous knowledge, unlike scientific knowledge, is locally produced, "unique to a given culture", passed down the generations and formulates a springboard in community decision-making. Like Warren, other scholars (Brokensha, Warren and Werner, 1980; Finnegan, 1970) have conceptualised such knowledge in binary opposition to scientific knowledge, based on the nature of its generation, management, administration and exchange, how phenomena are observed, studied and categorised. Because of its peculiar nature to be embedded in the local metaphysical, indigenous knowledge has been presented as an antithesis to scientific and rational knowledge. However, Pottier (2003) and Sillitoe (2002) prefer to examine indigenous and exogenous knowledges as part of one continuum of knowledge whose distinct characteristics are only observable under different contexts. This chapter, however, distinguishes knowledge (process of knowing) from information (the knowledge codes that allow transmission of knowledge between and among persons) (Mundy and Compton, 1995;

Tomaselli, 2006). Indigenous knowledge is not generated, brokered and sustained for the sake of it; it is rooted within the development of social cohesion and capital in that particular community. It constructs, explains and mediates questions of discipline and justice, law and order, rights and responsibility, citizenship and identity, politics and economics or the spirit and the real (Pottier, 2003; Sillitoe 2002). As such, indigenous knowledge systems are complex, plural, heterogeneous and display some non-linguistic characteristics, which makes them difficult to capture (Finnegan, 1970; Pottier, 2003).

Indigenous knowledge is not necessarily local knowledge. Local knowledge evolves reactively and experientially in response to specific challenges a people are facing in a particular geographical locale. All indigenous knowledge is, however, local, as it evolves organically within a specific time epoch, space, context and ecology. It is tied to the metaphysical and spiritual system of a specific people. Such that even when a people with shared indigenous knowledge practices are separated by time and space, they still retain almost similar traditions and norms, though they might modify some aspects to respond to the environment or context. Indigenous knowledge, therefore, builds on years of accumulated experience and passing down of that knowledge across generations (Pottier, 2003; Sillitoe, 2002). When perceived outside their context, indigenous knowledges appear backward, barbaric and retrogressive, but when rooted within their belief system, take on a deeper and important meaning (Finnegan, 1970, Marglin, 1990). This is an important consideration as it has implications for the debate on the epistemological validity and scientific objectivity of indigenous knowledges, which are, in part, shaped by "the outsiders' prejudice which leads to labels such as backward" (Marglin, 1990: 15).

From the perspectives of descriptive commodification and postcolonial perspectives, indigenous knowledge is created, modified, used and shared across the generations through a series of overt and covert communicative practices and performances known as indigenous knowledge communication systems. Mundy and Compton (1995) define such communication systems as the organically developed 'elaborate ways' through which society transmits technical and non-technical information among its members for purposes of informing, educating and entertaining them. For traditionalists, IKCS refers to those communication systems that exist outside of modernity or those that existed before the arrival of mass media (Mundy and Compton, 1995; Wang, 1982). Also known as indigenous communication systems (Adjaye, 2008), traditional systems of oral communication (Kamlongera et al., 1992), indigenous media (Ansu-Kyeremeh, 1994), oral literature (Finnegan, 1970) or oramedia (Ugboajah, 1985), IKCS have in-built media and communication systems that are rooted in orality, memory and narrative, such as folk media, village meetings, griot performances, poetry and storytelling, open market places, proverbs or drumbeating. These communication systems often perform positive or negative social functions within an indigenous knowledge system, mostly related to advancement of, especially within African contexts, ubuntu communitarianism, in which "humans depend completely on one another for their development", but at the same time, individuals are seen as part of the community whilst respecting their particular attributes (Christians, 2004: 243). In this case, then, individual freedom only exists insofar as it is used to help others advance (Christians, 2004). Whilst some of these communication systems informed by ubuntu communitarianism can be seen to be retrogressive and perpetuate subjugation and dehumanisation, others are empowering and offer space to the subaltern to contend and challenge the micro and macro forms of hegemony. For modernists, it becomes necessary to modernise media and communication systems in the global south in order to avoid a return to these indigenous systems of communication (that subsequently reject the liberal independent subject for the communitarian individual), which could hamper economic growth. For post-developmentalists (in entertainment-education, agriculture extension or public health), such communication systems can be harnessed to facilitate processes of mobility, especially in relation to adoption and diffusion of new knowledge and technology.

From the *descriptive commodification* perspective, IKCS ideally function to generate, transfer and share knowledge within that social system. Wa Thiong'o (1993) observes the centrality of indigenous communications emerging organically as people attempt to make sense of their immediate reality thereby allowing them to use such communications to share 'moral, aesthetic and ethical values'. Wang (1982) and Mundy and Compton (1995) contend that IKCS transmit technical information, entertain, pass on news, persuade and announce important events and exchanges. That means to understand IKCS, ethnographic research methods are required in order to comprehend what Malinowski (1926) and Kamlongera et al. (1992) describe as the complex arrangements and relationships in which culture is produced, administered, shared and maintained. Even these ethnographic approaches are continually being challenged by forces of nationalism and colonialism; hence, the very methodological approaches for engaging with indigenous knowledges are constantly being contested and challenged constantly (Shome and Hedge, 2002). Oftentimes, however, dominant systems and institutions have approached IKCS with a modernisation frame, conceiving them as unitary, unbounded, static, consensual, non-reflective, unscientific and traditional (Ascroft, 1974; Freire, 1972, 1996; Pottier 2003; Sillitoe 2002). The Western assumption is that, on their own, indigenous systems are not capable of explaining sociopolitical phenomena, unless repackaged within the lens of Western modernity (Ascroft, 1974; Fanon, 1960, 1965; Freire, 1972; Lerner, 1958; Schramm, 1964).

As a postcolonial perspective, indigenous knowledge allows us to go beyond the *organicness* of their development, but move towards the recognition of the constant *hybridity* between such knowledge and other forms of knowledge (including other indigenous knowledges). This offers an opportunity to question the role of indigenous knowledge in challenging the way we think about colonisation and power not just as linear processes, but also as contradictory processes that offer space for negotiation and subversion (Mbembe, 2001; Shome and Hedge, 2002) as well as achieving aesthetic 'extraversion' (Pejout, 2010), in which indigenous knowledges from one context are adopted and adapted by other indigenous knowledges in other contexts. A case in example is Kizomba, a sensual dance that evolved in Angola in the 1980s but has now been adapted and extraverted with Argentinean tango, European dancehall and Spanish salsa by young men and women of African, Caribbean, Brazilian, Portuguese and European heritage. As a postcolonial perspective, indigenous knowledge demonstrates that colonisation was and continues to be a contradictory process of subjugation, consent and compromise that sometimes renders both the coloniser and the colonised impotent (Mbembe, 2001).

Whilst the *descriptive commodification* perspective acknowledges the direct functional connection between IKCS and the immediate local community (local control and technology are developed locally and often serve local social objectives) (Mundy and Compton, 1995), the postcolonial perspective demonstrates that the process of brokering such knowledge is not confined to specific geographical locale (Mbembe, 2001; Wa Thiong'o, 1993). As is the case with Kizomba dance, indigenous knowledge exchange and utilisation is determined by their *aesthetic malleability*, that is, they are easily modified, recreated and re-brokered to suit other time and space contexts. What unites them is not the nature, form and objectives of performances and texts, but the centrality of the collective individual as defined within the ubuntu communitarianism (Christians, 2004). Kamlongera et al. (1992) provide an example of *gulewamkulu* initiation ceremonies in Malawi and the *egwugwu* in Nigeria, in which their indigenous communications mediate a tenuous relationship between ritual and theatre, the real and unreal, the global and the local, even though they are separated by time and space. Composers of indigenous texts or directors of performances remain unknown as individuals because communities do not attach much importance to individual authorship, and this has implications for debates on intellectual property rights within IKCS.

Three Forms of Indigenous Knowledge Communications

Available evidence suggests that there are three kinds of indigenous knowledges, which consequently generate three different indigenous communication forms. These three knowledge forms are: (*a*) *common knowledge*; (*b*) *technical* and *non-specialised* (governance); and (*c*) *privileged* and *specialised* knowledge.

Common Knowledge and Information: *Common knowledge* refers to information and messages produced and consumed within Wa Thiong'o's (1993: 25) 'particularities' and Mbembe's (2001) 'banality' of daily lived experience. These include open public forums such as announcements at the village headman's ground, children's games, public or private chatting, pounding, hunting, dancing, singing or working. Such knowledge is aimed at giving community members a sense of local identity and citizenship, by increasing their levels of social capital and thereby strengthening their social and knowledge infrastructure. It empowers individuals to increase their investment in their communities and help them to identify with a geographical and familial sense of community. For example, among the Afar people of north-eastern Ethiopia, there exists the *Dagu* system, an informal but a very 'sophisticated' communication process that has proved influential in disseminating local, national and global news (Menbere and Skjerdal, 2008). The *Dagu*'s unwritten rules oblige travellers and strangers to sit down, share a drink and any important news that must not be fabricated (Menbere and Skjerdal, 2008).

Likewise in Southern Africa, the tradition of *Kucheza* (Chichewa term for chatting) also functions as an informal system/process of mass news dissemination. *Kucheza* as a performance of communication operates at three levels: *Miseche* (gossip and twaddle), *Kuselewula* (joking/harmless flirting) and *Nkhani* (factual news). Participants in *Kucheza* may start off with *Miseche*, move on to *Kuselewula* (depending on the familiarity or friendliness of the other participant) and then wind up with more factual and serious news (*Nkhani*). The narration of *Nkhani* is marked by high or low vocal intonations to augment what Finnegan (1970: 6) describes as the "emotional intensity". The oral news structure and the content are very distinguishable from both *Miseche* and *Kuselewula* in that the oral narrative of news draws from folk media tools of *Mbalume* (coherence and accuracy), *Ndondomeko* (detailed and chronological) and even *Chining'a* (figurative speech that relies on proverbs or complex narrative tools). Even public transports are noisy *Kucheza* experiences, in which original strangers become acquaintances through sharing personal problems and deliberating sociopolitical developments. Public debates in hair saloons or market places have also become deliberative public spheres for sharing *common knowledge* and *information*. It should be highlighted here that such *Kucheza* sessions can consolidate extant social and class inequalities and relations as some voices are traditionally not allowed to be heard due to differences of gender, sexuality, ethnicity or class.

At the community level, public news dissemination is more organised and controlled through and by local political structures. For example, in southern Africa, *Mbera* system of communication requires that a member of the village governance committee stand on a high ground or walk through the village whilst beating a drum or an old aluminium pail and inviting the citizens to visit the village headman's ground urgently to listen to information and announcements from the leadership. Such announcements often comprise instructional information pertaining to community governance questions (regulating certain behaviours and practices) such as fishing, forestry conservation or general well-being. Similarly, among the Asante of Ghana, there is the *Dawurb* informal news dissemination custom, during which village announcements are signalled by a loud beating of a gong (Adjaye, 2008). The actual messages are then picked up through memory and repetition for the benefit of those who did not participate in the *Dawurb* (Adjaye, 2008). All these public announcements of news depend on the oratorical abilities of the public communicators (Finnegan, 1970).

Technical and Non-specialised Knowledge: Defined as 'indigenous technical knowledge' (Mansell, 2011), technical and non-specialised *knowledge* refers to the rules and binding regulations that ensure the organised *governance* of legislative, political, economic and social management of a community (such as marriage, punishment, disease/crime prevention or funerals) and its available resources (such as land, trees, water, grass). These rules and binding regulations indeed attach and liberate the individual to/from the community (Christians, 2004) and can, therefore, be both liberating or oppressive (Freire, 1972, 1996; Mbembe, 2001; Mohanty, 1991; Ochieng'-Odhiambo, 2010; Spivak, 1988). This knowledge exists in and operates at the levels of public and private spheres, and its generation and exchange is dependent on specific knowledge, capabilities, enabling technologies and political economic environment (Mansell, 2011). Public spheres refer to publicly available records in form of performances or texts such as rock drawings, songs, music, poetry, house murals, carvings, animal skin paintings or scrolls (Mundy and Compton, 1995). They contain information on political and economic governance, for example, land ownership, tax obligations, genealogies or histories about war (Adjaye, 2008; Mundy and Compton, 1995; Ochieng-Odhiambo, 2010). Adjaye (2008) refers to this governance attribute in his study of the institutions, personnel, procedures and mechanisms of diplomatic communication among the

19th century Asante of modern Ghana. The Asante indigenous systems of communication were at the centre of governance institutions and systems in the kingdom: the legislative, judicial, financial and political administrative faculties (Adjaye, 2008). The objective, therefore, is to maintain peace and order (even though such may be at the expense of individual liberties and freedoms); hence, the information and messages are concerned with the relationship among individuals and between the individual and the community (Christians, 2004; Ochieng-Odhiambo, 2010).

Such governance rules also extend to the private sphere, where messages are generated and tailored to speak to the needs of a private affair or ceremony. For example, in the wedding arrangements among the matriarchal and patriarchal societies of Southern Africa, a man will not, in an ideal situation, directly approach a woman he wants to propose. Instead, one will request their siblings to act as their adjudicators or representatives. The problem is that such rules and regulations oftentimes represent dominant narratives (while suppressing counter narratives) in society. In this case, the right to freedom of speech does not belong to any specific member of the community (as defined in Article 19) but rather belongs to the community as a whole and is only temporarily granted (as it can be withdrawn) to those who have to carry out specific responsibilities within the given structure of an IKCS. As observed in passing, the danger is that the communicative acts regarding technical and non-specialised knowledge are likely to perpetuate unequal power and class relations in favour of those monopolising power and its resources in society. Much as an individual has the right to fall in love and get married, they do not have the right to directly express that emotion and arrange their own wedding ceremony. That right exists in form of authority and is only reserved for uncles and aunts. It will be the same adjudicators who will be invited to help resolve a conflict when the marriage hits the rocks or make funeral arrangements in the case of the death of either or both of the marriage partners.

Technical and non-specialised knowledge is, therefore, functional in nature, consisting of written and unwritten obligatory rules and the 'chains of reciprocal services' or reciprocal reality (Christians, 2004; Malinowski, 1926; Ochieng-Odhiambo, 2010) that are socially binding in private and in public. The generation and brokering of this knowledge only takes place within the *private sphere*, in which symbolic power is heavily implicated in excluding certain social groups and elements through access to capacity, literacy, technology and resources. Generation/brokering constitute the initial production process in indigenous knowledge systems, when organic intellectuals and opinion makers such as traditional leaders, medicine men and elderly women advisors respond to a catalytic development such as a conflict, question, conundrum or social calendar event, and then authorise a relevant community institution to prepare a relevant response. It is only at the level of administering and sharing this knowledge that the rest of the community is brought in through public or private spaces. In this category, the relevant opinion makers and organic intellectuals evoke, administer and circulate appropriate knowledge and information through official/non-official records or performance for utilisation by the specific or wider sections of the community. This knowledge form is also made available in public spheres through structured events such as funerals, village courts or other organised policy consultation and implementing sessions. The same arrangement of *authority of speech* applies, in that no one has the right to speak on their own behalf, unless mandated by their age, traditional/social responsibility, family links or position in the clan.

Many Western-authored development projects have attempted to co-opt these technical and non-specialised knowledge resources and capacities in order to generate development from below interventions (Brokensha, Warren and Werner, 1980; Quebral, 1988; Servaes, 2008). Some community health development projects claim to have 'discovered' and introduced the 'Grandmothers-inclusive' health communication models that place elderly women at the centre of safe motherhood initiatives (Jonasi, 2007). Key to this strategy is the recognition and consolidation of the role of elderly women in challenging harmful traditional practices and strengthening those that promote community health, well-being and interpersonal and participatory communication (Jonasi, 2007). From the modernist perspectives, such specific IKCS enable elderly women to become honorary men in patriarchal societies, thereby enabling their advice, counsel and instruction to be accorded respect and weight, because by living longer, these elderly women earn the *authority to speak*.

The problem, however, is that within this knowledge category, the real power and decision-making responsibilities over whether customs can be practiced or discontinued lie in the specialised knowledge category. What this means is that there is a ladder of superiority of indigenous knowledge forms. Specialised knowledge forms are more superior to non-specialised knowledge forms. This is evident in the stronger degree of political parallelism (Hallin and Mancini, 2004) within specialised knowledge system than in the case of non-specialised knowledge. Whilst it is an attractive endeavour for Western community health development approaches to appreciate the importance of IKCS, there is need to understand the structures of power brokering, otherwise projects and initiatives may deal with institutions or individuals that, despite their ability to administer and share certain technical and non-specialised knowledge, have no real power in society. Elderly women in this case can administer technical and non-specialised knowledge and information, but the production and brokerage of such knowledge oftentimes lie in the hands of a complex political structure and network that rarely includes or involves these elderly women.

Specialised and Privileged Knowledge: *Specialised and privileged knowledge* mediates the relationship between the community and its Gods or spirit deities. This is the most important and superior form of knowledge because it affects the nature, procedures and the regulation of the other knowledge forms. The regulation of the community's relationship with its gods, ancestors and deities requires specialist knowledge brokers—the traditional leaders who are custodians of this privileged knowledge and hence are correctly defined as 'indigenous professionals' (Christians, 2004; Mundy and Compton, 1995; Ochieng-Odhiambo, 2010). The organisation of the structures of generating, brokering and managing such knowledge and the requisite skills is reserved for real power holders—the clique of few people (largely males) in the community, such as spirit mediators, healers, sorcerers, shamans, rainmakers and the initiation advisors (Kamlongera et al., 1992; Mundy and Compton, 1995; Ochieng-Odhiambo, 2010). For example, the organisation and administration of many initiation ceremonies are reserved for the knowledgeable institutional memory holders in the community, who are the trusted accomplices of the traditional leadership. Apart from participating in making collective decisions, they have the responsibility of being called upon during emergencies or the social calendar to lead the village/community in observing a certain ceremony and also imparting their treasured knowledge on to a particular social group (young people, pregnant mothers). The objective is to ensure continuity in the knowledge database of the community, as such, within IKCS, specialised knowledge is a natural resource that belongs to a community.

The generation of specialised knowledge, therefore, is the hub, the capital and the foundation of power production in the community/society as it also determines the nature and direction of the generation, dissemination and sharing of other knowledge forms. The whole epistemology and superstructure of a given society is organised around the power structures surrounding specialised knowledge institutions (Ochieng-Odhiambo, 2010). For example, the initiation ceremonies in some societies are organised around the dance/performance sects known as *gulewamkulu* (great dance) in Southern Africa or *egwugwu* among the Igbo of Nigeria. The organisation of *gulewamkulu* and *egwugwu* displays traits of political parallelism hence, such performances are closely linked to the local political and power structures. As institutions, performances and power mediators, *gulewamkulu* and *egwugwu* are the responsibility of the village executive committee, headed by the village headman himself (oftentimes a man), and has the delegation responsibilities in terms of choosing when and where the performance can take place (Kamlongera et al., 1992; Ochieng-Odhiambo, 2010).

In principle, the purposes of such performances are largely educational and instructional, as the masked performances and the accompanying music offer pathways on how to live and behave in the community (Kamlongera et al., 1992). At the psychoanalytic level, most of these performances provide emotional windows to let out the personality aspects which are sublimated by the society whilst claiming that the emotional outburst and expressions belong to the characters in the performance (Kamlongera et al., 1992). A performance then becomes an enculturation process defined as 'direct instruction' (Mundy and Compton, 1995). These performances have, in many instances, "become a medium through which ideas of opposition to the normal world or of the distortion of accepted human and social values are expressed" (Kamlongera et al., 1992: 40). However, feminist and postcolonist critical analyses of these performances reveal the consistent perpetuation of spectacles of representation that promote inequality, subjugation and moral violence against the subaltern (especially women and ethnic minorities).

The foregoing section has presented and critically analysed the three forms of indigenous knowledge communications based on the three knowledge forms of knowledges, namely: (*a*) *common knowledge*; (*b*) *technical* and *non-specialised* (governance); and (*c*) *privileged* and *specialised* knowledge. The indigenous communication forms ensure the sustenance of processes in which knowledge is brokered, generated, managed and exchanged to serve different social, economic and political objectives. In all these cases, such knowledge serves several utilitarian objectives including developmental objectives. The assumption by numerous donor or government-funded media for development initiatives is that indigenous knowledges have some positive elements, and these are the ones that have to be co-opted into the mainstream media for development approaches. What this section argues is that indigenous knowledge communications remain organic models of media for development and they can be studied and understood in their own right, not from prisms of external and orientalist development communication models.

AFTERTHOUGHTS

This chapter has introduced and examined the media for development approach as the first approach towards the study of media, communication and development. The discussion has presented and critically analysed the theory and practice of the three media for development strands, namely, (*a*) factual news and content, (*b*) creative and educational journalism, and (*c*) indigenous communications. The discussion on *factual news and content* has presented two key strategies by which mass media products on, in and about development are generated with the aim of informing and mobilising a range of target audience groups to make material and non-material contributions to development interventions that will benefit 'others'. The analysis of this strand brought in examples from *MindaNews* from the Philippines, *The Guardian* in the UK and of course, Western NGOs who use mass media to lobby and influence public and international policy on specific development crises in the global south. It has been pointed out that as a result of these attempts, there have been ethical questions raised regarding the representations of others in development discourse. For example, a study of the representation of the Rwandan Genocide in Western newspapers found a systematic orientalist discourse that constructed and framed Africans as inherently irrational, violent and tribalistic and that the West is the only hope for Africa's salvation (Wall, 1997).

The analysis of *creative and educational reporting* and communications has discussed strategic communications that are rooted in behavioural change theories that are produced by governments, organisations and media institutions so as to influence positive behaviour and social change in society. The established trend has been the co-optation of participatory research methods in the design and production of development messages and content, where some sections of targeted audiences are consulted to ensure the messages are culturally relevant and coherent. This section has presented social communication and theatre for development as case examples of creative and educational journalism. The first two of the three media for development strands (*factual news/content* and *creative and educational journalism/communication* share four similarities: (*a*) they are centralised, conceived and implemented within and by organisations and institutions that often live outside of development problems; (*b*) they are sometimes influenced by Western development and communication theories; (*c*) they are somehow external and involve minimal and little participation from primary stakeholders; and (*d*) they often rely on mass media and target mass audiences. Regarding the third trajectory of development reporting, that is, *indigenous communications*, the discussion has attempted to map out a media for development strand that evolves from the experiences and consciousness of living through a specific time and space. Unlike the other two strands, authorship of indigenous communications is collective and offers communities an opportunity to recreate the communications as time changes.

The major challenge that this discussion has raised with regards to the media for development approach concerns the continued co-optation of popular art forms, local knowledge and communication resources in order to uncritically celebrate dominant development discourses and epistemologies that have been seen to contribute to the deepening underdevelopment and poverty especially in the global south. The point of departure for media for development approaches should be to allow audiences to raise the question: whose development? Opening up citizen spaces for public communication of development issues, mobilising communities to uptake and adopt new knowledge and technology, do not make sense if the communication interventions do not deal with fundamental causes of inequality that have put communities in such positions. If people cannot eat healthy food, the root problem is not just nutritional knowledge—workshops on how to cook food will not solve the problem. The fountain problem could be lack of land on which to grow vegetables, the presence of a corrupt corporate buyer who buys all nutritious foods or the lack of income to buy such food because the local branch of a multinational corporation has laid off all the workers as it prepares to move the plant to another region where it can afford cheap or slave labour.

Radical approaches towards media for development (as in some TFD experiments) are often considered political and Leftist and if not banned by the government of the day, they die due to lack of funding, as development organisations have the tendency to argue that "such a proposal does not fall within our sectoral approaches". Media for development should, ideally, be a site, a communicative action and a discourse that empowers citizens to act as witnesses to the unmasking and demystifying of development policies and how they are implemented at the local level. As a major theoretical perspective in media for development, development journalism in all its forms has tended to provide a therapeutic treatment to development problems, encouraging people to take on best practices whilst living within the same political economy of development that is responsible for putting them in that situation. This approach, from the perspective of Mansell (1982), exemplifies superficial revisionism, in which the dominant paradigm is being masked with colourful notions of audience involvement and participation.

In theory and in practice, media for development focuses on the generation of content on and about socio-economic development targeted at primary, secondary or tertiary stakeholders. There are two groups of stakeholders who require different development content, hence the two MFD forms: the primary stakeholders and the secondary/tertiary stakeholders. On the one hand, primary stakeholders refer to interested constituents who directly live with development problems such as social exclusion, poverty, unemployment and other forms of marginalisation. In this case, MFD approaches oftentimes build on either general communication or behavioural change communication theories and models in order to inform and increase people's knowledge about particular development issues. On the other hand, secondary and tertiary stakeholders refer to policymakers, decision-makers, donor organisations and citizens and other partners from developed nations. These do not live through the development challenges in question, but nevertheless are implicated in the design and implementation of livelihood policies that affect the primary stakeholders. For them, MFD approaches are structured as forms of advocacy and agenda-setters so as to influence publics and policymaking structures within the "socio-political sphere of the audiences' external environment" (Singhal and Rogers, 1999: 9).

3

The Media Development Approach
Emphasis on Structure

THE PROBLEM

The chapter presents and critically analyses the second of the three approaches, that is, media development—which refers to externally or organically developed initiatives that are strategically designed to build media/ICT infrastructures, policies and capacities in both developed and developing nations as a way of consolidating good governance, free speech, political citizenship and sustainable development. The discussion is a postcolonial analysis in itself, attempting to demonstrate that the origin of media development approaches in the global south is rooted within four theoretical trajectories that all point to Webberian concepts of modernity. In all these approaches, Western organisations and institutions continue to implement what International Commission for the Study of Communication Problems (ICSCP) commissioners, Marquez and Somavia, described in the 1970s as a "Marshall Plan for the development of third world communications" with the intention of reproducing Western and neo-liberal values and transnational/corporate interests (UNESCO, 1980: 291). Whilst the chapter recognises the importance of media development in consolidating the processes of democratisation and good governance (Randall, 1993), concerns can be raised regarding the rapid co-optation of southern civil society institutions in implementing universalist media development indicators.

The chapter presents two key perspectives towards media development that are implemented in the global south, namely, the good governance and the community development perspectives. The discussion places political economy (Graham, 2005; Mansell, 2004) at the centre of media development. It does this by critically exploring the external and donor-driven models of media development through appraising the roles and responsibilities of international development organisations in relation to how the politics and economics of ownership, funding and control determine the debates on access, participation and sustainability of resultant projects. The discussion also employs political economy again as a facility for examining the endogenous and organic models of media development with or with minimal external and donor support. The central postcolonial argument, however, remains that media development debates in the global south have been designed in ways that give Western and "earlier experiences some universal validity" (Freire, 1978: 10). Nation states are being co-opted to adopt what Freire (1978: 10) describes as Eurocentric or Western-centric models that footnote indigenous knowledge communication systems, the southern concerns with cultural imperialism and the overemphasis on the minimalist model of civil society.

MEDIA DEVELOPMENT: TWO APPROACHES

In theory, in policy and in practice, media development refers to organised efforts at supporting and building the capacity of media institutions, policies, structures and practices as pathways towards consolidating citizenship and good governance, building fragile democracies as well as enhancing sustainable development initiatives. The approach aims to break up what Graham (2005) describes as 'knowledge monopolies' and closing digital divides through the provision of 'universal' access to media hardware and software. The assumption is that increased access to and participation in the public sphere strengthen civil society as a space where hegemony can be contested.

The intellectual framework governing the design and implementation of media development largely rests in four trajectories.

These are: (*a*) development sociology (Lerner, Rogers, Schramm); (*b*) North American political economy of communication (McChesney, Mansell); (*c*) enlightenment philosophy from the continent (John Locke, Immanuel Kant, deliberative democracy, reason, civil society, public sphere); as well as (*d*) international cooperation (UN institutions, access, participation). The development sociology trajectory emphasises the intensification of using media and communication to impart new knowledge and information to traditional societies in order to promote sustainable development. The North American approaches in political economy of communication emphasise the establishment of media and communication systems that would consolidate good governance and democracy. Associated with modernity, the continental enlightenment philosophy revolves around the celebration of reason, public spheres, independent and vigorous civil society as pathways towards strengthening deliberative democracy. The international cooperation approaches of organisations such as the World Bank promote the capacitation of media institutions from the global south as part of international commitments to peace, development and democracy. Co-operation also involves the collaboration of Western and southern media institutions. From the 1950s, when media development initiatives started being implemented in the global south, two distinct approaches have emerged and are being promoted by partners that have slightly different objectives. As named in passing, these two approaches are the good governance and the community development perspectives. The good governance models seem to have brought together the theoretical thinking from North American political economy of communication and the continental enlightenment philosophy. The community development perspectives seem to have combined the international cooperation approaches with development sociology.

Important to mention is that the design and implementation of most global media development initiatives are strategically led and funded by Western governments and development institutions such as UNESCO, BBC World Service Trust, Global Forum for Media Development, UNICEF, UNDP, World Bank and others. Only in a few cases, such as in South Africa, southern governments and institutions have, soon after successfully democratising, designed and implemented own media development projects as a way of consolidating citizenship, democracy and development.

At the global level, to ensure that the media in the global south are responding to the efforts at democratisation, media development indicators have been developed and used as instruments to monitor and evaluate country performances. Despite the different sociocultural, political and economic conditions, workshops with national civil society and government institutions have been organised in order to adopt the same five key indicators within the countries. Media development indicators refer to a universal framework for media practice and systems that enable the media to promote freedom of expression, good governance and sustainable development (UNDP, 2006; UNESCO, 1980, 2008). Such indicators have become benchmarks for measuring and categorising how media systems and structures, especially in the global south, perform in promoting good governance and democracy. All this work is carried out under the scientific and empirical paradigm known as media development.

Drawing on dominant, Western-centric development discourses and UNESCO's (1980) initiatives at developing media and communication systems, especially in the global south, and of course, building on the various international conferences on media development organised by Western governments and civil society institutions, two approaches towards media development can be identified. The first approach is the *community development* strand that promotes community engagement and empowerment as well as other micro-development objectives. The second approach is the *good governance* strand, which is rooted in Western neo-liberal democratic political theory and focuses on promoting good governance and democracy. What connects these two approaches is the question of power; hence, political economy becomes an imperative analytical tool for unpacking the question of media development.[1]

---

[1] A clear divergence in these two media development strands was empirically observed during the discussion sessions at the 2005 Sensitisation Workshop on Rural Radio for Policy and Decision Makers in East and Southern Africa, 26–29 April, held in Lilongwe, Malawi (SADC-CCD, 2006). The workshop had been organised by the FAO, CTA and the SADC Centre of Communication for Development, all of who emphasised the role of rural radio in promoting food security and sustainable livelihoods. The team from AMARC based in South Africa insisted the emphasis of the role of rural radio in promoting good governance and democracy.

Media Development, the Community Development Strand

As observed in passing, the community development strand owes its theoretical springboard in development sociology (Lerner's and Schramm's works on modernisation, and Rogers' scholarship in agriculture extension and communication) as well as international cooperation (especially UNESCO's efforts as proposed by the ICSCP). Some theoretical contribution has also come from community media and social change (Librero, 2004; Quebral, 1988; SIDA and Jallov, 2007).

Lerner, Rogers, Schramm and Technological Diffusionism

Technological diffusionism has been the dominant and technologically deterministic approach in media development. It is primarily rooted in Lerner's and Schramm's media modernisation proposals in which they called for the scaling up and scaling out of Western mass media systems, structures and regulatory policies in the global south (Lerner, 1971; Schramm, 1964). Writing in the 1950s, Lerner (1958: 38) attributes the West as the source of "the stimuli" that eventually "undermined traditional society in the Middle East". Like Schramm (1964), Lerner (1958) is referring to the inevitability of rapid economic growth that would transform the economies of scale in these 'other' worlds to replicate the West. He actually contends that "the western model is virtually an inevitable baseline" for development planning and implementation in the global south (Lerner, 1958: 39). Probably building on Lerner's work, Schramm (1964: 20) emphasises how Western media technology transforms a traditional family:

> No one who has seen modern communication brought to a traditional village will ever doubt its potency. Once in an isolated village in the Middle East, I watched a radio receiver, the first any of the villagers had ever seen, put into operation in the head man's house. The receiver promptly demonstrated that knowledge is power. It became a source of status to its owner; he was the first to know the news, and controlled the access of others to it. For him and all others who heard, the noisy little receiver became a magic carpet to

carry them beyond the horizons they had known. [...] Less quickly, less dramatically, the impact of communication is seen when a road is newly opened to a village. Strangers come in with good to sell and ideas and news to exchange. Villagers travel to the nearest city and bring back new standards and customs. And change begins.

Schramm's contention here appears technologically deterministic. In fact, in later chapters of the book, he makes it clear that "in the service of national development, the mass media are agents of social change" (Schramm, 1964: 114). For Lerner (1958) and Schramm (1964), therefore, Western media technology and its content facilitated the adoption of new customs and practices and the development of new social relationships. In the same vein, Rogers' (1962, 1976, 1993) theory of adoption and diffusion of innovation attempted to explain how individuals and societies embraced new knowledge and technology. Adoption for Rogers referred to the period between which the individual heard of an intervention for the first time and the actual time they adopted it—whilst diffusion entailed cumulative adoptions, that is, the way new knowledge and technology are introduced and accepted in a social system. In these processes (adoption and diffusion), the media are thought of as instruments for facilitating a rapid adoption/diffusion. On the other hand, agriculture extension/ communication has been largely concerned with the effective dis- semination of agricultural knowledge and research to end user, oftentimes the farmers (Librero, 2005, 2009). Considered together, Rogers' (1962, 1976, 1993) work in development sociology and of course, agriculture extension challenge media development ex- perts to establish media institutions and systems that are going to promote food security, adoption of new knowledge and technol- ogy and sustainable livelihoods.

Development, it must be noted, had been reduced to an eco- nomic phenomena by both Rostow's theory of economic growth and President Harry Truman's inauguration speech in 1949, in which the notion of "development meant nothing more than pro- jecting the American model of society onto the rest of the world" (Sachs, 1992: n.p.). Truman had, by describing the rest of the world as underdeveloped, homogenised the global south into a single category of 'underdeveloped' countries, whose only salvation lay in imitating and joining the West in moving along the same continuum of modernity for them to achieve development (Sachs,

1992). Central to this realisation of modernist development was greater production, industrialisation and technology (Escobar, 1995; Sachs, 1992). The financial institutions of the World Bank and IMF would immediately take the lead in 'advising' southern countries in how to develop. The first mission was sent to Colombia in July 1949, a team that comprised financial, engineering and other technocrat experts, who at the end of the mission recommended a relaunch of the country's whole economy (Escobar, 1995; Sachs, 1992).

Importantly, Lerner and Schramm argue that for modernisation to complete achieving sustainable economic growth, the individuals themselves have to be modernised as well. That there is need for traditional societies and people to abandon their native lifestyles and adopt modern living practices. These were processes that had already taken place in Western cultures, when "ordinary men found themselves unbound from their native soil" and moved "from farms to flats and from fields to factories" (Lerner, 1958: 47). In such a process, two factors are crucial: mobility and stability (social equilibrium); mobility referring to social dynamism that becomes an agent of social change, which is 'sum of mobilities' acquired by people (Lerner, 1971; Schramm, 1964). There were three kinds of mobility that individuals had to achieve in order to be modernised: geographical mobility, social mobility and psychic mobility. Geographical mobility implied unbounding man from his native soil to allow him to explore and migrate; social mobility required liberating man from native status to allow him to change his place in society; psychic mobility required the person to transform his native self in order to define a new personality worthy of his new situation (Lerner, 1971; Schramm, 1964).

Transforming individuals to achieve the three mobilities required the concerted effort of transformed educational system and the mass media (Lerner, 1971; Schramm, 1964). The role of the mass media was to bring new aspirations to people (Lerner, 1971) or new customs, practices and behaviours (Schramm, 1964). In fact, Lerner calls for the scaling up and scaling out of mass media: the mass media should "continue to spread around the world—inexorably and unilaterally" (1971: 870). The premise by Lerner is that the spread of mass media helps countries to establish Western-centric media systems to avoid "going back to an oral system of communication" (Lerner, 1971: 871). The modern mass media system must have the capacity to produce, distribute and consume the commodified information.

In media development initiatives, media itself is also an innovation to be adopted, to facilitate the transformation of Lerner's (1971) 'traditionals', the conservative self into the 'moderns', as such, diffusion becomes a strategy through which modern media systems and innovation are adopted and accepted through a social system (Rogers, 1962, 1976, 1993). Such diffusion becomes necessary considering Rogers' (1962: 57) concerns with "cultural resistances to new ideas". For Western organisations, the idea has been to bypass or overcome 'traditional norms' which Rogers (1962: 61) believes are characterised by 'less developed' technologies, agrarian economies, low level of literacy and in which "communication via word of mouth is more prevalent than by mass media". This was the traditional society Rogers (1962, 1976) and the early Rostowians attempted to modernise, to transform it into a "modern social system" marked by developed technology, urban behaviours of its citizens, literate, mobile industrialised, cosmopolitan social relationships, rationality and empathy (Lerner, 1958, 1971; Rogers, 1962, 1976, 1993).

Lerner (1958: 156) uses case studies from Turkey, Jordan, Syria and Iran to demonstrate the longing for modernity by the traditionals, transitionals and the moderns, as manifested through their longing for balanced news, more information about the world and their association of America with equality, high living standards and modernity. The major assumption, therefore, held by past and present diffusionists is that Western, modern and largely electronic media systems are the only reliable pathways, which governments can use to communicate to and with their citizens (Lerner, 1958, 1971; Rogers, 1962, 1993; UNESCO, 2008; UNDP, 2006). As such modern governments "cannot rely solely or even primarily on interpersonal communication to inform, activate or persuade the millions of individuals and thousands of organizations and groups that they must somehow reach" (Lerner, 1958: 236).

The International Cooperation Approach

By the 1970s, however, there were tenuous and confrontational debates raging among UNESCO member countries regarding huge inequalities in the political economy of international media and communication. In response to these concerns and debates, the UNESCO General Conference held in Nairobi, Kenya, in 1976, decided to establish a commission to look into the problems of international media and communication, resulting to the establishment of the International Commission for the Study of Communication Problems (UNESCO, 1980). Led by the Irish, Sean MacBride, the Commission (UNESCO, 1980: 42) was tasked with carrying out four specific tasks:

> To study the current situation in the fields of communication and information and to call for fresh action at the national level and a concerted, overall approach at the international level. [...] To pay particular attention to problems relating to the free and balanced flow of information in the world, as well as the specific needs of developing countries [...] To analyse communication problems, in their different aspects. [...] To define the role which communication might play in making public opinion aware of the major problems besetting the world.

Responding to this call, UNESCO and specifically the ICSCP tasked a number of researchers to carry out studies on various aspects of communication and information would be used as background material in discussing and compiling the report. Very relevant to the discussion of media development is Part III, which presented 'Problems and Issues of Common Concern' that had been identified by member countries and respective studies. It will be these problems and issues that would form the springboard of the media development initiatives that would be carried out by UNESCO and other international development organisations under the soon to be formed International Programme for the Development of Communication (IPDC). There were five problems and issues: flaws in communication flows; dominance in communication contents; democratisation of communication; images of the world; and the public and public opinion (UNESCO, 1980). A critical analysis of these problems shows that the theory and practice of media development today rests in resolving these conundrums.

Under the *first problem* of flaws in communication flows, the ICSCP noted the problematic concepts of freedom of information, free flow of information, balanced flow of information and free access to the media. Under this general problem, four problems were identified. These were: physical and ideological constraints against *free flow* (such as repressive legislation, intimidation and harassment of journalists), *one-way flow* (dependencies, disparities, imbalances and inadequacy in global information flows), *vertical flow* (unidirectional flow of information, concentration of communication resources and information overload) and *market dominance* (commercialisation of communication content, massification, commercialised pluralism and commodification of audiences) (UNESCO, 1980).

The consequence is that policymakers and planners focus on establishing media and communication systems that mirror Western models, since it is unproblematically assumed that such Western-centric and Eurocentric models reflect deeper democratic cultures. As such, transplanting the models that have been successful at consolidating democracy and good governance in the West will also consolidate the same in the global south. Such media development projects then focus on strengthening public service broadcasters (transforming them from state broadcasters), developing regional press and promoting the involvement of the market in media business. For much of the global south, where two economies coexist antagonistically alongside each other (first world, globalised economy versus third world, informal economy), promoting the involvement of capital in media development only results in various forms of convergence—in which the powerful classes end up controlling both media and politics. With the exception of South Africa perhaps, for Africa, media ownership patterns reflect the notion of 'political parallelism' mentioned by Hallin and Mancini (2004).

Regarding the *second problem* of dominance in communication contents, the key concern was the "lacunae and distortions in information" resulting to the public, the government and institutions being ill-informed, uninformed or even misinformed (UNESCO, 1980: 156). Such a problem emerged as a result of other smaller problems such as: *distortion of contents* (lack of news accuracy, deliberate distortion, silence on facts or events, problematic news values, decontextualisation and dehistoricisation), *cultural alienation* (increased external content, introduction of new media, threats against cultural and natural identity, dominance of foreign language content and marginalisation of multiplicity), *external influence* (fostering endogenous cultures and languages, unlimited external content, commercialisation of culture and transnational media ownership) and the need for *shared responsibilities* (in eradicating the many shared deficiencies in national and international communication systems). The implication of dealing with this specific problem is that national media legislation and policy have ended up specific quotas regarding content. In such processes, national regulatory authorities, under the influence of political actors, have been able to deal away with critical programming, especially if it comes from or is associated with the West.

On the *third problem* of democratisation of communication contents, UNESCO (1980) presents the factors that impact on this lack of democratisation, namely, barriers to democratisation, breaks in barriers, critical awareness and the right to communicate. Democratisation of communication is defined here in terms of audience participation and partnership in communication processes and institutions, the increase in message exchange and the depth of social representation in communication (UNESCO, 1980). The barriers to communication include inequalities in wealth distribution, digital divide, lack of good governance, lack of representation in public policymaking, social exclusion and illiteracy. The breaks in barriers refers to initiatives undertaken to reduce these barriers, such as broadening popular access to the media, participation of non-professionals in content and message production, development of alternative, participation of the community and media users in management and decision-making and decentralisation of the mass media. On critical awareness, UNESCO (1980) observed the need to develop critical attitudes on the part of the audience towards programming and content (and the need to empower citizen groups to demand access to and participation in the communication system). On the right to communicate, was also the demand for a two-way flow, for free exchange, for access and participation in ways that satisfy human communication needs (UNESCO, 1980). Solving this specific challenge has seen the intensification of efforts to establish alternative and community media within the global south, in new democracies and especially among marginalised groups.

Unfortunately, this attempt to achieve democratisation of communication has, often, but not always, ignored two crucial aspects: sustainability of media projects outside donor funding, and also democratisation of communication in relation to the behaviour of media institutions themselves. When it comes to issues of sustainability (financial, social and institutional), most donors have rushed to establish national or community media projects without undertaking necessary business research. When the donors in question feel they have achieved key objectives, they hand over these media projects to national bodies, which are often underprepared to sustain the projects, especially in hostile or financially arid business environments. This has resulted to total or partial closure of media development projects that started off successfully—just because donors felt they had to move on and focus on other projects. In relation to democratisation, again, governments and institutions have focused on establishing an increased number of media spaces, which it is assumed will increase public participation in national dialogues. An aspect of democratisation that has been totally ignored is the behaviour of senior media staff—most of whom are used to undemocratic approaches and practices from the *ancient regime* and bring these with them in the new democratic dispensations.

On the *fourth problem* of images of the world, the crucial factor identified was the construction of representation and the role of the media and communication in "awakening the conscience of, and sensitizing public opinion to the major problems confronting the world and in helping towards their solution" (UNESCO, 1980: 175). Such major problems include(d) war and disarmament, hunger and poverty, the colonial gap between the north and the south, the east–west interface, violations of human rights, equal rights for women, interdependence and cooperation. On the *fifth problem* of the public and public opinion, there was a concern on the lack of understanding of the public and the different forms of public opinion (such as national and world opinion) (UNESCO, 1980). Addressing the last problem has seen media development projects being established to promote ethnographic and development journalism approaches that offer an opportunity for the journalists and the public to critically engage with specific challenges. Cases in point include the emergence of the development journalism movement in South East Asia and Asia, as well as the civil journalism movement in the US in the 1980s. Other projects addressing these problems include establishment of pollster organisations, journalists associations, relevant training courses and workshops to build the capacity of journalists.

Resulting from the identification of these problems, UNESCO (1980) immediately indentified and proposed strategies for 'development of communications' (media development) that focused on three aspects: infrastructure, technology and policies. It is this section of the proposals that has received scathing attacks from academics, researchers and policymakers alike for being Eurocentric and technologically deterministic. Whist such criticism may be valid in some respects, what is often forgotten is that the other media development proposals presented in this report are very much valid today and have been taken up by most media development organisations and institutions. The major proposed media development strategies comprised building the capacity and professionalism (standards and integrity) of journalists, strengthening independence of self-reliance of the media and communication, democratisation of communication, fostering international cooperation and establishing enabling law, regulation and policies (UNESCO, 1980). By the end of 1980s, UNESCO would, as a result of the ICSCP recommendations, establish the IPDC to lead the organisation's efforts at developing media and communication, especially in the global south. The next section, therefore, examines the role of IPDC and other major organisations who are developing media and communication systems and structures as part of consolidating democracy and development in other places, especially the global south.

The Community Media Perspective

Community media, sometimes known as citizens' media, refers to the structure, process and content of media owned by and serving the interests of geographical or ideological communities (including communities of practice). This media provides alternative perspectives, rejects commercial and corporate agenda setting, is oftentimes antagonistic towards the state and the market and positions itself with independent civil society institutions (Bailey, Cammaerts and Carpentier, 2007; Carpentier, Lie and Servaes, 2003). The functional objective of such citizens' media is well captured by a former station manager of an African community radio station, who observed that a local broadcaster that had been established with the financial and logistical support from UNESCO was a "development radio" (Manyozo, 2012).

> This [development radio provides villagers with] *mphamvu zambiri* (a lot of power). [Such] radio is guiding traditional leaders about development, and reminding them not to politicise development as well as reminding people about their roles and responsibilities in development. [Motioning with the hand holding the two tapes] Before this radio, we village people were nothing to government officials, but today, when I visited the government offices to follow up on the proposal for a local development project, I was received as an important person, because this radio has given us an identity, that we are people with important ideas too. We are now known and now we are able to go through complicated bureaucracies and meet senior officials we couldn't meet before this radio was established. Even women are able to speak on radio.

What this community radio practitioner refers to here is the existential focus on community development (minus political issues such as democracy). For organisations such as FAO, Farm Radio International or the Technical Centre for Agricultural and Rural Co-operation (CTA), the focus on development issues was always a strategic move on their part, especially in the 1960s/1970s, when many countries in the global south attained independence from European powers but ended up as political dictatorships. Any attention paid to governance or democracy issues would have been restricted by national governments, and hence, by only focusing on depoliticised 'development' issues, these international organisations were able to meet their sustainable livelihoods objectives but also ensured they did not conflict with the newly established political dictatorships.

In the community development strand, media development initiatives aim to strengthen citizen access to and participation in local community development initiatives including traditional governance systems. These are governance systems that are not based on cyclic elections, but rather trust, personal relationships, networks and social capital. These are governance systems that have chiefs who are not elected through popular elections, but nominated, anointed and confirmed through patronage systems that are rooted in indigenous knowledge communication systems and not radio, television or newspaper. As such, they require a completely different set or category of indicators.

There are three fundamental aspects of this media development strand that distinguish it from the good governance (deliberative democracy) strand. First is the promotion of self-management as the highest form of participation (Quebral, 1988; Servaes, 1996; SIDA and Jallov, 2007). Building on the postcolonial critique of modernisation paradigm by the thinkers from the dependency school of development at the Economic Commission for Latin America (Escobar, 1995; Hedebro, 1982), this strand of media development has rejected the continued dependence on donor and government funding as a reliable mechanism for achieving financial sustainability. In fact, Quebral (1988: 80) highlights the need for political independence by suggesting that such media be removed from "political propaganda" by "housing them in universities". She goes further to refer to this "micromedia" that will "make themselves part of the structure of each local human settlement, that will identify with its inhabitants and steep themselves in its affairs so that they will speak in its idiom, and more important, articulate its interests" (Quebral, 1988: 81). The emergence and consolidation of the community media movement has demonstrated that the most effective models of media development are those that are owned and managed by local communities. This is only possible if, during the establishment of media projects, the communities establish clear and comprehensive mechanisms for sustaining the initiative financially, which in the end enables the community to strengthen the two other forms of sustainability — social and institutional sustainability (Ilboudo, 2003). In this case, media development indicators should ideally be examined in relation to how a media project has achieved financial, social and institutional sustainability. Is there a clear and pragmatic business model that enables the financial sustainability? Are there enough local institutions that are supporting the media project in questions? Is the local community supportive of the media project? And, do they identify with it?

The second aspect of this community development strand is the centrality of IKCS. In chapter 2, the discussion provided examples of IKCS such as *Dagu* from Ethiopia and *Kucheza* from Southern Africa, which obligate participants to share latest news and gossip as well as dialogically discuss latest social and political developments within the available public spheres, such as public transport. In this case, media development refers to communication development — as such, focus is not on developing the (digital) media instruments and related capacities and capabilities, but rather on developing interpersonal communication processes, or what UNESCO (1980) referred to as 'communication between people'. For example, Kamlongera (1988, 2005), Valbuena (1986) and Mda (1993) discuss the development of indigenous folk arts as instruments of social mobilisation within development projects. In the Philippines, Valbuena (1986) discusses the development of community skills and capacities in using indigenous and folk media (such as the *Zarzuela, Cancionan, Balagstan, Balitao* or *Bantanyon*) to develop short skits and dramas based on local music, satire and dramatic conflicts in order to promote local development and social change.

The third factor of this media development strand is the importance of media projects in improving social capital, local livelihoods and local development (SIDA and Jallov, 2007). This explains why these media projects are promoted and implemented even in countries with poor governance records, because they are seen to support the development activities of the government of the day. It has often been argued that when development communication emerged in the Philippines and South East Asia in the 1960s, numerous Western scholars confused the paradigm with government propaganda (Librero, 2009; Quebral, 1988). The implementation of these media initiatives has, therefore, been largely based on 'non-political' local development challenges. The indicators that are used as benchmarks for measuring positive change revolve around improved gender relations, sustainable usage of forestry and natural resources, improved living standards, increased levels of social capital and stronger decision-making structures (SIDA and Jallov, 2007).

Regarding media development indicators that capture the community development strand, the aim would be to document the cost-effective impact of a media project in reducing/eradicating poverty through providing relevant information, increasing local institutional transparency and accountability as well as challenging people to actively contribute to development policy formulation, implementation and management (Manyozo, 2012; SIDA and Jallov, 2007). Therefore, unlike the good governance (deliberative democracy) perspectives that focus on promoting freedom of expression within Western neo-liberal concepts of democracy, the community development strand aims to validate the *participatoriness* and *effectiveness* of *mediated* local development interventions (Jallov, 2005; Manyozo, 2012).

The evaluation methodology known as the Most Significant Change (MSC) has been employed as a participatory assessment instrument in evaluating media development projects in East Africa (SIDA and Jallov, 2007). The indicators upon which MSC is used to evaluate these media projects attempt to capture three development narratives, namely, (*a*) *exposure* (listenership to, usage and ownership of development content), (*b*) *adoption* (implementing best-bet development practices) and, importantly, (*c*) *active participation* in media and development projects. Capturing media development in this strand, therefore, requires a completely distinct set of indicators (from the governance strand). Table 3.1 builds on the MSC methodology in proposing the indicator categories that could possibly capture media development from the perspective of the community development strand.

Table 3.1: Proposed Draft of MD Indicator for the Community Development Strand

Category	Key Indicator(s)
Category 1: Exposure to development information and communication	a- Increased awareness of sectoral development issues b- Increased changes in people's perceptions and attitudes c- Increased and consolidated interpersonal and intra-community dialogue on development issues
Category 2: Adoption of development practices	a- Increased adoption of best sectoral strategies in development b- Improved uptake of best innovations and practices in public health, agriculture and other development sectors c- Stronger local systems and structures of accountability and transparency
Category 3: Active participation in media and development projects	a- Increased involvement of local people in self-management of media and development projects b- Independent mechanisms for financial sustainability of media/development projects c- Stronger community support for media projects (social sustainability) d- Local institutional support for media/development projects e- Development and availability of locally generated evaluation instruments for measuring impact of media projects

(Table 3.1 Contd.)

(Table 3.1 Contd.)

Category	Key Indicator(s)
Category 4: Indigenous knowledge communication systems	a- Availability of indigenous knowledge communication systems b- Presence of indigenous institutions (such as initiation schools) that are responsible for passing on indigenous knowledge to young people c- Existence of traditional performances, ceremonies and activities that observe indigenous knowledge d- Traditional laws and regulations that govern the operations and management of a community and its resources e- Indigenous knowledge and communications mobilise community members towards development projects

Source: Author.

The Good Governance Strand

As argued in passing, the design and implementation of this strand finds theoretical foundation in a combination of enlightenment philosophy as well as political economy of communication. The ulterior objective by Western governments and media institutions is to strengthen the nation state in the global south along the models characterising liberal democratic polity. At the level of policy, this media development strand is informed by political liberalism theories of, among others, John Stuart Mill, Immanuel Kant, Jurgen Habermas, Hegel, Gramsci, John Keane and Robert McChesney. All these theorists, in one way or the other, emphasise the separation of the state, the private and the civil society institutions and spaces. The assumption in this strand is that independent (free from the state and of course, the market) and pluralistic media have promoted good governance and democracy in the West, and it will also promote the same in the global south.

Political economy as a critical perspective finds itself at the centre of this strand, in which policymakers and public intellectuals attempt to find the best system that will promote good governance and democracy in the global south. The central philosophical tenet driving this strand is 'freedom of expression' as articulated in Article 19 (Universal Declaration of Human Rights) and in Anglo-European libertarian philosophy of John Locke, John Asgill, Mathew Tindal, John Milton, Ferdinand Tonnies, Walter Lippmann, among others. The rationale for this principle of freedom of the press has, according to John Keane (1991), four reasons: the theological reasons, the prominence of rights of individuals (above other rights), the theory of utilitarianism and the idea of attaining truth.

Largely informed by John Milton's *Areopagitica* (1764), the *theological basis* for this principle was rooted in the belief that God as the Sovereign Authority granted reason to His subjects which they must use to pursue, develop and test their virtues—and this can only be possible by a free press (Keane, 1991). With regards to the primary importance of press freedom as a human right, John Locke's treatise, *Epistola de Tolerantia ad Alarissimum Virum* (1689), Matthew Tindal's *Reasons Against Restraining the Press* (1704) and John Asgill's *An Essay for the Press* (1712) provided an intellectual enlightenment for this school of thought (Keane, 1991). The utilitarian theory of the press rejected state (and commercial) censorship of free speech and public communicative acts as a basis for dictatorship and an impediment to the attainment of the maximum happiness of the maximum number of citizens (Keane, 1991). For William Goldwin and James Mill, the right of individuals to freely express their opinions override the other rights, as it is this right that forms the basis of good governance. Finally, the fourth justification for freedom of the press would be the right to search for and attain the truth, a philosophy which has its roots in the enlightenment philosophies of Joseph Priestly (1768), Immanuel Kant's *Critique of Pure Reason* (1781), Thomas Paine's *The Rights of Man* (1791), Thomas Erskine's (1793) legal defence in support of Thomas Paine, John Stuart Mill (1859) and, more recently, Jurgen Habermas (1962). It was John Stuart Mill's (1859/2003) collection of essays, *On Liberty*, that would provide a comprehensive justification for positioning the media as a key instrument of good governance and attaining public happiness. In *On Liberty*, Mill (1859/2003) observed:

> If all mankind minus one were of one opinion, and only one person were of the contrary opinion, mankind would be no more justified in silencing that one person, than he, if he had the power, would be justified in silencing mankind. [...] The peculiar evil of silencing

the expression of an opinion is that it is robbing the human race;
posterity as well as the existing generation; those who dissent from
the opinion, still more than those who hold it. If the opinion is right,
they are deprived of the opportunity of exchanging error for truth:
if wrong, they lose, what is almost as great a benefit, the clearer
perception and livelier impression of truth, produced by its colli-
sion with error.

For Mill, the attainment of truth would only be possible if public spaces were open to debates, allowing opposite views to clash
agonistically. Years later, Jurgen Habermas (1962) would build on
such enlightenment conceptualisation of media and democracy to
propound the theory of the public sphere that referred to an ideal
and normative site, space and moment in social life when communities and societies came together to dialogically and rationally
debate issues affecting them and propose action solutions. The
public sphere displayed attributes that enabled the mediation of
both the private and public authority spheres through facilitating the transformation of public reason and public opinion into a
public action (Habermas, 1962). Probably building on Habermas,
both Rawls (1997) and Cohen (1997) observe that the attainment
of truth in these public spheres should be a guiding principle of
all forms of deliberative democracy, as this allows the extensive
harnessing of the deliberative capacities of rational beings.

It is for this reason that the media development initiatives
and indicators located within the good governance strand usually build on the concepts of free press and deliberative democracy and thus focus on three crucial aspects, which distinguish
them from the community development strand: the first is that
media development initiatives are designed and implemented in
line with each of the three dominant phases of democratisation.
Randall (1993) introduces the three phases of democratisation
as being the origins, the transition and the consolidation phases.
Each of these phases is characterised by different media systems
and models—and therefore, requires different types of media development interventions (Randall, 1993). For example, in the first
phase, focus may be on introducing enabling regulatory and policy mechanisms and frameworks, introducing new media outlets
or even new media/digital technology; whilst in the consolidation phase, focus maybe put on building the capacity of journalists to carry out investigative journalism or on media literacy or

even strengthening press laws to protect rights of journalists and media practitioners. As will be discussed later in the chapter, the problematic of this approach is that the question of governance is often conceptualised without critical consideration for two factors, namely, the theory of the state (and state formation) and the changing models of governance, especially in the global south.

The second aspect of this good governance strand is that initiatives attempt to promote the Western-centric minimalist model of civil society, in which emphasis is on establishing and strengthening media systems and institutions within the space of the civil society. Cammaerts (2008) distinguishes the Hegelian model of civil society (maximalist) from the Gramscian model (minimalist), in that the latter displays distinction among the public, private and civil society spaces. In fact, it is probably within this minimalist civil society space that Jurgen Habermas (1962) would locate his concept of public sphere, away from the influence of both the state and the market—and when this did eventually happen, he would use the concept of *refeudalisation* to describe the phenomenon. The civil society, for both Cammaerts (2008) and Habermas (1962), constitutes that space, that site—where independent citizens and institutions contest and challenge hegemony and dominant ideologies. However, the ad hominem assumption is that the civil society is the only space which promotes freedom of expression. Evidence from the global south, however, suggests that there are many scenarios of investigative journalists being threatened by corrupt NGOs or other civil society institutions when such journalists write critical pieces exposing such corruption. The consequence is that media development organisations have avoided working with government departments of information and communication—when actually it is these same departments that are responsible for designing and implementing national information/communication policies.

The third aspect of the good governance approach to media development is that the design, implementation and evaluation of media development today revolves around media development indicators (UNDP, 2006; UNESCO, 1980, 2008), which are the tools for cost-effectively measuring the actual characteristics that link free, independent and pluralistic media to good governance and democratic processes. The first framework for media development indicators evolved from within two organisations. The UNDP (2006) released *The Guide to Measuring the Impact of the*

Right to Information Programmes that aims to measure four principal outcomes. These areas are: the legal regime for the right to information; implementation of right to information legislation by
government; use of the right to information by the general public
and civil society; and the use of the right to information by marginalised groups (UNDP, 2006). Permeating through these indicators are gender and pro-poor interests.

The media development guide by UNDP (2006) focuses on information only, in fact, information as a commodity. It leaves out
other areas of media development, such as media ownership and
control as well as larger questions of access and participation.
These issues are then picked up by the IPDC, which developed
a draft of a media development framework that would be taken
though a 'vast consultation' process involving organisations and
institutions around the globe. Eventually, UNESCO would adopt
the indicators in 2008. The five principal categories of indicators comprise: (*a*) a system of regulation conducive to freedom
of expression, pluralism and diversity of the media; (*b*) plurality and diversity of media, a level economic playing field and
transparency of ownership; (*c*) media as a platform for democratic discourse; (*d*) professional capacity building and supporting institutions that underpins freedom of expression, pluralism
and diversity; and (*e*) infrastructural capacity is sufficient to support independent and pluralistic media (UNESCO, 2008). Each
of these five categories has a series of indicators that in turn have
their sub-indicators.

From these five categories, three issues stand out: pre-eminence
of information (as a commodity), the emphasis on media as vehicles
for achieving free speech and the centrality of Western models of
governance. This chapter examines these three issues in order to
demonstrate that there is an assumption by media development
organisations that such categories and indicators "could be applied unproblematically anywhere" (Hallin and Mancini, 2004: 2).
Even in cases where region-based organisations have developed
their own indicators as in the case of the African Media Barometer
(AMB), the new categories themselves have ended up replicating
the ones developed by UNDP (2006) or UNESCO (2008).

These universal indicators are largely construed from Habermas'
(1962) rendition of the public sphere, which is a critical theory
developed to explain ideal and normative conceptualisations
of communicative action within public spaces. In *The Structural*

Transformation of the Public Sphere, Habermas (1962) traces the factors and processes leading to the emergence of the bourgeois public sphere in Western societies from around the 18th century. As an idea, the public sphere has its intellectual origins in the renaissance philosophy, especially in relation to reason and rationality, two notions that would form the backbone of the Habermasean public sphere. For Habermas (1962), the public sphere was a space where people met and held rational-critical dialogues, exercise public reason on matters of public interest. What is important in Habermas' conceptualisation of the *Öffentlichkeit* is the interpersonal nature of the dialogue, the immediacy of feedback, the reign of rationality and reason and the reciprocal relationships and knowledge that participants had about/with each other within these spaces (Calhoun, 1992).

The ideal and normative model of the public sphere has received criticism from a number of scholars, especially in the way it overlooked questions of power, inequality, passion and unreason, marginalisation and social exclusion (Calhoun, 1992; Mouffe, 1999). The concern for Habermas was the 'refeudalization' of the public sphere, the restitution of knowledge monopolies, a development that took place "when the laws of the market governing the sphere of commodity exchange and of social labour also pervaded the sphere reserved for private people as a public, rational-critical debate had a tendency to be replaced by consumption" (Habermas, 1962/1989: 158). The growth of mass media as an industry attracted business interests, which were only interested in selling both the content and the audiences as commodities (Calhoun, 1992; Mouffe, 1999; Graham, 2005). In the process, the media lost their public service role as mediators of rationalistic public reason and chose instead to serve the interests of the state and the private spheres (which were one and the same anyway) (Calhoun, 1992). In a way perhaps, Habermas was pointing out two models of a public sphere, the *refeudalised* market model (representing private and state interests), as in the US public service broadcasting model, and the rational-communicative-dialogical model (representing public interests), as in the UK or European public broadcasting models (Calhoun, 1992).

Whilst the public sphere idealism of Habermas has been heavily criticised (Calhoun, 1992; Cohen, 1997; Mouffe, 1999; Rawls, 1997), media development initiatives today seem to have revived such idealism by trying to establish and consolidate media models that lie outside the influence of the state, that is, in the sphere of the civil society. It is assumed that within this sphere, the media can then be independent, be free, be pluralistic, be diverse and be a vibrant watchdog of the state, which is how Habermas (1962/1989) originally envisaged the public sphere. Carpentier, Lie and Servaes (2003: 58) draw on Thompson (1995) to define a civil society as "as a group of intermediate organizations, separate from the privately owned economic organizations operating in the market economy, personal and family relations and from the state and quasi-state organizations". Carpentier, Lie and Servaes (2003) and Bailey, Cammaerts and Carpentier (2007) note that civil society models vary the world over, but still attempt to replicate the neo-liberal market economy model in both their form and structure. This is what Bailey, Cammaerts and Carpentier (2007) and Cammaerts (2008) term as the Gramscian minimalist model of civil society.

Drawing from these Western models of civil society, most media development initiatives today celebrate pluralism and diversity unproblematically and uncritically. The assumption is that as long as the media are located outside the spheres of the state, they will automatically become plural and diverse. Karppinen (2007), however demonstrates that fluidity of these concepts in the examination of European media policy. Karppinen notes that access and participation are fundamental in any mediatised public sphere, but notes two different models of diversity. The first is public sphere or policy diversity model, which is similar to Habermas' dialogical model of the public sphere, one that offers diverse public interests, opinions, media outlets, content and actual content (Karppinen, 2007). The second kind is the market diversity, which is competitive and "diversifies program types and genres to the public but simultaneously reduces the diversity of political views or cultural representation or even excluding some contentious issues altogether" (Karppinen, 2007: 14). In the end, Karppinen (2007: 24) prefers a combination of the two, but one in which media development widens "social access to public debates" through supporting and enlarging the "principled opportunities of structurally underprivileged actors of the public sphere. This creates a room for critical voices outside the structures of the market and state bureaucracy, aiming to increase inclusiveness and openness of the public sphere to various forms of contestation".

For example, in South Africa, the pre-1994 apartheid system of governance preferred to allocate and regulate media resources and institutions to white businesses and enterprises. The end of apartheid did not undo these racial inequalities overnight. The 'transformation' of South African media is a process that should ideally involve a number of strategies—and this includes the major media and communication training institutions and philosophies, ownership and control of media businesses, and of course, transforming and democratising the newsrooms (SAHRC, 2000). Even the government-sponsored media development initiative, the Media Development and Diversity Agency (MDDA) (MDDA, 2007) recognises the existence of racial inequalities in media ownership and control, and hence, it attempts to "encourage ownership and control of, and access to, media by historically disadvantaged communities, historically diminished indigenous language and cultural groups". In fact, writing in one of his weekly columns, 'Letter from the President' in the online *ANC Today*, President Jacob Zuma (2010: n.p.) asks critical questions regarding the dilemma of transforming and rescuing the country's media systems and structures from apartheid frameworks:

> What is the role of the media in the promotion of our country's human rights culture and the Bill of Rights? Does it have a role in promoting nation building? Does it have a role to play in the promotion of the country's prosperity, stability and the well-being of its people? Is it a spectator, or does it have vested interests and an agenda, political and commercial, that it cherishes and promotes? [...] The media has put itself on the pedestal of being the guardian. We, therefore, have the right to ask, who is guarding the guardian? [...] Can a guardian be a proper guardian when it does not reflect the society it claims to protect and represent? [...] When a person from ku-Qumbu in the Transkei opens a newspaper in the morning, does he or she see himself or herself in it? [...] Are editors under pressure to sell their papers and to increase their circulation figures at whatever cost, including at times relying on unchecked and unverified smears in order to boost sales and circulation? What protection does an ordinary citizen who cannot afford lawyers have when their rights have been violated? How can they compete with powerful business interests who control the media either through ownership or advertising spend? [...] Is the media a mirror of South African society? Is it in touch with what the majority of South Africans feel and think? [...] Is there alienation with the post-apartheid democratic order and thinking?

Through these questions, Zuma is raising two crucial points in relation to the political economy of media development: first, he is arguing that within freedom of information, information is not neutral, as it can be (and has been made) to speak with "vested" interests and agendas (Zuma, 2010: n.p.). The neutrality of information is an assumption made by both approaches in media development, in which the media are thought of as market places of ideas. Years before Zuma raised his critical questions about 'vested interests', in 1976, the Latin American Institute for Transnational Studies (ILET) observed that 'alternative' development required another type of news, in which information is not just about facts but about the social phenomena (UNESCO, 1980). The ILET also observed that "information is a social right, not an article of merchandise", and it "should be an instrument of liberation" that aims to "make people more aware, to give them a full understanding of the economic and political situation of their problems on both the national and the international plane and of their ability to participate in the decision-making process" (UNESCO, 1980: 157). The notion of freedom of information has been left to the interpretation of the market, which prefers the mercantile conceptualisation that unfortunately footnotes important facts that cannot be sold (UNESCO, 1980).

Second, Zuma is challenging the civil society to develop media development indicators that reflect the South African material context in lieu of its apartheid past. The media or the information society reflects the modes of material production. The media reproduces the economic and social relations and structures, and in the case of South Africa, it would refer to the class interests that still dominate South Africa's economy. Or, to put it in other words, transitioning democracies with special historical experiences and needs require *special indicators* in order to transform their media and communication systems and structures. In fact, Allen and Stremlau (2005) ask the pertinent question, "should media freedom be an essential aspect of peace building, or does peace building necessitate the restriction of dissent—in other words, censorship?" Their argument is that media institutions should not be developed quickly in post-conflict states as they may actually hinder long-term peace objectives (Allen and Stremlau, 2005). In the case of South Africa, this would involve generating a category or categories of indicators that monitor whether transformation is indeed taking place in the media and whether the media are 'reflecting' the South African society, so that when "a person from ku-Qumbu [in the Eastern Cape] in the Transkei opens a newspaper in the morning", they should be able to identify themselves in it (Zuma, 2010: n.p.). Of course, a point to be highlighted is that Zuma assumes there is one homogenous society that can be represented by one homogenous media. It must be mentioned that the criticism levelled against Zuma's proposal was that the governing African National Congress was intending to introduce a Media Tribunal to police the activities of the country's press. Nevertheless, the MDDA's (2007) super-objective of transforming media ownership and representation to include 'previously marginalised groups' still warrants a special category of media development indicators.

Based on the minimalist model of civil society, in which Carpentier, Lie and Servaes (2003), Bailey, Cammaerts and Carpentier (2007) and Karppinen (2007) locate pluralistic and diverse media, Western media development initiatives aim to consolidate democracy and good governance, that is, to consolidate the minimalist model of civil society in the global south. Such governance is described in terms of elections, electoral processes, representatives and civil society. This is governance in the Western style and usually disregards hybrid and traditional forms of governance. However, the Economic Commission for Africa (ECA) (ECA, 2007) acknowledges that in much of the global south, traditional systems of governance operate alongside these Western models. Because of the "inherent institutional duality" of the African, Asian or Latin American political cultures, the challenge for political scientists has been to establish pathways for 'incorporating' traditional leadership and governance within 'modern' systems of government (ECA, 2007). Unfortunately, within modernisation, traditional governance systems are the very issues that Lerner (1958) proposed they be abandoned, and their indigenous knowledges and indigenous knowledge communications systems were considered by Wright (1959: 45) as "rather limited" and by McLuhan (1964: 91) as a "tribal trance of resonating word magic and the web of kinship". They just had to be abandoned.

Despite this duality in terms of governance systems, media development indicators have only tended to cater for the modernised governance systems, leaving out the traditional systems and

their indigenous knowledges. That means that the good governance strand of media development tends to ignore theory of the
state formation in the global south, which rests heavily on traditional governance systems. The media are being defined from the
perspective of Western literacy, that is, in terms of radio, television, newspapers and internet. There is no reference to indigenous
knowledge communication systems, perhaps in fear of "going back
to an oral system of communication" (Lerner, 1971: 871). Ample
evidence seems to suggest that even under the most of oppressive
dictatorships, when radio and television were under total control
of the state and its ideological and repressive apparatuses, indigenous knowledge communication systems have been able to draw
upon the multi-accentuality and multiplicity of meanings in order
to criticise the ruling politburos.

THE ROLE OF INTERNATIONAL/WESTERN ORGANISATIONS

The International Programme for Development of Communication[2]

The IPDC has been described as a 'multilateral forum' comprising representatives from different countries and organisations organised within the UNESCO system with the responsibilities of
mobilising the international community to 'discuss and promote
media development in developing countries'. The structure or forum was established in 1980 in Belgrade as an Intergovernmental
Council of the IPDC. Central to the work of the council is the support for media projects as well as the environment that allows for
the flourishing of a free, healthy, independent and pluralistic media in development countries. The media development initiatives
that have been prioritised, supported and funded revolve around

---

[2]The material used in this section draws upon text available at the website: http://
portal.unesco.org/ci/en/ev.php-URL_ID=18654&URL_DO=DO_TOPIC&URL_
SECTION=201.html (accessed on 12 April 2012), which has been posted at various
times. Specific references are unavailable.

three sectors: infrastructural development, capacity development and advocacy. Such initiatives include promoting media independence and pluralism, development of community media, radio and television organisations, modernisation of national and regional news agencies and training of media professionals. All of the IPDC's initiatives are premised on the concept of free flow of information (Article 19) as a fundamental precondition to good governance and democracy. Today, the council sees its responsibilities as lying in the:

> Betterment of the flow of free information [at international and national levels], promotion of literacy and contribution to the establishment of public spheres that are important for democracy also at the grassroots level. [...] promotion of freedom of expression and media pluralism; development of community media; human resource development; promotion of international partnership. [Promotion of a] wider and better balanced dissemination of information with no obstacle to freedom of expression; [and] strengthen[ing] communication capacities in developing countries.

To achieve these objectives, the IPDC has funded and implemented media development projects in partnership with other development organisations and local civil society partners. For example, in 1998, a Media Development Project was launched in Mozambique, as a collaborative initiative of UNESCO and UNDP, aimed at strengthening democracy and governance through development of the media in a country that has suffered brutal effects of a civil war between 1975 and 1992. The Project was designed to support the processes of decentralisation, pluralism and independence of the media and to build the capacity of journalists and editors (Jallov, 2005; Manyozo, 2012). It supported the emerging independent print press; helped communities to establish and sustain community radio stations; and provided support to the national public broadcaster; strengthened the role of women in the media; and provided capacity building in development journalism, especially in HIV/AIDS reporting (Jallov, 2005; Manyozo, 2012). In the community radio sector, the Media Development Project focused on five main objectives: emphasising community ownership of the stations, training and capacity building of communities to ensure technical sustainability, developing a financial partnership strategy, development of local content with the community and participatory evaluation (Jallov, 2005; SIDA and Jallov, 2007).

The BBC Media Action[3]

Another development organisation at the heart of media development is the British Broadcasting Corporation (BBC) Media Action (which used to be known as the World Service Trust), an arm of the BBC, which is a global charity employing media and communication to mobilise social groups, civil society organisations and governments to reduce poverty and promote human rights, and enable people to build better lives. The WST receives funding via grants and voluntary contributions from such organisations such the UK DFID, the European Union (EU), various UN organisations and the BBC. Its aim is to design and implement media development initiatives in the global south, especially in developing and transition democracies. These initiatives include the establishment of an 'independent and vibrant media'.

The Media Action's media development initiatives are aligned to the Gramscian, minimalist model of civil society, in which individuals, social groups and civil society can contest hegemony, using media and communication to build active citizenship, political agency and social development. Multi-stakeholderism (Cammaerts, 2008) is central to the achievement of the Media Action's media development approaches based on partnership with civil society, media and governments. The strategic objective of the WST's media development initiatives is to strengthen development and democracy. In India, the Media Action has implemented one of the largest media development projects since 2001. The projects have encompassed training provision in health communication and journalism. The media development initiatives of the Media Action in the subcontinent encompass the following:

> Partner[ing] with civil society, the media and governments in over 30 countries to build long term development solutions by: Assessing the information needs of individuals and communities [and] producing innovative and strategic content on all media platforms

---

[3]The material used in this section draws upon text available at the website: http://www.bbc.co.uk/mediaaction/ (accessed on 12 April 2012), which has been posted at various times. Specific references are unavailable.

(including new media) that informs and engages audiences around key development issues; extending the reach and impact of our programmes through listening clubs, learning groups and other outreach activities; building the capacity of government and civil society organisations to use media for development; strengthening the media sector to address development issues effectively; applying rigorous research so that we can measure impact and value for money, and produce information that informs the development of our work.

Building on the above described approach, the BBC Media Action would produce health education programmes on HIV/AIDS, reproductive health, leprosy or social relations—some of which involved collaboration with Bollywood stars such as Shilpa Shetty. An important aspect of the Indian media development project involved providing journalism training, especially in relation to building the capacity of local journalists and media in areas of peace journalism, disaster risk reporting, environmental journalism and HIV/AIDS reporting. In response to the Kashmir conflict, the Indian media development projects have involved:

A journalism training project delivered in partnership with the University of Kashmir. Held in 2008–2009, the programme provided students with professional skills to cover a wide range of social affairs and development issues. Workshops created a pool of professionals to teach and mentor current and future students, who were taken out of the classroom and into the community to cover real life stories. [...] Between 2006 and 2007, we mobilised two pillars of civil society, the media and NGOs, to raise public awareness of the environmental realities in India and push these issues higher up the news agenda. We provided training and mentoring for journalists and NGO staff in nine states and created opportunities for dialogue between them. The workshops covered how vested interests can shape environmental news coverage and the ethics of journalism, including objectivity and reporting a plurality of views, finding and authenticating sources and interview techniques. [...] In 2007, our 'Reporting Society' project partnered with three leading journalism schools to train media students and develop new courses on social affairs reporting. The training covered the ethics of representative and balanced reporting, sensitivity to audience needs, and the media's role in stimulating informed debate.

By building the capacity of local journalists and media structures, the BBC-Media Action was laying the ground for institutional sustainability, especially after the cessation of their funding in the country and beyond. The Media Action's approach in India mirrors those approaches adopted by international development organisations in much of the global south—where emphasis is on especially under the transition and consolidation phases of democracy, building media and communication systems and structures that address the immediate national development goals. These are the same approaches employed by NGOs under the umbrella of The Global Forum for Media Development.

The Global Forum for Media Development[4]

The Global Forum for Media Development (GFMD) is considered more of a process than a structure which brings together global practitioners in media development from over 500 organisations in order to support the planning, design and evaluation of media development initiatives that are independent and free at the community, nation state and regional levels. Like the IPDC, the work of the GFMD includes: sharing of knowledge, research and best practices in media development; facilitating the interaction of media development practitioners with other stakeholders; lobbying policymakers and decision-makers to prioritise media development as a facility for democratic governance and sustainable development. The forum's work also involves promoting, conducting and sharing impact research on the impact of media development; establishing common practices, standards and ethics for media development.

As in the case of most media development institutions and processes, GFMD has been mostly funded by Western governments and development organisations, such as National Endowment for Democracy, John S. and James L. Knight Foundation, Open

---

[4]Most of the material used in this section draws upon text available at the website: http://gfmd.info/index.php/about_gfmd/ (accessed on 12 April 2012), which has been posted at various times. Specific references are unavailable.

Society Institute, Lodestar Foundation, USAID, UNDP, UNDEF, UNESCO, OSCE, Council of Europe, CAF Latin America, Avina Foundation, Lebanon Press Club, Norwegian Foreign Ministry, the government of Greece, and the City of Athens. With such funding, the forum has been able to organise campaigns, test toolkits (such as the media landscape toolkit) as well as promote and develop media development manuals and publications. For example, the forum has been recently testing a media landscape toolkit in Ghana, with financial assistance from the Washington-based Centre for International Media Assistance. This largely quantitative facility allows for the identification of data gaps in the media landscape, thereby enabling the coherent assessment and evaluation of the media landscape, information on which is then used as baseline survey for the development of relevant and country-specific media development initiatives.

International Freedom of Expression Exchange (IFEX)[5]

The International Freedom of Expression Exchange (IFEX) is a Canada-based international organisation, established in 1992 by the Canadian Journalists for Free Expression (CJFE), which manages the programme from Toronto. It was established soon after the fall of the Berlin Wall that resulted in the establishment of multiparty democracies in Africa, Latin America and Asia. Central to multiparty democracy is media liberalisation, in which freedom of expression becomes a central instrument that allows citizens to hold their elected leaders accountable. The coming together of these organisations was the recognition of the need to create a "coordinated" mechanism and strategy that would expose the violation of this inviolable right (of freedom of expression) globally.

The work of IFEX comprises running the freedom of information service, building regional capacities for defending and promoting free expression (through funding, training and other

[5]Most of the material used in this section draws upon text available at the website: http://www.ifex.org/what_we_do (accessed on 12 April 2012), which has been posted at various times. Specific references are unavailable.

forms of support), leading and facilitating campaigns and advocacy and, finally, building free expression communities through deliberative and participatory forums where members plan and implement strategies and actions. The guiding light to the work of the network is the UN Article 19 of the Universal Declaration of Human Rights, which states that "everyone has the right to freedom of opinion and expression; this right includes freedom to hold opinions without interference and to seek, receive, and impart information and ideas through any media and regardless of frontiers". As such, IFEX works with other similar organisations that defend this right such as the UK-based Article 19.

Article 19[6]

This is a registered UK Charity, one of the earliest human rights organisations established in 1997 with the aim of defending and promoting the right to free speech, freedom of expression and freedom of information the world over. It has field offices in Senegal, Kenya, Bangladesh, Mexico and Brazil for easy urgent and timely coordination of regional campaigns and initiatives. The organisation is founded on the principle of Article 19 itself. Even during the height of the most oppressive dictatorships in Africa, Asia and Latin America, the organisation was able to provide details of secret nation state operations against its opponents, including arrests, torture, harassment and murder. Over the years, its work has encompassed monitoring, researching, publishing, lobbying, campaigning, setting standards and litigating on behalf of individuals, groups or even policies anywhere else in the world. The work of the organisations goes beyond media and communication and includes other sectors such as democracy, development, health, education or gender.

Such work involves: partnering with 52 national organisations with the aim of achieving institutional, cultural and social change; monitoring threats to freedom of expression in different

---

[6]Most of the material used in this section draws upon text available at the website: http://www.article19.org/about/index.html (accessed on 12 April 2012), which has been posted at various times. Specific references are unavailable.

regions of the world and using these reports to develop long-term strategies to address them; advocating for the implementation of the highest standards of freedom of expression, nationally and globally. The work also encompasses developing legal standards which strengthen media, public broadcasting, free expression and access to information, and promoting these standards with regional and international intergovernmental organisations; developing legal analyses and critiques of national laws, including media laws so as to provide requisite assistance to civil society organisations and governments in developing appropriate national standards of protection. The organisation undertakes litigation in international and domestic courts on behalf of individuals or groups whose rights have been violated and, importantly, provides legal and professional training and mentoring to national actors and stakeholders. It also lobbies national governments, international and regional bodies to bring national laws in line with international standards and then, finally, conducts cutting edge research and develops policies in relation to free speech and democracy.

United Nations Development Programme[7]

The UNDP has a huge Democratic Governance Programme under which media development initiatives are implemented. The Programme's areas of work include access to information and e-governance; access to justice and rule of law; anti-corruption initiatives and human rights; electoral systems and processes; local governance and parliamentary development; public administration; and women's empowerment. The aim is to achieve civic participation of even the most marginalised social groups (such as women and the poor) and also to consolidate governance systems that are accountable, transparent, inclusive and responsive. A major component of these initiatives is media development, through which the UNDP attempts to strengthen democracy and electoral

---

[7]Most of the material used in this section draws upon text available at the website: http://www.undp.org/oslocentre (accessed on 12 April 2012), that has been posted at various times. Specific references are unavailable.

processes including the administration of the elections and cultivating vibrant democratic governance in the global south. In some countries, this has involved funding public broadcasters to produce programmes that encourage participatory democracy, especially in relation to empowering citizens to engage with government and service providers. In other countries, UNDP's media development initiatives have encompassed supporting the development or consolidation of legal and regulatory framework for a free, independent and pluralistic media. A very good example is the Media Project in Mozambique discussed in passing, which UNDP and UNESCO funded and supported. Such work has involved strengthening the work of civil society organisations, especially those working on promoting freedom of information and the increment of opportunities for citizens to access reliable, balanced and timely information. The central ethos in UNDP's media development programmes is that freedom of information is central to the achievement of economic, political and social development the world over.

Regional Initiatives: Media Institute of Southern Africa[8]

The Media Institute of Southern Africa (MISA) was established in 1992 soon after the end of communism and apartheid and the civil war in Mozambique, thereby heralding a new era of democracy and good governance in the region. Countries such as Malawi and Zambia would immediately become multiparty democracies afterwards. MISA is an NGO comprising of member organisations from all the 11 countries in the Southern Africa Development Community (SADC) region. Central to the work of MISA is the 1991 Windhoek Declaration on Promoting an Independent and Pluralistic African Press, assented to by African media representatives and later adopted by UNESCO, which had actually funded the conference. There are 19 statements in the Declaration,

---

[8]Most of the material used in this section draws upon text available at the website: http://www.misa.org (accessed on 12 April 2012), that has been posted at various times. Specific references are unavailable.

perhaps a signifier to the organisation's commitment to uphold Article 19 in the print press. Radio and television media were left out, despite the fact that radio is the most accessible media on the continent. It could have been strategic considering that most countries in the region were still transitioning to democracy and electronic media were still under state control. It is for this reason that statement 17 called on UNESCO and IPDC to speed up organising a similar conference for radio and television media professionals. The African Charter on Broadcasting would be adopted in 2001 in Windhoek. The declaration itself reveals that media development is central to the achievement of democratic governance. There are four issues that stand out: the recognition of the transitory nature of SADC Africa's democracies; the repressive mechanisms against the media and professionals; the centrality of the civil society in developing an independent press; the role of UNESCO in implementing media development initiatives.

Today the work of MISA involves facilitating and coordinating five programmes: freedom of expression, broadcasting, media monitoring, gender and media support and legal support. The *freedom of expression* programme is a SADC media law reform initiative that aims to advocate and campaign for a repeal of the laws and regulations that limit or hamper the media from being free, independent and pluralistic. Leading such initiatives is the campaign to lobby SADC governments to enact the Access to Information (ATI) legislation. The broadcasting and ICT programme aims to campaign for a three-tiered broadcasting system (public, community and private) that emulates the principles of Windhoek Declaration and also promote universal access to ICTs as a vehicle for sustainable development, guided by the African Charter in Broadcasting. Regarding *media monitoring*, MISA observes and documents developments in the media in the SADC countries, especially violations of press freedoms. Such monitoring is carried out in line with the African Media Barometer (AMB), a self-assessment facility used by African civil society organisations to describe and measure national media systems and environment. The original 2005 AMB initiative was initially funded by the Southern African Media Project of the Friedrich-Ebert-Stiftung.

The *gender and media support* programme aims to streamline gender issues within the media through initiatives such as strengthening the capacity of media women's associations, media monitoring of gender perspectives and representations, building the gender and media capacity of civil society organisations as well as carrying out of gender and media studies in the region. The *legal support* initiative centres on a media defence fund and the Media Law Network, the aims of which are to engage in legal challenges to defend practitioners charged with breaking draconian censorship, publications and other media laws. The MISA's legal support initiatives have become even more important with the rise in state attempts to stifle free and independent media.

AFTERTHOUGHTS

The chapter has discussed the theory, policy and practice governing the second approach towards the study of media, communication and development, that is, the media development approach. The discussion has traced the roots of the approach to three sources. First is in the works of Lerner (1958) and Rogens (1962), who conceptualised media development as a strategy for replacing traditional means of communication with modern media systems and institutions that would contribute to the modernisation of individuals and societies. Second is in the work of the ICSCP (UNESCO, 1980) whose study raised evidence-based factors that contribute(d) to global inequalities in international media and communication. Emerging from this study, the IPDC was established to scale-out and scale-up media development in the global south. Third is the role played by international media development organisations that design and implement media development initiatives. These are organisations that continue to advance the modernisation objectives of consolidating market-friendly models of media systems in the global south, even though such models contribute to overdependence on external aid and inequality in the political economy of international communication (UNESCO, 1980; Mansell, 1982; Manyozo, 2012).

The discussion has also carved out two major models of media development that sometimes are in perpetual tenuous relationship to each other: the good governance (deliberative democracy) model and the community development blueprint. The chapter has argued, on the one hand, that the good governance strand has its roots in enlightenment and utilitarian philosophies and principles, especially in relation to freedom of expression as a central tenet in achieving deliberative democracy. In fact, organisations and institutions promoting this model base their approach on the media development indicators, developed by the IPDC and being adopted by media institutions the world over. The processes through which such adoption and adaptation are taking place still raise a lot of questions regarding the notion of local context and multi-stakeholderism. On the other hand, the community development strand provides an opportunity for media projects to be implemented with the aim of promoting national or local development goals.

What the last part of the discussion has demonstrated is that media development indicators oftentimes aim to achieve this goal, of ensuring a governance model that promotes market liberalism as conceived in the West. There is, however, another community-based model of traditional governance that the Western media development indicators ignore completely. Even in the cases where southern organisations and institutions have developed their own media development indicators (as is the case in the African Media Barometer, which is still media-centric), indigenous knowledge communication systems are visibly absent. This is because governance theory has been conceptualised in Western terms, marked by elections, the media, elected representatives and formal economy institutions. The indigenous and traditional forms of governance and their informal economies have not found a place.

It is for this reason that the chapter has called for a proper contextualisation of the media development debate. Consulting different national actors and stakeholders prior to adoption of the indicators has only resulted in the adoption of the same universalist indicators. This implies two things—either the consultation processes are flawed or the consultees are not familiar with the ideological implications of adopting externally authored media development indicators. This discussion, therefore, calls for a radical rethink of media development not an instrument of modernisation, but as an instrument that, as was originally intended in the UNESCO's study of ICSCP, attempts to eradicate global and local inequalities in media and communication. The global south faces increasing problems of poverty, inequality, social exclusion and underdevelopment. Media development initiatives should be designed, implemented and monitored with the aim of addressing these severe and immediate development conundrums.

4

The Participatory Communication Approach
Emphasis on Process

THE PROBLEM

The chapter interrogates the third approach to the study of media, communication and development, namely, the participatory communication approach (that is also being referred to as the community engagement approach), which ideally and normatively refers to how communication features in the grass-roots development approaches (Willis, 2005). The approach thus refers to the organised decentralisation of decision-making structures and processes that focus on the community as a collective unit of policy design and implementation at the local level. Such processes do not necessarily rely on the media but on what UNESCO (1980) described as 'communication between men', or interpersonal communications that are used in the generation, exchange and utilisation of development knowledge. As community engagement, participatory communication employs deliberative processes and collective decision-making mainly to foster improved livelihoods, safer communities and sustainable environment (Manyozo, 2012; Willis, 2005).

This enables citizens and communities to "have the maximum influence, control and ownership over decisions, forces and agencies, which shape their lives and environments" (UK Government,

2008: iii). The chapter builds on notions of grass-roots development (Arnstein, 1969; Bessette, 2004; Taylor, Wilkinson and Cheers, 2008; Willis, 2005) and power (Scott, 2001) in order to expound a community engagement blueprint that stresses collaborative decision-making and empowerment within community development initiatives. The exposition contends that participatory communication as in grass-roots development is fraught with power contestations, largely because it is oftentimes located within social capital and social relationships.

The discussion builds on and discusses two structural models of participatory communication (or community engagement), namely, the systems and empowerment approaches (Kilpatrick, 2009). It interrogates the communicative practices governing the politics of democratic decision-making in development policy formulation and implementation both in the north and the south. Through comparing and contrasting the two major participatory communication (community engagement) approaches, the chapter investigates how the theory and practice of participation becomes elusive if not considered within specific power structures and relationships. The chapter also recognises the multiplicity of disciplinary backgrounds that informed the emergence of community engagement.

COMMUNITY ENGAGEMENT AS PARTICIPATORY COMMUNICATION

In development practice, community engagement is located within grass-roots approaches that, since the 1970s, have continued to emphasise the basic needs (BN) approach (Willis, 2005). The BN approach emerged in response to the failure of the trickle-down effect as propagated by the classic economic growth models — emphasis was on the most salient development needs such as food, shelter, clothing, essential services, paid employment and other qualitative needs (Willis, 2005). Key to the implementation of this approach was the decentralisation and devolvement of governance and development structures and processes. Willis (2005: 106) actually observes that in the "market-led economies, there was a tendency to move away from central government activities and decision-making to a more decentralized approach". Such a strategic approach brought in cost-effectiveness and allowed local communities to decide on what kind of development they wanted.

In this case, therefore, community engagement would emerge as a key development practice in deliberative democracy that allowed development industries to reduce donor dependency, increase local participation and ownership of interventions as well as provide the relevant political economy in which grassroots participation took place. Today, community engagement has emphasised maximising community capability and strength as building blocks of sustainable development (Hickey and Mohan, 2004; Taylor, Wilkinson and Cheers, 2008). It has been shaped by dominant development thinking. The modernisation strategies have perceived poverty and underdevelopment as immediate upshots of backward traditional practices in much of the global south. As a consequence, community engagement, has been structured within integrated rural development programs, and incorporates external, donor-driven and co-opted praxes of participation and consultation. Participatory development has, in contrast, emphasised the heteroglossia of voices. As such, development entails participatory social-economic and political change processes, in which citizens and societies are challenged and empowered to assume greater control over their lives, environment and destiny (Rogers, 1976, 1993; Servaes, 2008). At the centre of engaging communities in grass-roots development is the question of communication at the community level.

Community communication refers to the participatory and grass-roots forms of communication that have a "program of motivation and activation, in which the final goal is the improvement of the quality of life for those living in the community" (Kivikuru, 1994: 408). Informed by participatory action research, Freire's critical pedagogy, agricultural extension and the knowledge management and dissemination models, participatory and community communication offer an opportunity for consultative, collaborative and collegial forms of participation (Krohling Peruzzo, 2004; Tufte and Mefalopulos, 2009). The concept thus refers to communication processes (stories, proverbs or orality) taking place within communities with or without the mediation of media instruments. The media's role in this case is to facilitate access and participation not just for the sake of it, but in order to allow for informed, participatory and inclusive decision-making in relation to the formulation of the development agenda (Kivikuru, 1994, 2005; Krohling Peruzzo, 2004; Tufte and Mefalopulos, 2009).

Oftentimes, communication for development is confusedly equated with participatory communication. What the three approaches (proposed in chapter 1 and discussed in the subsequent chapters) have shown, however, is that participatory communication is a major strategy towards community (and stakeholder) engagement that is based on dialogue, respect for local knowledge and collective decision-making. Development organisations have attempted to develop bottom-up strategies and models in inclusive development, such as participatory communication (Tufte and Mefalopulos, 2009), the communication for social change model (Figueroa et al., 2005) or the participatory rural communication appraisal (Anyaegbunam, Mefalopulos and Moetsabi, 1998; Willis, 2005). At the community level, the structure and process of participatory communication require dialogical processes to enable local people to exert a level of commitment, ownership and control of a development process (Tufte and Mefalopulos, 2009; Willis, 2005). Similarly, the integrated communication for social change model refers to a grass-roots mobilisation that brings together local and external stakeholders to deliberate relevant development interventions with the aim to improve local livelihoods, achieve sustainable environment and meaningful development (Figueroa et al., 2005; Willis, 2005). In the same vein, the Participatory Rural Communication Appraisal (PRCA), developed by FAO, is a community-centred participatory action research strategy, in which communities establish their communication needs prior to developing a communication intervention (Anyaegbunam, Mefalopulos and Moetsabi, 1998). The objective of employing participation as a means and an end is to enable effective grass roots–led research (that allows for a better understanding of a community) to allow communities to set the agenda, increase and equalise social capital levels, strengthen the efficiency of development project delivery and, importantly, to increase levels of community investment and self-efficacy (Taylor, Wilkinson and Cheers, 2008; Willis, 2005).

Bessette (2004) proposes significant elements of a community communication process as comprising establishing relationships with local communities; understanding local settings; involving a community in identifying development questions and concrete initiatives; identifying relevant stakeholders; building partnerships; collaboratively developing, pre-testing, self-managing, implementing and evaluating initiatives; and importantly, sharing and utilisation of results. Operating through all community engagement levels should be decision-making, which is a deliberative and rational communicative action, through which communities analyse their situation, and using available evidence, choose a public action that will address the root causes of a local problem. At the level of the community, participatory communication thus becomes a "continuous cycle of action and reflection, in drawing conclusions, applying them in practice and then questioning them again" (Bessette, 2004: 26).

In this process, the role of the facilitator is to help participants to make informed, clear, economically pragmatic, ecologically compatible and socially acceptable decisions. This is a participant-facilitator who motivates communities to unpack complex development conundrums. The communicative facilitator ideally understands the praxis of living with the people if they are to effectively help communities to *speak and unspeak* their world (Freire, 1996). Living with the people is a process that requires tools and a comprehensive understanding of the local setting and subjects (Bessette, 2004). It also requires a communicator's understanding of indigenous knowledge systems, to enable them to *speak and unspeak* alongside local people (Freire, 1972, 1996). Such a facilitator is a progressive and democratic advisor who respects the people's expertise, asking critical questions, motivating them to think beyond their horizons and come up with solutions (Freire, 1972, 1996).

Participation

In communication for development, there are two conceptualisations of participation, the pragmatic view and the Marxist perspective. To the pragmatists, participation is an education and research strategy for including or taking on board constituent and stakeholder needs and interests within a proposed project or development initiative (Manyozo, 2002). On the other hand, Marxists view participation as a form of class struggle for social justice, a process in which power redistribution looms large. Tufte and Mefalopulos (2009), however, point out that even if the scope, methods and objectives may differ, at the centre of participation is the understanding that primary stakeholders should be at the heart of an intervention. There is, therefore, no singular normative of participation. The various "gradations" of participation (Arnstein, 1969; Hickey and Mohan, 2004; Willis, 2005) find a theoretical confluence within three fundamentals: participation implies minimal or total liberation from oppressive power relations; it implies access to decision-making processes; and it implies communicative relationships. Communication as participation, therefore, explains a holistic, collective and dialogical process that brings together relevant stakeholders, engaging them in critical deliberative dialogues about a development problem (Bessette, 2004; Hickey and Mohan, 2004; Willis, 2005). Ideally, the praxis should be inclusive, as it requires creating sustainable collaborations with local communities, without manipulating them to accept outsiders' thinking on solving particular problems (Hickey and Mohan, 2004). For Bessette, participation involves the integration of community needs in development policies, during which relevant stakeholders "learn together through joint action and reflection" (2004: 26). The procedural challenges facing this form of deliberative participation include sectarianism, incoherence, injustice and irrelevance (Cohen, 1997).

Drawing on Northern American political science frameworks, Arnstein (1969: 217) presents and describes three key forms of participation, which are *citizen power, tokenism* and *non-participation* or the "empty ritual of participation". Likewise, Tufte and Mefalopulos (2009) describe four major forms of participation, namely, passive participation, consultation, functional participation and empowerment participation. These categorisations are largely based on the levels of power distribution between powerful elites and communities. *Citizen power* (Arnstein, 1969) or *empowerment participation* (Tufte and Mefalopulos, 2009) refers to processes in which the politically and economically marginalised are involved in discussing, sharing information, problematising their situation, developing plans and then owning and controlling managerial decisions on programme implementation. At this level, communities exercise self-management of the political economy of structures and processes of participation (Servaes, 1996, 2008). Participation as in participatory communication then becomes a process of *becoming* in itself, in which "nobodies are trying to become somebodies with enough power to make the target institutions responsive to their views, aspirations and needs" (Arnstein, 1969: 218).

Arnstein's (1969) *tokenism* encompasses informing, consulting and placating citizens, who may feel they have been heard. Yet, due to the unequal power relations, their views and aspirations remain proposed contributions; after all, powerful elites "retain" the decision-making powers and responsibilities (Arnstein, 1969). This is what Tufte and Mefalopulos (2009) refer to as participation by consultation or participation by collaboration, in which stakeholders are invited by outside experts to contribute to projects with predetermined objectives. Equally, Arnstein's (1969) *nonparticipation* or *passive participation* (Tufte and Mefalopulos, 2009) entails therapy and manipulation, and, in practice, involves powerful elites manipulating communities into thinking grass-roots concerns have been captured, when in reality, such views are not used to redirect policy decisions. In both tokenism and non-participation, participation is integrated as a rubber stamp or letterhead strategy where powerful elites deliberatively distort participation to "engineer" community support for irrelevant programmes and policies. This is what Freire (1972, 1996) refers to as the banking form of education, a public relations showpiece of advising and persuading communities to take up certain policy decisions. This is carried out through irrational means such as sourcing signatures, filling out questionnaires, voting for policies, which Cohen (1997) and Rawls (1997) reject as they believe they compromise the normative essence of deliberative democracy.

Power

As community engagement, participatory communication is a political strategy of bringing a community into decision-making processes requiring the development and implementation of acceptable policies in government, institutions and the community

(South Australia Government, 2008). As power, participatory communication has, in practice, become a strategic and participatory process in which institutions and elites or the 'principals' share power with the 'subaltern' (Scott, 2001: 2), the communities, thereby strengthening local democracy. This enables people to "have the maximum influence, control and ownership over decisions, forces and agencies, which shape their lives and environments", argues Hazel Blears in the UK Government White Paper, *Communities in Control, Real Power, Real People* (2008: iii). This is both causal and capability power (Scott, 2001). Causal power is a Lukesian (2005) conceptualisation, which implies agency in "bringing about consequences" and "producing specific effects" at the local, societal or global levels, despite certain constraints (Scott, 2001: 1).

To exercise power that produces causal consequences, communities must have this power first. As such, there is a difference between exercising and holding power (Scott, 2001). After acquiring this power, communities will still have it even when they are not exercising it (Scott, 2001). This act of having power is referred to as a dispositional capacity, the "ability that actors have to facilitate certain things" (Scott, 2001: 6). Probably informed by Gramscian concepts of hegemony, Althusserian concepts of ideological state apparatuses and the Habermasean concept of public sphere, Scott's (2001: 9) concept of power displays "facilitative or productive" characteristics, marked by collective and communal mechanisms through which consensus is achieved within a community. Power relations are developed though communicative acts, cultural and social upbringing and interactions as well as shared social values (Scott, 2001). For communities, engagement is a process of collective mobilisation that builds a sense of solidarity, enabling members to acquire the 'community spirit' and of shared understanding, allowing people to establish a consensus and legitimate collective decisions on specific courses of actions (Scott, 2001; Taylor, Wilkinson and Cheers, 2008; Willis, 2005).

In this case, then, participatory communication is fundamentally a process of sharing power equally within the community by increasing the level of social capital (Putnam, 2000) as well as sharing power between this community with shared values and experiences and the principal power holding institutions (Gibson and Woolcock, 2007; Willis, 2005). An important feature of participatory communication is deliberative dialogue, which, normatively is rational and democratic and ideally comprises rational considerations, corrective influence and persuasion (Cohen, 1997; Rawls, 1997; Scott, 2001). Cohen (1997) argues that democratic dialogue follows an ideal deliberation procedure allowing for collective decision-making around conceptions of public good. As a form of deliberative democracy, participatory communication should involve independent, free, rational and pluralistic deliberations. Rawls (1997: 96) similarly underlines a deliberative democracy framework based on public reason, "which is the reasoning of citizens, and its nature and content is public". Through public reason and deliberative contestations, participatory communication processes identify problems, assess local situation, bring out disagreements, solve conflicts, plan and agree on solving development challenges (Cohen, 1997; Rawls, 1997). Such dialogues are carried out in situated and *mediated* public spheres, for after all, democracy is dialogue (Freire and Horton, 1990).

As a strategy for giving communities causal power, participatory communication allows communities to make and influence decisions that characterise their world view. Arnstein (1969), however, fears that in the absence of equal power relations between powerful institutions and elites (the principals and subalterns), communities cannot "insure" that policy directions include their concerns. This could result in situations where communities make decisions that cannot, or may not be, and oftentimes, are not implemented. Even at the community level, hierarchical power relationships do exist, as some elite groups with access to financial or material resources tend to be more powerful. Without adequate sharing of power at the community level, communities may only "participate in participation itself" (Arnstein, 1969: 220).

This could result from powerful individuals preventing real community concerns being articulated through 'non–decision-making' (Lukes, 2005), enabling such elites to illegitimately speak for the community and implement private rather than public policies (Scott, 2001). Lukes (2005) uses the notion of non–decision-making to describe these manipulative processes through which the interests of those exercising power prevent the real interests from being articulated. This is done through the control of the political agenda, in which the powerful elites latently influence and shape the real interests. Perhaps fearing non–decision-making in participatory communication, Arnstein (1969) as well as Willis (2005) argue for the equalising of social capital and power relations as a precondition for implementing any engagement exercises, just to 'insure' that policy directions capture real community interests.

COMMUNITY ENGAGEMENT AS PARTICIPATORY COMMUNICATION IN THE GLOBAL NORTH

Discussions of communication for development tend to assume that the theory and practice are only relevant to the global south. Growing social exclusion, poverty and other forms of economic inequalities have shifted the debate to include the global north. The only difference is in strategic approaches. In the global south, community engagement has oftentimes been applied to development projects, where the largely financially weak governments have no clear engagement policies, and it has been left to NGOs to design and implement their own models. In the global north, however, community engagement seems to be a key political discourse in the running of local government and is guided by coherent government policies (and white papers). For example, in launching the *Big Society* at Liverpool Hope University on 19 July 2010, the British Prime Minister, David Cameron, described three strategies of social action, public sector reform and community empowerment that would place the citizen at the centre of government. He argued that:

> The *Big Society* [...] is about liberation. [The *Big Society* is] — The biggest, most dramatic redistribution of power from elites in Whitehall to the man and woman on the street. [...] For years, there was the basic assumption at the heart of government that the way to improve things in society was to micromanage from the centre, from Westminster. But this just doesn't work. [...] We've got to get rid of the centralised bureaucracy that wastes money and undermines morale. [...] We need to create communities with oomph — neighbourhoods who are in charge of their own destiny, who feel if they club together and get involved they can shape the world around them. (Watt, 2010: *Guardian Online*)

Cameron's *Big Society* idea does not seem very new to the UK. In fact, the Labour government that Cameron replaced had already, in 2008, developed and released the White Paper, *Communities in Control: Real People, Real Power* (UK Government, 2008). Like Cameron, the White Paper recognises the concentration of power within central and local government institutions, and proposes that communities should control and exert influence over the political economy of local democracy and decentralised development (UK Government, 2008). Building on both the White Paper and Cameron's concept of *Big Society*, part of this chapter investigates how the political economy of participatory communication as community engagement consolidates communication, cohesion and collective decision-making within impoverished urban communities.

'Passing power' to communities requires understanding the nature of both power and the communities; the need to mobilise the communities in order to give them increased confidence and self-esteem to participate in community activities; and to empower them to make social, ideological and cultural investment in their institutions and communities (Fulcher and Scott, 2007; Taylor, Wilkinson and Cheers, 2008; UK Government, 2008). Otherwise, power may go to groups that have neither interest nor investment in the community (Taylor, Wilkinson and Cheers, 2008). It is important to understand the ownership and exercise of power at the community level and ways through which "it can be diffused throughout the communities" (UK Government 2008: 12). In practice, efforts should be made to understand community as a place, defined by social relationships, interaction and interdependency among its members (Fulcher and Scott 2007; Taylor, Wilkinson and Cheers, 2008). Understanding communities of place allows for the employment of community participation, involvement and empowerment concepts that are reflective of and dependent upon community values, attitudes and knowledge (Fulcher and Scott, 2007; Taylor, Wilkinson and Cheers, 2008).

The White Paper discusses the significance of community engagement strategies such as participatory budgeting, scrutiny committees, petitions or public presentations of petitions that articulate a collective view and put pressure on those in power (UK Government, 2008). Within unequal power structures, petitions achieve little, considering that "less than a third of councils guarantee a response to petitions" and the "number of councils who make details of their petitions scheme available to the public is even smaller" (UK Government, 2008: 64). The major problem with the White Paper is it only focuses on building citizenship and does not deal with the operationalisation of devolving power. The assumption is that access to decision-making structures would automatically empower people; that opening up public life opportunities would involuntarily pass power to communities, even within unequal and hierarchical power relationships. The implication is that community engagement is then conceptualised as access to decision-making spheres rather than the decentralisation of the actual causal and capability characteristics of that power.

Like the White paper, another policy guideline, *Community Engagement to Improve Health* (NHS-NICE, 2008) defines engagement as a strategic process involving communities in decisions that affect their health and well-being. This entails enabling people to participate in the planning and delivery of acceptable, relevant and appropriate health services (Communities Scotland, 2007). The communities in greater need of engagement processes comprise individuals and groups with severe and special health needs, those experiencing difficulties accessing health services or people living in impoverished areas known as Super Output Areas (NHS-NICE, 2008). The guideline acknowledges that community engagement approaches ideally "help communities to work as equal partners or which delegate some power to them, providing them with total control" in developing and implementing sustainable public health services (NHS-NICE, 2008: 6).

Debates on involving communities in public and community health recognise that involving people in decision-making in health service delivery creates healthier, liveable and stronger communities (Communities Scotland, 2007; Kahssay and Oakley, 1999; NHS-NICE, 2008). Governments and organisations have attempted to understand the institutional, structural, cultural and ideological frameworks of communities as a platform for conceiving empowerment models that could increase social capital, community strength and cohesion (Taylor, Wilkinson and Cheers, 2008). Primary Health Care (PHC) was conceptualised as a strategy for enabling people seek better health locally, prevent disease and injury, shape and manage their health environment (WHO, 1994).

In fact the 1978 Alma Ata Declaration on PHC highlighted the need for socially acceptable health care, meaning well-being and healthy life cannot only be achieved by hospitals, medicine and availability of well-qualified professionals, but through sanitation, health education, improved housing standards, nutrition, clean water, affordable and clean energy and liveable and safer communities (WHO, 1994). Community health has, therefore, become a social responsibility of the community. The World Health Organisation (WHO) eventually developed *Guidelines for Rapid Participatory Appraisals to Assess Community Health Needs*, giving rise to the praxis of Community Involvement in Health Development (CIH).

The CIH approach now "involves both a commitment to promote better health with people and not merely for them" (Kahssay and Oakley, 1999: 8). Ratified by WHO's meeting in Yugoslavia in 1985, CIH relies on the involvement of communities in formulating decisions and actions affecting their health. It is believed this builds community esteem and responsibility, breaks local dependence and ensures that health services appropriately meet local needs (Kahssay and Oakley, 1999). It is within this context that the policy, *Community Engagement to Improve Health* was developed. This specific policy does not really conceive community engagement as a process of *becoming* in itself, in which powerless subalterns assume power, reinforce their social capital and mobilise to collectively plan and implement health services that are "responsive" to their aspirations. Engaging communities to improve health requires the actual trust, delegation and capacity provided to communities in planning and designing the delivery and governance of health and well-being initiatives. The objective is to improve health literacy and the appropriateness, cost-effectiveness, sustainability, accessibility and uptake of health services (NHS-NICE, 2008). What are the important aspects of this health guideline?

First, there is an emphasis on strengthening community organising and cohesion through democratic leadership and building on existing community groups. Second is the emphasis on public consultation and collaboration, which focus on involving communities in making decisions on local health policy and service delivery. Third is the need to systematically evaluate the effectiveness of community engagement approaches (NHS-NICE, 2008). Prior to implementing community engagement processes, there is need to understand objectives and expected outcomes, content, methods and processes, the participants, target audiences, resources, expected challenges, proposals for implementation and evaluation (NHS-NICE, 2008). Fourth is the need for effective facilitators with skills in helping participants to make informed decisions. Fifth is the minimal concern with power relationships. The guideline encourages identifying the forms and distribution of power in relation to decision-making, resource allocation and defining project objectives (NHS-NICE, 2008).

Sixth is capacity building—training that should develop the knowledge and skills of public sector agencies, NGOs, communities and other stakeholders. Ideal training should cover community engagement, community leadership, organisational change, communication and negotiation, conflict management, partnership building, accountability, business planning and financial management, participatory research and evaluation. The *Community Engagement to Improve Health* guideline, therefore, provides important logistics for bringing the community into the decision-making process in health service delivery. However, barriers to engagement still comprise hierarchical cultures within statutory organisations, top-down ideologies and approaches characterising professional and institutional organisations, conflicting priorities and visions, inadequate community engagement skills for public service staff and lack of knowledge of and interest in community engagement approaches (NHS-NICE, 2008).

COMMUNITY ENGAGEMENT AS PARTICIPATORY COMMUNICATION: SYSTEMS VERSUS EMPOWERMENT APPROACHES

Kilpatrick (2009) presents two major approaches towards community engagement: the *systems* discourse and *empowerment* discourse. The *empowerment* discourse, conceptualised by Taylor, Wilkinson and Cheers (2008) as community empowerment and developmental approaches, allow communities to achieve greater control of agenda setting and decision-making. In contrast, the *systems* discourse, defined as the contributions and institutional approaches by Taylor, Wilkinson and Cheers (2008), refers to externally driven engagement in which participation is an administrative apparatus for soliciting consumer perspectives towards improving community health, services and well-being. The empowerment approach builds on theoretical thinking from alternative development, emancipatory participation, liberation theology and participatory action research (Hickey and Mohan 2004; Kilpatrick, 2009). It is characterised by attempts to improve the participation of communities in producing development from below. Kilpatrick (2009) again argues that within the empowerment approach, key factors are personal development, consciousness raising and social action. Empowerment requires partly passing power to communities and then removing constraints to allow them to exercise this power.

On the other hand, the systems (or institutional) community engagement (Kilpatrick, 2009) has intermittently been employed to legitimise unpopular decisions, allowing organisations to achieve pragmatic objectives. In such processes, 'professional developers' employ "consumer and community involvement as interventions designed to achieve positive outcomes for communities" (Taylor, Wilkinson and Cheers, 2008: 88). The political economy of such structured processes oftentimes resides with external agents—the very reason Arnstein (1969) worries will lead to communities being co-opted to rubber stamp illegitimate institutional agendas. Systems engagement is, therefore, considered a form of 'networked governance' that extends democracy into the community and consolidates institutional capacities to respond to local needs and improve service delivery (Queensland Government, 2005).

The Systems Approach as Community Governance

This approach mainly refers to the decentralisation and devolution of governance structures and can be traced to some strands of North American political sciences, which emphasise political participation as being central towards building citizenship (Hickey and Mohan, 2004). Also conceptualised as community organising or grass-roots advocacy, the community governance approach has been largely employed as an advocacy strategy in Western liberal democracies and encompasses the strengthening of civil society coalitions in challenging economic and political hegemonies to improve social services (Arnstein, 1969; Hashagen, 2002). Informed mainly by concepts of participation in community action programmes, a community governance approach is seen as an ideal strategy for educating communities about government functions, systems and bureaucracy. It is seen to address concerns with low levels of trust and confidence in government, community expectations for a responsive and accountable government, increased social exclusion and the inability of government to solve all challenges (Arnstein, 1969; Queensland Government, 2005; Willis, 2005). Community engagement, in this case, becomes a form of "networked governance" that aims at strengthening government capacity to respond to community needs, whilst facilitating citizen participation in government decisions (Queensland Government, 2005: 4).

For most developing nations, community/local governance has become an imposed condition for obtaining foreign aid and debt. The assumption by consolidated liberal democracies and donor institutions is that community governance, decentralisation and devolution pave the way for economic growth, transparency, poverty reduction and good governance. Many democracy consolidation programmes have established citizenship initiatives such as study circles and leadership building initiatives to strengthen civil society participation and involvement in democratic processes. In transitional democracies, governance approaches threaten sustainability of one-party hegemonies that are clinging to power through vote buying, ethnic mobilisation and corrupt electoral systems.

Consolidated democracies have institutionalised community engagement programmes that link boroughs, councils and municipalities to local communities. These encompass programmes such as participatory budgeting, sustainable communities, anti-racism initiatives or local assemblies. Community policing, for example, aims to improve neighbourhood safety using local and community intelligence to transform policing from being a police activity to a form of citizen involvement and engagement. Likewise, Scotland's Inclusive Regeneration Programme employs functional participation towards influencing policies and services, a practice Arnstein would have described as tokenism or co-optation (Arnstein, 1969; Hashagen, 2002). In the US, Arnstein (1969) provides American examples of Citizen Advisory Committees, Community Action Agencies and the Model Cities Advisory and Planning Committees as cases of institutionalised participation in local governance, especially in ghetto neighbourhoods. The objective of such structures has been to link citizens to the political processes of making governance work at the local level. Similarly, Hashagen (2002) presents Scottish 'models' of community engagement, three of which are political and inform this governance approach: community organising, public participation and the community democracy model, all of which aim to stimulate governance at the grass-roots level. In such approaches, institutional power structures employ consultation and public participation strategies to obtain grass-roots perspectives, needs or responses to proposals. This is, therefore, an attempt to "extend" democracy into the community, by establishing an "informal tier" of government (Hashagen, 2002: 7).

To implement these structured engagement strategies, such institutions and governments have established Departments of Communities, mandating them to initiate and implement effective community engagement practices across the public sector. Community engagement has then become an instrument for involving citizens in government planning and decision-making in order to achieve policy legitimacy and *publicness* (Queensland Government, 2005). The community governance approach has been used to create government–community collaborations on policy and service questions (Arnstein, 1969; Hashagen, 2002). Oftentimes this type of engagement avoids addressing questions of unequal power relations. The objective lies in only enabling governments to elicit diverse perspectives as a way of improving the quality of its decisions, as such communities end up participating in participation (Arnstein, 1969). But as Willis (2005: 115) observes, the systems approach towards engagement is fraught with problems of participation. Four reasons are cited to support this observation:

> The time and energy requirements for local people to participate; the heterogeneity of local populations meaning that community participation does not always involve all sectors of population; just being involved does not necessarily lead to empowerment; focusing at a micro level can often lead to a failure to recognize much wider structures of disadvantage and oppression.

It is clear from Willis' critique that though the concept of participation is always flagged around in relation to grass-roots development interventions, not all primary stakeholders are involved. In fact, one aspect Willis left out was information—a subject Quebral and Gomez (1976) as well as Gibson and Woolcock (2007) have highlighted—observing that citizens cannot be fruitful and critical participants if they do not have the relevant information about an issue at hand. It is possible, therefore, that adequate consultation mechanisms may be employed in ways that take into consideration the local power and social relations. But if information is not made available to participants, citizens may only end up participating in participation itself.

There are many engagement approaches employed at different stages of the systems approach, but the basic premise is that the communication processes are controlled by governments and institutions. Willis (2005) provides four dimensions within which participation is conceived, namely, appraisal, agenda setting, efficiency and empowerment. The systems community engagement processes, therefore, ideally take place in four phases or levels— planning, strategy development, implementation, feedback reporting and evaluation (South Australia Government, 2008).

From these phases, emerge four major engagement levels: information, consultation, involvement and collaboration. *Information* is marked by a one-way transfer of information using printed and electronic media to help stakeholders to access appropriate information, enabling them to make informed contribution to the engagement process (Queensland Government, 2005). Even though the community might suggest certain items on the agenda, the information provided is decided upon by the institutions supporting the engagement process and agenda. As will be shown in the discussion of the Lewisham Assemblies later in this chapter, the *consultation* level is ideally a two-way and oftentimes a mediated process of seeking and receiving citizen views on pertinent issues. This takes place before or during structured meetings, which from experience, end up including and excluding certain groups in society. In fact, community engagement, if not carefully planned, ends up capturing the voices of the same groups over and over again and then excludes certain groups repeatedly. As such, if not reflexively implemented, community engagement ends up being a process of capturing the voices of the *engageable* groups—those that are always available, those that are always active in community events, those that believe have consolidated historical memory of the community. For Arnstein (1969), Willis (2005) and of course, Taylor, Wilkinson and Cheers (2008), these processes of *information* (provision) and *consultation* are usually structured within unequal power relations, as such, if not carefully thought out, what eventually transpires is merely tokenism and placation.

The *involvement* level encompasses using engagement instruments of printed and electronic media, open house discussions, information contact, interviews, surveys, workshops and field trips (South Australia Government, 2008). Again this is often problematic, because these communication instruments might not suit certain groups in society. It is possible, for example, to produce communication tools that are only used by certain elite groups and thereby marginalise the very groups that the involvement level seeks to capture. The involvement level ideally challenges citizen juries, deliberative polling or mediated and negotiated dialogues to become part and parcel of decision-making (South Australia Government, 2008). These engagement levels allow government and communities to collaborate in agenda setting, policy dialogue and the development and evaluation of policy (Queensland Government, 2005). The *sites* where all these engagement levels are employed include regional parliament, internet broadcasting of parliamentary proceedings, ministerial regional community forums, community cabinets, ministerial regional community forums, negotiation tables, smart service, online engagement through websites or community renewal programmes (Queensland Government, 2005; UK Government, 2008). Again, in the absence of equal power relations, communities cannot guarantee that policy directions will integrate their concerns (Arnstein, 1969; Willis, 2005).

A governance approach, therefore, seeks to bring together organisations and departments to work together in encouraging communities to support working partnerships with their local governments, thereby improving the delivery of public service (Arnstein, 1969; Queensland Government, 2005). It also attempts to allow communities to contribute towards government policy development and decision-making. The approach is seen as a strategy for meeting the expectations of communities whose citizens seek government collaborations in tackling local challenges (Queensland Government, 2005). In this case participatory communication could be considered a partnership between governments and communities in developing local solutions to local problems, as was the case in the Tara engagement process in regional Australia.

The Tara engagement process encompassed collaboration between an Australian community of Tara with government/nongovernment service providers so as to promote local leadership, increase citizen consultation and build local capacity (Cruickshank and Darbyshire, 2005). Tara used to exhibit symptoms of a declining community, marked by increased numbers of people residing on rural subdivisions, over-reliance on local services, high unemployment, crime and insecurity, domestic violence, disability and health (Cruickshank and Darbyshire, 2005). The Tara Community Action Team (TCAT) was established in 2001 to solve local problems using local solutions through transparent communications and engagement with government institutions (Cruickshank and Darbyshire, 2005). The TCAT brought together multi-sectoral government managers, the Tara Shire Council and the Tara Neighbourhood Centre. The engagement process comprised three cycles, involving observation and reflection, planning and action.

Borrowing from the CFSC model (Figueroa et al., 2005), it can be demonstrated that the *catalysts* were the Chinchilla community, which unsuccessfully applied for funding to build an alternative educational centre, and the inefficient Education Queensland official who had concentrated on funding Chinchilla, neglecting the larger Tara community. All of these factors enraged community members (Cruickshank and Darbyshire, 2005). The outrage generated a rational communal *dialogue*, which raised questions about building a better Tara. The process of dialogue involved situational analysis, diagnosis of community problems and generation of possible solutions. The *community action* brought together government managers, Tara Shire Council and Tara Neighbourhood Centre, creating the TCAT. Planning of action encompassed identifying and selecting appropriate solutions, trial and evaluation. The resultant engagement process would generate "purposefully designed" and planned change such as a Housing Policy, active community relationships, new projects, respect for government workers and increased education opportunities (Cruickshank and Darbyshire, 2005). Implemented in other parts of Australia and Western democracies, are various kinds of community governance. Stehlik and Chenoweth (2005), for instance, introduce the 'transformative and innovative community building' model, which emphasises the resilience capabilities of communities in executing community-strengthening projects despite challenges and constraints. Central to the sustenance of this model is a progressive facilitator, the Local Area Coordinator or small community practitioner, who is an advocate of the people (Stehlik and Chenoweth, 2005).

Systems Engagement under the Brockley Assembly, Lewisham Council,[1] UK

As in Australia, the local government system in the UK is partially structured to improve service delivery at the local level. In most of the London's boroughs, the highest unit in local governance is the Council, which is headed by the Executive Management Team comprising a Chief Executive Officer and five directors. To improve citizen participation in local governance, citizens elect a Mayor to lead the Council in proposing the budget and making effective policies. The Council itself is subdivided into Wards, each of which established a Local Assembly as a deliberative unit that enables neighbourhood citizens and their elected councillors to come together to decide on how to regenerate and improve their local areas. Assembly members are those that live, work or study in the area. In Lewisham Council, South East London, each Local Assembly meets four times a year. Lewisham Council observes that the Assembly sessions are "friendly relaxed meetings" that comprise "open discussion and debate about what matters in your area" in order to "make a real change to your area". There are 18 Local Assemblies in Lewisham, one of which is Brockley. The meetings are chaired by one elected Councillor with the support

---

[1]The material used in this section draws upon text available at the website: http://www.lewisham.gov.uk/CouncilAndDemocracy/ElectedRepresentatives/Councillors/LocalAssemblies/ (accessed on 12 April 2012), which has been posted at various times. Specific references are unavailable.

of a Local Assemblies Coordinator who works for the Council. To facilitate the community engagement and involvement in local development planning and implementation in the Assembly, the Locality Fund and the Mayor's Fund are allocated.

The £10,000 annual Locality Fund is largely for community engagement events that allow communities to come together and forge a sense of *community-ness*. Examples of events and activities include fun run, open markets, upgrading open spaces and parks, arts festivals, cultural exchange events, workshops, street tree planting, youth panels, food festivals. On the other hand, the £50,000 Mayor's Fund requires that Assembly members plan local projects towards improving the community but are not necessarily required to carry them out themselves. Such initiatives are often times carried out with other service providers. Examples of projects include buying additional waste bins, decorating recycle bins, communal gardens, filming or music equipment, sports equipment or dance sessions (Brockley Local Assembly, 2009).

Community Engagement and Consultation

There are three main consultation and engagement sessions in the Brockley Assembly: (*a*) the Ward surgeries that are held on the second and fourth Saturdays of each month by the three councillors; (*b*) the Coordinating Group meetings which plan the agenda for the Local Assembly; and (*c*) the Local Assemblies themselves, during which participatory budget sessions are also held. Participatory budgeting is a fundamental facility suggested in the White Paper, through which citizens exercise greater power and responsibility over how local budgets should allocated and invested. The structure and process of consultation is based on Lewisham Council's (2007) strategic guidance towards *Communication, Consultation* and *Engagement*. Consultation and engagement are ideally expected to be timely, diverse, carried out before introducing new initiatives, based on listening to grass roots and based on clear procedures. In terms of standards, the engagement and consultation have provided accurate information to consultees regarding the venue, rationale, objectives, expected outcomes and the consultation itself will respect the rights and privacy of individuals, be ethical, dialogical and allow communities to access the results of the consultation exercise (Lewisham Council, 2007). To evaluate the effectiveness of such engagement and consultation processes, the Council developed three sets of indicators, namely, keeping residents informed, involving residents in making decisions and listening to residents (Lewisham Council, 2007). To meet these goals, Lewisham Council (2007: 10) set up the Communication and Consultation Board, which is expected to:

> Co-ordinate and approve communication, consultation and community engagement activity undertaken on behalf of the authority. [...] Promote best practice and encourage the co-ordination of communication and consultation both within the Council and with our partners. [...] Audit and review communication, consultation and related community engagement activity. [...] Advise on the development of the corporate Communications and Consultation Strategy. [...] Advise officers on effective communication, consultation and related community engagement activity. [...] Establish sub groups or processes to review proposed consultation or communications activity.

From a participatory communication perspective, it is very clear that the idea of the *Big Society* is not new, the emphasis being on building "neighbourhoods who are in charge of their own destiny, who feel if they club together and get involved they can shape the world around them" (Watt, 2010: *Guardian Online*). Lewisham's engagement and consultation provide pathways for the creation of Cameron's *Big Society* through the dialogical and deliberative policy formulation, through strategies such as print publications, street publicity, press and the media, partner organisation communication, face-to-face engagement, consultation (through service user forms, surveys and polling, deliberative sessions) and online communication (Lewisham Council, 2007). The challenge is that most community engagement strategies are structured. Informal engagement such as saloon chats would contribute much to the strengthening of policymaking from below. The expectation is that the consultation and engagement endeavours are supposed to be informative and allow for the strengthening of intra-community partnerships that enable citizens to control local development.

To prepare members to be well informed of impending consultations during Assemblies, the Coordinating Committee plans and prepares an agenda, that includes, among others, detailed concept notes of project proposals submitted for funding to the Mayor's or Locality Funds. Brockley Assemblies always feature agenda items revolving around projects proposed by different local associations. The discussions involve brief updates on the developments taking place within the localities, the possible local partners to help with project implementation and the collective decisions over whether the proposed projects warrant the proposed budgets. The Assemblies allow project proponents to make an oral presentation on the rationale, objectives, budget lines and community benefits of the initiatives. Members then raise questions before participating in open voting over granting funds to projects. Sometimes, projects being preferred by the community require approval at the cabinet level, bringing up tensions between deliberative and representative democracies. The 'rational' discussions do not necessarily involve everyone—as there are more knowledgeable, confident and outspoken members than the rest.

For Taylor, Wilkinson and Cheers (2008), the group of individuals who have lived in a community for a long time and are familiar with each other expend and share more community investment and narratives than most members. Through charity work and other activities, such community members have been able to develop and strengthen their social infrastructure, thereby acquiring higher levels of social capital (Putnam, 2000). The concept and practice of collective and participatory decision-making then is challenged by the unequal distribution of social capital among the members.[2]

Therefore, the implementation of the ideas of *Big Society* and the White Paper requires a priori equalisation of power relationships at the local level, in order to stabilise the levels of social capital among diverse demographic groups in the community. Otherwise, such implementation will rest on the shoulders of

---

[2]For example, even though I felt I had something to say in the Assemblies I have attended so far, I have not been able to because I do not know many residents. It was also frightening to see people like Stuart or Lorna demonstrating a detailed awareness of places and historical developments going as back as six or 10 years. It was only when I volunteered to join the smaller Assembly Coordinating Group that I began to feel more confident to make minor deliberative contributions because I could identify with one or two community narratives.

those with much deeper community narratives, investment and social infrastructure. Social capital has also been a significant factor even in the process leading to the Assembly's organisation and holding of the World Food Festival at Friendly Gardens on 17 July 2010. Unlike the South Acton Food Festival, the food was prepared and contributed by various community members, who celebrated their knowledge of healthy eating and nutrition by bringing dishes from Pakistan, India, Jamaica, Malawi as well as England.

The Empowerment Approach as Community Development

This approach largely builds on theoretical thinking from dominant and alternative development discourses. It is characterised by attempts towards improving the relationship and the participation of rural and regional communities in producing development from below—from the viewpoint of people whose experiences are often footnoted in the dominant development paradigms and narratives. The approach seeks to involve communities experiencing marginalisation, poverty and underdevelopment. In the mechanistic interventions implemented under the first two development paradigms, there was dishonesty, arrogance and disregard for knowledge and experiences of massified constituents (Ascroft, 1974). Though local people have had specialised knowledge, institutional experts and the traditional power holders disregarded its supposed irrelevance and incompatibility with scientific development models (Ascroft, 1974; Kamlongera, 2005). The community development approach emphasises empowerment as constituting emancipation from structures of oppression (Hickey and Mohan, 2004). In critical pedagogy, Freire (1972, 1996) distinguishes banking education from emancipatory education. Banking education is deterministic and mechanistic, in which individuals are treated as dehistoricised and depoliticised subjects, without any agency to change their world (Freire, 1996). Liberatory education, as is the case in this empowerment perspective, problematises the future, challenging participants to use the word or dialogue to intervene in the reconstruction of their world (Freire, 1996). A case in example of this approach in practice is the Kecamatan Community Development Project in Indonesia.

Resulting from the criticism of the modernisation and dependency paradigms, most developing countries embraced Western-recommended economic programmes called social dimensions of adjustment. This would translate into poverty alleviation interventions and become a significant feature of development strategies in many developing countries. To guide the design and implementation of these strategies, Western financial institutions authored a Poverty Reduction Strategy Paper (PRSP), a template which developing nations, especially the Highly Indebted Poor Countries adapted to their contexts. The poverty alleviation programmes would integrate participatory communication as a pathway for addressing the sustainable development, through dispensing funds for execution of projects conceived in and managed by communities. Indonesia, for instance, established the Kecamatan Development Project (KDP) in 1998 to directly dispense block grants of between US$60,000–US$110,000 to its rural sub-districts known as the Kecamatan (Gibson and Woolcock, 2007).

The funds have been largely used to construct infrastructures and establish socio-economic activities. It must be realised that for very impoverished communities, development is understood existentially—it must be seen, it must be eaten, it must be touched, it must be felt. The KDP have attempted to integrate community engagement as an operational philosophy, allowing communities to "convene a series of facilitated meetings at the hamlet, village, and *kecamatan* level to encourage and institutionalise broader community participation in decision-making and priority setting" (Gibson and Woolcock, 2007: 6). The development planning process should ideally involve a series of processes that depend on village-level collaboration with the project bureaucracy. Through deliberative dialogues facilitated by elected village facilitators, communities develop, contest and fine-tune proposal ideas (Gibson and Woolcock, 2007). The assumption by Gibson and Woolcock (2007) is that these development projects allow for citizen delegation, when power itself becomes a subject of negotiation between the traditional power owners and citizens. Questions, however, could be asked about the way in which citizen participation in these projects is structured and doctored though limited budgets, hierarchical bureaucracy, politicisation of decision-making procedures and the limited deliberative spheres where communities can challenge institutionalised approaches towards project conceptualisation and implementation.

The KDP community engagement approach has allowed for *deliberative* and *mobilisational* forms of contestation in formulating pragmatic and collective decisions (Gibson and Woolcock, 2007). Deliberative contestations rely on Rawlsian-like (1997) public reasoning to challenge powerful elements (Gibson and Woolcock, 2007). When Biting Village received a KDP grant for road and market construction projects, the village management team discarded the transparent planning procedures by inadequately socialising the village facilitator, who brought in friends and relatives (Gibson and Woolcock, 2007). In the ensuing conflict, non-elite groups deliberatively contested proposals by the governing elites (Gibson and Woolcock, 2007). Mobilisational contestation, in contrast, captures the "strategic negotiations" and other tactics used in "circumventing dead-end bureaucratic channels" to bargain for power sharing (Gibson and Woolcock, 2007: 9). The District Legislative Assembly inaction over a leaky dam in Ponorogo District resulted in villagers mobilising and organising a public protest that brought in a wide "web of actors" (Gibson and Woolcock, 2007).

The community development approach should be seen as a communicative arbitration, in which stakeholders engage in agonistic and antagonistic confrontation as a form of communication, and as spelt out in Rawl's (1997) and Cohen's (1997) notions of public reason, eventually arrive at some sort of negotiated settlement. Participation is measured by the extent to which communities drive the engagement process, are heard and have their contributions implemented (Arnstein, 1969; Taylor, Wilkinson and Cheers, 2008). Participation in development is thus manifested through community support, ownership and contribution towards initiatives (Taylor, Wilkinson and Cheers, 2008). Hickey and Mohan (2004) lament the dominance of the instrumental, top-down, organisation-driven form of development participation that is ecologically irrelevant and de-emphasises collective and community-driven decision-making. This occurs when outsiders settle the consultation agenda, exclude certain ethnic and demographic groups, and insist on implementing consultation systems inconsistent with community communication structures (Taylor Wilkinson and Cheers, 2008). Resultantly, there emerges some incongruence between preferred community consultation techniques and external development plans. This discussion, however, seeks to demonstrate that the empowerment approach to community engagement rests on two strategies: the knowledge and management model (which integrates the institutional approaches with empowerment models) and the community development model (in which local development planning is the prerogative of communities).

A COMBINATION OF SYSTEMS AND EMPOWERMENT APPROACHES

One case study which demonstrates the increased combination of both systems and empowerment approaches towards community engagement can be found in modern approaches towards agriculture extension. Knowledge Management and Dissemination (KMD) evolved as an agricultural extension approach within the modernisation contexts, primarily to generate and transmit scientific agricultural research to farmers. Though numerous critical analyses of the paradigm continue to label it top-down, agriculture extension has become more participatory considering that PAR has now become a central feature of its praxis. Through numerous affiliate institutions, FAO has pioneered and tested many participatory approaches towards agriculture extension, as is the case in PRCA—the participatory rural communication appraisal (Anyaegbunam, Mefalopulos and Moetsabi, 1998). Through the infusion of new thinking by the Consultative Group for International Agricultural Research (CGIAR), emphasis is supposed to be placed on community involvement in the knowledge and technology generation within specific contexts, though such involvement can be contested. The CGIAR institutes continue to establish KMD programmes, premised on the deduction that relevant research, knowledge and technology can assist farming communities in achieving food security, poverty reduction and preservation of natural resources.

The CGIAR institutions employ participatory community engagement strategies centred on farmer-based experimentation of knowledge and technology. The Adaptive Collaborative Management, for instance, is a KMD model for empowering people to identify local problems and solutions as a fundamental towards managing landscapes for sustainable livelihoods (CIFOR, 2005). In this process, the role of the facilitator is to help participants to develop practical action strategies. This is a participant-facilitator, a communicative mediator who understands and appreciates the praxis of living and engaging with the people. The Forestry Research Institute of Malawi (FRIM) emphasises the role of community engagement in enabling and promoting the participation of local communities and the private sector in forest conservation and management (FRIM, n.d.). To achieve meaningful and sustainable agro-forestry, the institute employs a community participation philosophy that involves:

> Enabling and promoting the participation of local communities and the private sector in forest conservation and management, eliminating restrictions on sustainable harvesting of essential forest products by local communities [...] Empowering rural communities to manage forest resources, forester ownership and rights to trees and ensure that such trees are utilised sustainably [...] Ensuring that men, women and the youth's role in forest and tree resource utilization and management is promoted. (FRIM, n.d.)

The important factor in these participatory communication or community engagement approaches revolves around participatory research that brings on board local communities even before new knowledge and technology have been introduced. This is what the model of PRCA developed by both FAO and the SADC Centre in Communication for Development advocates—the co-researchership between communities and scientists. Likewise, the International Centre for Agricultural Research in the Dry Areas (ICARDA) implements a KMD model geared at achieving proper management of knowledge research generated from science and technology and its linkage into use by local farmers in dry areas.

The KMD processes are seen as strategies that help farmers put generated agricultural knowledge and innovation into practice and develop their experimental and innovative capacities.

They are perceived as being able to strengthen the up-scaling and out-scaling of innovation and technology among farming constituents (ICARDA, n.d.). To understand KMD as a community engagement strategy, studies should locate the encounter points between indigenous knowledge and scientific research; the role of indigenous knowledge communication systems; the production of informal and non-formal education content for rural media and ICTs; the pilot pretesting of generated innovation; and developing relevant evaluation instruments. The KMD blueprints offer possibilities for grass-roots research and engagement through which largely rural and economically marginalised communities collaboratively generate, manage, share and utilise relevant knowledge and technology towards improving rural livelihoods and reducing poverty. The aim is to empower these communities to achieve sustainable development, food security, stronger communities and increased levels of social capital for all groups. The KMD model, therefore, implies democratising knowledge brokering processes, through motivating local people and scientific experts to collaboratively and innovatively improve productivity, food security, livelihoods and strengthen their communities.

Enabling Rural Innovation as KMD

Like ICARDA's community engagement approaches, the Enabling Rural Innovation (ERI) was developed by the International Centre for Tropical Agriculture (CIAT), in order to help rural farming communities to improve human capital, gender equality and natural resource management (Kaaria et al., 2008). The ERI approach aims at redirecting agricultural markets towards poverty reduction through increased agricultural productivity, cheaper food prices and the generation of economic opportunities in the non-farm sector (Kaaria et al., 2008). Central to ERI processes are participatory and decentralised research and development, that include stakeholder engagement, participatory assessment of opportunities and assets, establishment of farmer research committees and the identification of agro-enterprise options (Kaaria et al., 2008: 55). The ERI approaches integrate farmer participatory research, rural agro-enterprise development and natural resource management (Kaaria et al., 2008). The ERI principle is built on four people-centred principles, namely: a resource-to-consumption framework featuring two-way linkages between community assets and their production; balancing food security activities with those that generate income through market-oriented production; building a community-based market culture; and using participatory approaches to decentralise control of the research and development agenda, thereby empowering farmers to experiment with new practices and strengthening their analytical abilities (Kaaria et al., 2008).

In Uganda, CIAT only came in to support the Nyabyumba Farmer Field School in area-based participatory marketing after the potato members had dialogically mapped the actors in potato production and marketing systems (Kaaria et al., 2008). From the perspective of the social change model, the ERI process was initiated by a local *catalyst*—the increasing prices of potatoes and the subsequent need for new markets. The CIAT teams only trained the farmers in rural agro-enterprise development, group dynamics, leadership and conflict management (Kaaria et al., 2008: 57). *Community dialogue* involved identifying new markets, business partners and changing farming and production practices. They negotiated a business deal with Nandos, a multinational restaurant, specifying supply, quality, variety, prices and payment terms. Through an enterprise-planning meeting, the farmers collectively understood the need to transform their production system to meet the market demand (Kaaria et al., 2008). *Community action* involved supplying to Nandos, negotiating with markets independently, initiating internal savings and loan mechanisms (Kaaria et al., 2008). The ERI approach has strengthened farmers' abilities and capabilities to test new varieties and has helped farmers solve problems, it has increased the bargaining power of farmers' groups and strengthened shared household decision-making (Kaaria et al., 2008). In participatory communication therefore, community engagement is about collaborative learning experiences and the involvement of community-based stakeholders in knowledge brokering, exchange and utilisation. As such, community engagement should be seen as a necessary stage in the agriculture extension programme, in which farming communities critically analyse the available information, and with the help of extension agents and researchers, they draw upon available resources to make decisions on whether to adopt the best-bet practices or other Technological, Institutional and Policy Options (TIPOs).

A Revised Agro-knowledge Management and Dissemination Model

This chapter argues that it is possible for a supposedly top-down process of KMD to adopt participatory research and communication strategies. Unlike scholars (Melkote and Steeves, 2001; Morris, 2005; Quarry and Ramirez, 2009; Servaes, 2003, 2008) who conceive diffusionist and systemic approaches in binary antagonism to participatory and bottom-up perspectives, this section demonstrates that practitioners have been able to find a compromise between the two positions. The dissemination instruments (such as radio or television) can be transformed into engagement approaches by bringing in participatory ethos. For instance, rural radio forums offer a Habermasean public sphere for citizens to conduct deliberative development dialogues in response to a disseminated radio programme. Such forums are then transformed into a more participatory communication instrument, requiring communities to generate radio content and simultaneously run supporting development endeavours, as is the case in the Development through Radio (DTR) projects.

The ICARDA's model (see Figure 4.1) could be taken as representative of most CGIAR Institute models and it makes a lot of assumptions: indigenous knowledge is not modern; conflates learning with dissemination; conflates community engagement with dissemination; and perceives end users as beneficiaries. The revised model that this chapter is presenting here portrays KMD as a cyclic process that begins and ends or rather continues with research, since learning is a continuous process.

In this model, focus in not only in transmitting knowledge products such as TIPO-packages, best bet practices (BBPS), knowledge dissemination methodologies, innovations and skills. Rather, it is in improving the learning environment within which the process of knowledge utilisation takes place. It is a conducive learning environment in which the farmer engages with new knowledge and technology that will strengthen the farmer's resolve to make

Figure 4.1: Knowledge Management and Dissemination Model

Knowledge Management

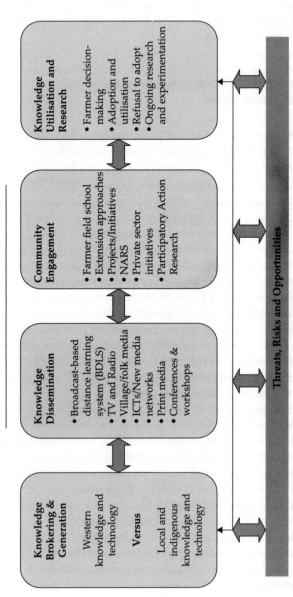

Knowledge Brokering & Generation	Knowledge Dissemination	Community Engagement	Knowledge Utilisation and Research
Western knowledge and technology **Versus** Local and indigenous knowledge and technology	• Broadcast-based distance learning system (BDLS) • TV and Radio • Village/folk media • ICTs/New media networks • Print media • Conferences & workshops	• Farmer field school • Extension approaches • Projects/Initiatives • NARS • Private sector initiatives • Participatory Action Research	• Farmer decision-making • Adoption and utilisation • Refusal to adopt • Ongoing research and experimentation

Threats, Risks and Opportunities

Source: This KMD model has been adapted from ICARDA's KMD model available in their website (www.icarda.org).

pragmatic decisions taking into consideration the constraints as well as the available resources and supporting environment. This model, therefore, has three key processes: *knowledge generation and brokering, knowledge management* (linear and non-participatory methods versus community engagement approaches), *knowledge utilisation and research* (encompassing farmer decision-making and refusal to adopt knowledge and technology). Even with this model, without a coherent implementation strategy, participatory communication becomes another term for spicing top-down initiatives. A good example is the Malawi Rural Growth Centre Project.

Participatory Communication and Development Decentralisation: The Rural Growth Centre Project

Malawi became independent in 1964 but immediately became a dictatorship under the one-party government led by the Malawi Congress Party (MCP) up until 1993, when the country adopted pluralistic politics that enshrined multiparty governance. During the period of high economic growth in the 1970s, the Malawi government embarked on a radical rural development plan that involved the establishment and building of Rural Growth Centres, funded by the German government and the EU. A rural growth centre is a rural market centre within a geographical area that provides a market for local products, social services such as health, education, postal and government business services (Ministry of Local Government and Rural Development, 2008). The Centre is meant to link local subsistence production system to national and regional production systems.

The Ministry of Local Government and Rural Development (2008) observes that the initial MRGC Project attempted to achieve three objectives: to create focal points of development in remote and underdeveloped areas by providing social and economic services and facilities according to needs; to contribute to the decentralisation of administration and foster community development and social participation; and to contribute to the integration of development activities on the local, district and central government levels. There were 14 centres constructed during this period (1977–1990). The pilot phase of the Rural Growth Centres Programme covered

10 centres and came to an end from 1986 when a national programme called National Rural Centre Programme (NRCP) was established (Ministry of Local Government and Rural Development,
2008). The NRCP managed to construct four centres out of the intended 50 centres largely due to aid suspension to the government,
as international pressures against the Malawi Congress Party–led
government intensified. This phase of centre construction was also
criticised for emphasising social service infrastructure and not
production, processing and manufacturing; political interference
in the choice of centre sites; and the failure by local development
committees to maintain the infrastructure (Ministry of Local Government and Rural Development, 2008). It was also established
that most services were underutilised largely because communities were not forthcoming, and in some cases, not interested at
all. Community communication and engagement activities such
as theatre for development were organised by the government
to mobilise communities to use the services (Kamlongera, 1988,
2005).

As part of public sector reform, the Malawi government developed the National Decentralisation Policy and then enacted
the Local Government Act in 1998. The objective was to institutionalise decentralised development planning and consultative implementation by the District Assemblies in liaison with
grass-roots institutions. Around 2006, a new government in the
country reintroduced the MRGC Project, following the Integrated
House Survey of 2005 that revealed increasing rural poverty in
the country. The understanding was that communities and local
development committees would be at the centre of their design
and implementation (Ministry of Local Government and Rural
Development, 2008). This is how the government has conceived
the new Rural Growth Centre Project. The MRGC Project has
been implemented as part of the Growth and Development
Strategy and the Integrated Rural Development Program, whose
principal aim has been to build human, economic and political
infrastructure and capacity that supports rural and regional
development. For the Malawi government, technological deter-
minism notwithstanding, the construction of social service infrastructure is central towards stimulating economic development
in remote and rural Malawi (Ministry of Local Government and
Rural Development, 2008).

Bureaucratic Decentralisation of Local Development Planning

As part of the decentralisation programme, the planning and implementation of development programmes was supposed to have been the prerogative of the District Executive Committees (DECs). The District Development Planning Process takes place at three levels. The Village Development Committees (VDCs) on the ground develop and send their Village Action Plans (VAPs) to the Area Development Committees (ADCs), who prioritise the most important VAPs and then send them to the DEC, which is a technical and advisory body of the District Assembly (Malawi Government, 2001). The VDCs and ADCs are structures that aim to empower local communities to participate in decision-making, management and governance of local development planning and implementation (Malawi Government, 2001). These committees rely on and carry out regular VAP processes to ensure that 'the correct and desired project components are chosen for development' whilst ensuring sustainability and local ownership (Dowa District Executive Committee, 2006). The DEC prioritises the grass-roots development plans and produces a District Development Plan. The DEC comprises the District Commissioner (Chairperson), Director of Planning and Development, Ministry representatives at district level, heads of Assembly departments, NGO representatives and a few co-opted members.

The District Development Planning Committee (an arm of the DEC) conducts desk and field appraisals, to assess whether the community's proposed project is in line with government policies as well as establish the possible community contribution to the proposed development project in terms of labour and natural resources. The irony is that one duty of the DEC is to build the capacity of the VDCs and ADCs in technical, leadership and management faculties (Malawi Government, 2001). In the absence of such capacity building, the continued centralisation and bureaucratisation of local development planning within the DEC ensures, in Lukes' (2005) third view of power, that the subjective interests of government officials and politicians override those of the VDCs and ADCs. One initiative that is supposed to benefit from this decentralised development planning is the revamped Malawi Rural Growth Centre Project.

About 15 new Centres were planned to be built in the country, with funding from the government itself, the Clinton-Hunter Foundation and the German Government, at a cost of between MK95 and MK120 million each (Ministry of Local Government and Rural Development, 2008). The National Decentralisation Policy (1998) and the Local Government Act (1998) mandate local communities to lead the design, implementation and management of development initiatives including the MRGC Projects (Malawi Government, 2001). The problem, however, is that the 'ownership and championship of the vision' for the centre project is the prerogative of the Headquarters of the Ministry of Local Government and Rural Development (Ministry of Local Government and Rural Development, 2008). In this complex matrix of development bureaucracy, the notion of effective engagement with VDCs and ADCs is non-existent and so is an engagement policy. One Centre that has been faced by centralised planning is the Nambuma Rural Growth Centre Project, whose construction is funded by the Clinton-Hunter Foundation.

A meeting of Dowa District Executive Committee was held in February 2006 in relation to the government's revival of the MRGC Project. The meeting had two objectives: to discuss the recent field appraisal conducted by the District's Director of Planning and Development in the community and to discuss the construction of a Rural Growth Centre at this community (Dowa District Executive Committee, 2006). According to the meeting, Nambuma Rural Growth Centre would have two key components: a reliable road network between the main M1 Road and the Centre (as it would open up accessibility to the Centre), a road that is still dusty and almost impassable during the rainy season; and the construction of structures based on the village action plan process (Dowa District Executive Committee, 2006). The construction of this Centre would also include electricity, water, internal road network, telecommunications, produce market, public health facility, police unit, magistrate court, commercial and residential areas ownership (Dowa District Executive Committee, 2006).

The Nambuma Rural Growth Centre Project raises numerous questions regarding the commitment of the central government to decentralise its authority in economic development planning and project implementation. The Nambuma Area Development

Committee believes the consultation process has not been engaging, since:

> What actually happened here was *umbanda* (robbery) because the government officials just came and told us that they had interesting plans for this place and they needed our support. We were not engaged with on what we thought was the best way to build the rural centre. In fact, we can see that the government people are avoiding the grassroots development committees because they don't want accountability. If they have any plans, they only inform their front-line officers without informing our development committee. And when they do come, we are not prepared for their visit. (Manyozo, 2012)

There are two interesting points regarding Lukes' (2005) conceptualisation of non–decision-making that emerge in this observation. The first point regards the tension between representative democracy and electoral democracy. As elected representatives, Malawian politicians are under extreme pressure to be seen to be bringing 'development' into their constituencies. In the end, they exert pressure on both the central and districts governance systems to implement development projects rapidly, and that oftentimes involves cutting through the red tape of the bureaucracy of local development planning. If addressed, the concerns raised by local development committees would delay 'development', with devastating consequences at the next ballot. Subjective political interests of politicians and the central government end up overriding the real interests of the VDCs and ADCs on the ground.

The second point is the deliberate non–decision-making by District Executive Committees. By not properly informing the community development committees of visits or any impending development plans, the government–community interactions are structured in a way that prohibit local concerns from being integrated within development plans. For Arnstein (1969), community development committees end up being out-thought, out-witted or even out-voted because they are not adequately informed of specific policies or plans. In the end, community engagement becomes a session during which government officials lecture communities about the necessary development in that area. In the case of Nambuma, the area development committee wanted a hospital to be built first, but the construction started on the market and a community centre hall, "things that were not a priority" (Manyozo, 2012). Nambuma communities have ended up 'participating in participation' itself, which is a major strategy used by the 'principals' (government officials) to implement non–decision-making (Arnstein, 1969; Lukes, 2005).

What also poses a challenge to decentralised development planning and implementation in Malawi is the increasing latent conflict among development implementing organisations (Lukes, 2005). Such institutions disregard the decentralised planning framework as their primary objective is to 'outsmart each other' in order to "project their institutional perspectives, ideals and agendas onto rural communities" (Chinsinga, 2005: 537). Consequently, such competitiveness has led community development organisations to use financial incentives in soliciting the help of extension workers to build quicker project–community relationships. As communities seem motivated to engage in financially rewarding projects implemented by NGOs, volunteerism on government-led development projects is perceived as slave labour, thereby "diminishing the appeal of participation in local government structures" (Chinsinga, 2005: 537). There is a popular assumption that "development is rich and pays very well, as such, everyone wants to be paid for any local development project" (Manyozo, 2012). Rural development has thus become a flourishing market, dominated by Western organisations, most of whom have no confidence in the accountability mechanisms within local government development structures.

A PARTICIPATORY COMMUNICATION MODEL

The proposed community engagement blueprint includes five processes of mobilisation, research, dialogue, decision-making and empowerment (see Figure 4.2). Cross-cutting through all these elements, processes and procedures are the engagement strategies of informing, consulting, involving, collaborating and building partnerships. The entry point is the *catalyst*, a borrowed idea from the CFSC model, but in this case it is a disagreement or prospect, which initiates an engagement process. Taylor, Wilkinson

Figure 4.2: Proposed Model of Participatory Communication as Community Engagement

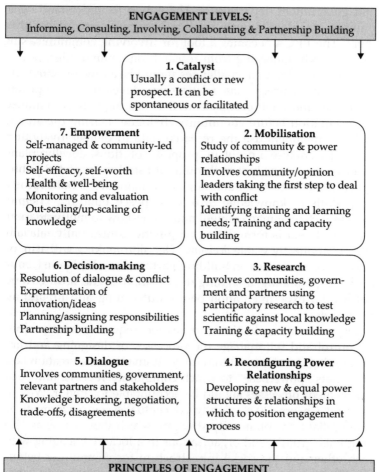

and Cheers (2008) describe the catalyst as being spontaneous or facilitated. *Mobilisation* emerges as a response to the conflict or prospect, usually bringing together opinion and community leaders to explain the problem, providing a rationale for research and dialogue.

Through a series of consultations, a *research process* is executed in collaboration with research institutions, organisations and government departments. The aim is to understand communities of place, power relationships and networks within them. The PRCA becomes a tool for involving communities in this research. Emerging from research on communities, power and local development challenges should be a process of *rethinking and reconfiguring power relationships*, developing new power structures and relationships as well as dealing with community representation before community dialogue. During *community dialogue*, members use the research data to deliberatively and rationally analyse a problem, propose solutions, develop plans and assign responsibilities through physical or mediated public spheres. Facilitators moderating such dialogues should ideally have skills in knowledge brokering, peace building, systems thinking, change management and know-how to motivate communities towards formulating pragmatic, contextually relevant and economically viable *decisions*. Decision-making will also involve making choices on building partnerships, budgeting, raising funds, planning, assigning responsibilities and how to carry out a pilot experimentation before out-scaling and up-scaling the process.

Empowerment is another progression requiring communities to control and self-manage the processes of designing and implementing development initiatives. It involves the creation of a grassroots "powerbase" to which community representatives in engagement processes should be accountable to. Taylor, Wilkinson and Cheers (2008) rightly conceptualise empowerment as being reliant on community strength, which they define as "individuals, groups, and organisations in a locality engaging with each other and the social infrastructure for community betterment". Community strength, combined with community capabilities and community resources, formulates the building blocks of empowerment, and consequently participatory development, thereby enabling communities and their partners to determine the direction of an intervention (Arnstein, 1969; Bessette, 2004; Taylor, Wilkinson and Cheers, 2008). Importantly, permeating through all these levels and elements of the engagement process are principles of value-led, clarity, transparency, sense of agency as well as capacity building and legacy.

AFTERTHOUGHTS

The chapter has demonstrated the third approach towards to the study of media, communication and development—the participatory communication (community engagement) approach. From the perspectives of development theory, participatory communication is an interpersonal communication mechanism that allows for stakeholders to take centre stage in the design, implementation of development plans. From political science perspectives, participatory communication implies the building of networked governance, in which democracy is extended into the local communities, allowing for the creation and sustainability of Cameron's *Big Society*. In both cases, participatory communication implies the strategic and coordinated decentralisation of decision-making processes and structures within institutions, governments and communities.

As an approach to the study of media, communication and development, participatory communication allows for the examination of the field in the site and spaces where the media are playing a footnote role. The first two approaches (media for development and media development) attempt to demonstrate the media-centric critique of the media's role in consolidating good governance and sustainable development. What this chapter has demonstrated is that there are other communicative pathways that do not depend on the media. The discussion has drawn from case studies from the north and south in order to explicate the importance of the MCD debate to both worlds.

The UK Government White Paper, *Communities in Control: Real People, Real Power* (2008), recognises the concentration of power at different levels, hence the need to devolve or pass on power into the hands of citizens. The objective is not just to involve or collaborate with communities but to eradicate the unbalanced power relationship between the principals (the government and local governments and institutions) and the subalterns (citizen and community groups and representatives). This can only be achieved by ensuring that the wretched of the earth have "the maximum influence, control and ownership over the decisions, forces and agencies which shape their lives and the environments" (UK Government, 2008).

From power perspectives, "maximum influence, control and ownership" would imply something much more than substantial or total control—it implies the abolishment of the hitherto hierarchical relationship that characterised principal–subaltern power relationship as well as the repositioning of subalterns as the new principals. It now requires radical rethinking of power relationships to pave way for principal communities who, according to Freire (1996), are in a position to speak and unspeak their world—to critique and intervene in it, to reshape and redesign their world according to their aspirations, needs and world view. The danger, as Freire (1996) cautions, is that the new principals could oppress the subaltern within themselves or the older principals and, consequently, continue the cycle of power concentration. To avoid this, there is need for the current subalterns to liberate both themselves and their current principals so that their assumption of dominant power position should not result in the further centralisation of power, authority and decision-making again. Otherwise, the process of devolution and decentralisation will have ended up in creating alternative concentrated, centralised and oppressive power structures, the very factors that the engagement process intended to eradicate in the first place.

The foregoing has attempted to define community engagement from a communication for development perspective, which has communication, power and participation at its centre. Participatory development entails the active involvement of the citizenry in the design and implementation of policies affecting their lives. The modernisation and dependency approaches assumed diffusionist perspectives towards community engagement through propounding top-down, external and culturally irrelevant participatory approaches. As a strategy of integrating participation in development, community engagement has been 'letter-headed', that is, co-opted and manipulated by organisations and governments, which have all too often implemented policies without adequate consideration for constituent knowledge, aspirations and power relations. Sociocultural dimensions of development are vital, as such, multiplicity paradigms place much emphasis on authoring development from below. Community engagement then becomes a significant strategy for authoring that kind of participatory development.

Participatory communication requires a progressive facilitator who should help people problematise, *speak* and *unspeak* development in their own contexts. The process provides that springboard for community-reliant and managed development interventions as decision-making becomes decentralised. The effect of this decentralisation, however, depends on the amount and level of power allocated to the marginalised constituents. The empirical cases show that local power is embedded in personal and interpersonal relationships, social capital and networks. The difference exists, however, in the institutional and the empowerment approaches. On the one hand, in the institutional (systems) approaches, decision-making processes and structures are commandeered by external stakeholders, who may not necessarily have the interests of the local community at heart. Empowerment approaches, on the other hand, originate from the community, in which local people and grass-roots associations delegate plan and their implementation. Whether systems or empowerment approaches, the participatory communication approach towards the study of MCD shows that the media are just instruments aimed at facilitating the communicative practices surrounding the design, implementation and management of development interventions. In other cases, such media are not needed and the community engagement approach provides that theoretical instrument for studying media, communication and development.

5

Power, Participation and Policy in Media, Communication and Development

THE PROBLEM

This chapter attempts to achieve three objectives. First, it attempts to tie together the three approaches discussed in Chapters 2–4. Second, the chapter proposes a matrix for rethinking the theory and practice of media, communication and development based on an adapted typology of knowledge for development propounded by Mansell (2012). Third, the discussion summarises the key debates and concerns facing this field, for policymakers, practitioners and educators alike. The chapter itself and the ensuing discussion are being construed as a response to invitations by governments, international media and development organisations requesting developing world countries and their partners to develop coherent and ecologically relevant communication for development policies, approaches, methods and training programmes (Balit and Ilboudo, 1996). Based on this last point, the chapter seeks to demonstrate that academic training programmes have the responsibility to respond to the changing approaches and praxes on the ground (led by international and local NGOs) but, at the same time, they also have to provide intellectual enlightenment to the field.

This requires, in part, to holding sustained critical discussions with policymakers and practitioners and at the same time, building teaching philosophies and content on the empirical case studies—since communication for development or MCD (as defined in this book), according to Librero (2009), is as an applied form of communication and at the same time, a transformative endeavour. The chapter, therefore, does not just offer critical perspectives for the sake of it, whilst fantasising impractical blueprints and solutions, but rather involves communication thinkers abandoning the comfort zones of their academic cocoons—and going out in the real world, to test their ideas with real practitioners, on real issues and with real people. The aim is to improve individuals, communities, societies and the environment. This 'improvement' is considered development in some quarters, which is viewed as social change in others (Quebral, 1988; Servaes, 2008). In this case, therefore, the challenge of developing coherent theories and methodologies for the field does not lie solely in the hands of academics and intellectuals but rather at the space of interaction that brings in together theory and practice—hence that space is the site of policy. In an applied communication field like this one, policy can, therefore, be defined as a dialogue, a conversation, an intercourse and of course, an agonistic conflict between theory and practice.

The chapter and the book in general recognise that in the absence of coherent distinction among the three approaches characteristic of previous literature in the field, the debate on and about policy has been dominated by international (Western) organisations who specifically focus on one or two approaches and usually disregard the 'others'. This demonstrates that policymaking in the field is political, as the process has become a site of ideological conflict between international organisations that either prefer media-centric or livelihoods-centric policies—or between academic institutions (who believe the policies lack theoretical basis and are descriptive) and practitioners (who believe that the theories in the field do not pay attention to the 'facts on the ground').

THE GENESIS OF POLICY DEBATES IN MCD

The very first coherent policy questions in the field can be traced to three sources: the Second Vatican Council, Asia/South East Asia and UNESCO. The first source was the Second Vatican Council

(1962–1965), which among other decrees, passed a very important development communication policy that was known as *Inter Mirifica: Decree on the Media of Social Communications* (Second Vatican Council, 1963), which challenged media and communications programmers, producers and other experts to use these instruments to liberate the spiritual and material lives of the public (and specifically the underclass) from the slavery of poverty, underdevelopment, marginalisation and modernism. Other similar documents would be released by this Second Vatican Council in support of the *Inter Mirifica*—and would contribute to the emergence and consolidation of the liberation theology in the Catholic Church, especially in Latin America.

The second source of these policy debates can be traced to Asia and South East Asia, in the 1950s, when national governments and international (largely Western) development institutions mobilised for the integration of media and communication strategies within national development plans (Kumar, 1981; Manyozo, 2012). For example, the Indian government had, by the 1950s, successfully piloted and scaled out/up farm radio forums. Building on this experience, the government would again, in 1959, introduce a national development policy, within its Third Five Year Development Plan, so as to establish 15,000 radio forums by March 1966 (Rogers, Braun and Vermilion, 1977; Rogers, 1993). The successful implementation of this radio forum programme would become a model for similar projects in Africa. By the 1970s, India would introduce two fundamental initiatives—the rural television projects of the Satellite Instructional Television Experiment (SITE) and the Kheda Communication Project. The most important policy development was the Verghese Committee of 1978, whose findings and Report underscored the need for "decentralised and participative development from below" (Kumar, 1981: 221).

Likewise in the Philippines, the Marcos government would launch the 'Bountiful Harvest' campaign, *Masagana 99*, in the 1970s as a countrywide and extensive rice production scheme with the aim of creating self-sufficiency in rice as the staple food in the country. The Ministry of Agriculture launched a food production initiative which involved a 'complete package of technology', a comprehensive credit system without collateral, a market system and a communication campaign that largely depended on radio (Librero, 1985). The community radio station based at the

University of the Philippines, Radio DZLB, was tasked with the testing and refining the *School on the Air* model. In 1976, the station would run a two-month radio school on rice pests and diseases, after which it also organised and conducted several radio schools, at the end of which, students received Certificates of Graduation (Librero, 1985, 2004). In the same vein, Quebral and Gomez (1976) critically examine the country's 1970s Four-year Development Plan of the Philippines, which primarily aimed at uplifting the general well-being of every individual citizen, and they observed that development communication topics automatically emerge from the national development policies.

To achieve these development objectives, Quebral and Gomez (1976) outline the requirements for the kind of communication that can bring about desired change. They distinguish advertising and propaganda from development communication, in that the latter educates for purposes of greater social equality and larger fulfilment of the human potential. As discussed in Chapter 2, a major objective of development communication is transmitting and mediating knowledge that will inform people of significant events, opportunities and dangers, and will also provide a public sphere where issues affecting national or community life may be deliberated. The incorporation of communication policies within national development plans would be adopted by most countries in Asia and South East Asia. It would be the same period that development journalism would be invented and consolidated as a journalistic practice aimed at sensitising, educating and mobilising primary, secondary and tertiary stakeholders on important development questions.

The third source of these debates was UNESCO. By the 1970s, the international community had come to realise the importance of both communication policies in support of development and national communication for development policies. This would result in the 1976 Nairobi General Assembly of UNESCO mandating the organisation to examine problems facing global communications. UNESCO (1980, 2008) would bring global partners and stakeholders to rethink the role of media and communication in good governance and democracy. As discussed in Chapters 1–3, the recommendations of the ICSCP Report (UNESCO, 1980) provided a policy platform for rethinking the political economy of media, communication and development. The questions on policy would indeed loom large, especially considering the ideologically charged environment of the cold war in which the commissioners carried out their work.

THE CENTRALITY OF POWER IN MCD POLICY DEBATES

In a presentation to the Institute of Development Studies, University of Sussex, Mansell (2011) proposes the relocation of the dominant and oftentimes *Western-centric* knowledge for development debate. She observes that past and current research in ICT for development has been largely framed within two axes:

> The first is a producer/user axis, at the extremes of which research is either strongly technology-driven with little regard to the local contexts of its use or it is highly situated in specific contexts without attention to the broader power relations that influence its use. The second is a top-down/bottom-up axis where research is concerned either with programmatic institutional strategies (donor agencies, governments, business) or it is focused on bottom-up participatory initiatives that often lack funding and continuity. [...] Research targeting issues at the nexus of these two axes is largely absent. (Mansell, 2011: 2)

At the interface between these two axes is power, a critical appraisal of which is necessary to allow for the generation of counter-narratives and the subsequent deconstruction of the dominant narrative that promotes a "neoliberal view of markets, a deterministic idea of technology, and a neutral view of information or knowledge" (Mansell, 2011: 3). Drawing on Mansell's critical knowledge for development typology that places power as a key concept in challenging the dominant knowledge-based society/economy models, this chapter is likewise proposing a critical-empirical matrix of media, communication and development that identifies power as a critical and analytical facility that determines the way projects are conceived, executed and evaluated. In this case, power should become a significant critical perspective in MCD studies, projects and experiments.

Regarding the first axis (producer/user), much literature was written in the field after the 1980s, when the discourse of participation became dominant (Gumucio, 2001; Mansell, 2011; Quebral, 1988; Servaes, 2008; Melkote and Steeves, 2001). These writings emphasise that policy debates in the field, especially in the global south, have been designed by Western international development organisations in ways that, according to Freire (1978: 10), provide Western and "earlier experiences some universal validity". Countries and institutions are being co-opted therein to adopt "packaged and prefabricated" policies that have been designed outside specific contexts. This has often resulted in the lack of sustainability of the resultant initiatives and strategies. The literature written before 1980s emphasised scaling up/out of media technology in order to build modern media systems that would be key to transforming the social, psychic and geographical mobilities of the traditional and underdeveloped global south (Lerner, 1958; Rogers, 1976; Schramm, 1964; UNESCO, 1980).

The second axis (top-down/bottom-up) is again extant in these literatures. The trend has been that such studies that build on participatory approaches (post-Freirean/postmodernisation) have undermined the top-down, institutional and mechanical approaches whilst celebrating bottom-up philosophies (Mansell, 2011). For these scholars and studies, the lessons from the failure of the modernisation paradigm to eradicate poverty and underdevelopment demonstrate that the "idea of a Marshall Plan for the development of third world communications is inappropriate", as it will "reproduce western values and transnational interests" and eventually "reinforce minority power structures within third world countries" (UNESCO, 1980: 281). Likewise, Ansu-Kyeremeh (1994) and Freire (1978) caution that development (and by implication, communication) initiatives should not be transplanted but rather be reinvented and, in this case, national governments and stakeholders should have both the power and control to drive the policy formulation and implementation exercise. But, at the same time, these Western-centric studies and scholars that have celebrated the producer-led approaches have also promoted the top-down and institutional strategies and philosophies. This can evidently be seen in media development, in which Western organisations and government promote media and communication systems and models that advance Western concepts of democracy and civil society, without any appreciation of the contradictory and tenuous coexistence of dual governance/civil society models in much of the global south. But this has not been a black and white case, as top-down institutions have claimed to be employing participatory approaches in their work. This is evident in the co-opted consultation praxes that Western and transnational media development organisations employ to encourage national governments and civil society institutions to adopt.

Since the flow and contestation of power is critical in the design and implementation of interventions in media, communication and development, Mansell's typology becomes relevant, as it challenges us to think of the political economy of decision-making. Again, Mansell's typology opens up the field to a critical theoretical trajectory that is missing in the key and monumental work in the field, political economy (Gumucio, 2001; Hemer and Tufte, 2005; Quebral, 1988; Servaes, 2008; Melkote and Steeves, 2001). For Mansell, the debates should not focus on which project was participatory or not, which project was top-down, producer-led or driven by technology or whether it was contextualised—rather, the important questions should be about the power, as in decision-making—in both the structures and processes of development and whether media and communication were employed sufficiently to decentralise these power structures and processes and whether they undermine the political economy of the dominant development discourse.

In the figure below, the three Ps, that is, Power, Participation and Policy, constitute the glue that holds together the three strands/ approaches in media, communication and development. This chapter and this book in general reject the dominant approaches of examining research and projects from the two dominant binary oppositions of diffusionist and participatory approaches that characterise the field (Morris, 2005; Servaes, 2008). In Figure 5.1 this proposed matrix adapted from Mansell's knowledge for development typology challenges scholars, experts and planners to think how each of the three Ps influences the way each of the three MCD approaches floats around the interface of the two axes (the Top-down/Bottom-up and the Producer/User). Figure 5.1 elucidates as to how the contestation of power figures at the confluence of the two axes in media, communication and development.

For example, in the *media for development* approaches, discussions have oftentimes focused on how producers, funders and

Figure 5.1: Two Axes for Rethinking Knowledge in Development

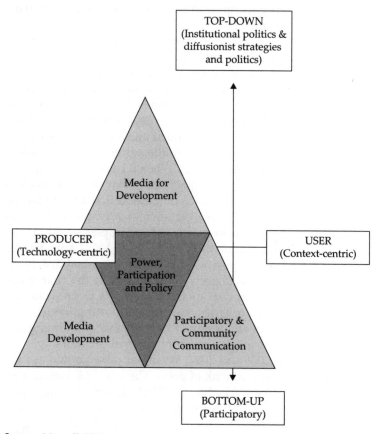

Source: Mansell, 2011.

subject-matter specialists research and produce culturally relevant educational and informative content that will inform and educate people about specific development challenges but at the same time motivate them to act upon that knowledge. The typology above allows us to break down this perception at three levels. At the level of power, it is no longer a question of who controls which processes—but rather how the institutional and knowledge infrastructure (that includes politics of donor aid, organisational politics, professional capacity, digital/media literacy, development and communication policies) work together to influence how primary stakeholders participate in the design and production of the development content.

With regards to *media development*, the general understanding has been a focus on how governments and institutions collaborate to develop media and communication systems that consolidate new democracies. Power as an analytical praxis again looms large, because it enables us to focus on how media and communication systems of donor countries influence and determine the kind of media projects that are funded and supported as well as the level of multi-stakeholderism in the design and implementation of media projects and policies. When it comes to *participatory and community communication*, again, the praxis of power enables us to think of how development, communication and donor aid policies influence the way the instrumental or empowerment approaches to participation are conceived and implemented.

In fact, a careful examination of the three MCD approaches/strands in relation to power shows that organisations interested in improving livelihoods (as spelt out in the first seven MDGs)[1] oftentimes support or implement MCD projects that are non-political and oriented towards supporting livelihoods. In this case, projects are designed in cooperation with and implemented in countries governed by political dictatorships. For example, around 2006 and 2007, Myanmar (also known as Burma) experienced an outbreak of polio. The UNICEF liaised with Myanmar's Ministry of Health, the World Health Organisation, the Centres for Disease Control and the Japanese Government Committee on Vaccines for the Children of the World to organise and implement an intensive immunisation campaign from 2008. This immunisation initiative involved training over 16,000 community health workers, mobilising 32,000 volunteers, public communication campaign (that comprised messages on white street banners, village announcements as well as community communications provided by health workers). When it comes to

---

[1]There are eight Millennium Development Goals, namely: (*a*) eradicate extreme poverty and hunger; (*b*) achieve universal primary education; (*c*) promote gender equality and empower women; (*d*) reduce child mortality rate; (*e*) improve maternal health; (*f*) combat HIV/AIDS, malaria and other diseases; (*g*) ensure environmental sustainability; (*h*) develop a global partnership for development.

media development initiatives, organisations such as UNICEF stick to the provision of technology and skills/capacity to enable marginalised groups join the information society which consequently enables them to participate in the knowledge economy. A good example is FAO, which since the 1980s has helped national governments and local development organisations to establish media projects that are specifically aimed at supporting national development policies.

On the other hand, there are organisations that specifically approach MCD as a political tool in which focus is on building and strengthening democratic cultures in regions and countries. As explored in the discussion of media development in Chapter 3, organisations and institutions working within the political economy of communication perspective (such as IFEX, UNDP, UNESCO, GFMD) have introduced media development projects to strengthen the civil society space in new and transitional democracies. The assumption has been that a stronger media consolidates democratic governance (Keane, 1991). By focusing on the civil society space, these organisations/institutions have overlooked the fluidity of civil society organisations (some of whom threaten investigative journalists who expose the organisations' corruption) as well as underestimate the importance of the state in media and communication policy formulation and implementation. This book, therefore, proposes the active involvement of the government departments of information in media development. The challenge such organisations face is that they cannot work without state involvement and cooperation in countries where democratic governance is tightly controlled, such as China, Burma, Zimbabwe, North Korea and other countries with similar political attributes.

Regarding the *participatory and community communication* strand, power considerations allow us to rethink the institutional/ systems approaches in relation to the empowerment perspectives and discourses. The centrality of power enables a re-examination of the praxis of participation, in which self-management is the most ideal and normative form of power, that is, from the perspective of the primary stakeholders. At the heart of participation (within the framework of this strand) is dialogue. Power perspectives do not just focus on the existence of dialogue, be it within a radio listening club or within a participatory budgeting meeting. It is a question of who is speaking. How are they speaking? To whom are they speaking? And importantly, who is listening? (Or, in other words, is this communicative act of speaking contributing to the *meta* dialogue on the issue?) And for those that are not speaking, the questions would be: who or what is preventing them from speaking? Do they want to speak? Have they ever spoken? Then there are cases of dialogues beneath the dialogues or the actual dialogues versus the imagined dialogues, or the dialogues that never take place even if the said group has spoken.

Actual dialogues refer to the actual conversations, during which participants speak and listen to each other. But some of these actual dialogues are spoken outside the procedures and forums for dialogues because of so many constraints. This is captured well by Spivak (1988) in her examination of the conundrums facing the production and articulation of subaltern speech. A good example comes from some patriarchal societies in the global south in which women, for example, may not be accepted to speak in certain forums and dialogues. During family meals, however, these women are able to advise their husbands or male relations on what to say in the relevant public forum. Considering that most of these 'backstage' contributions are brilliant, in most cases, the male dialogue participants do indeed pass them on, but as their own, without actually acknowledging where they are coming from. The problem arises when these ideas are challenged in these forums—they cannot be defended properly because the actual speakers are not allowed to speak in real time. Thus, an essential element of dialogue—that is, an honest critique and challenge of the communicative act (Calhoun, 1992; Habermas, 1962)—this praxis of public reason (Rawls, 1997) never takes place, as the participants who could defend their ideas are prohibited from presenting and defending their dialogue. In other contexts, such constraints go beyond gender—they include class, literacy, wealth status, level of social capital and other social trajectories.

The mention of social capital and relationships is also important, because it has a huge bearing on the manner in which dialogue is constructed, challenged and appreciated. At the levels of bridging and bonding social capital (Putnam, 2000), the important consideration is the impact of the wealth of connections (*social wealth*) that an individual has. Chapter 4 gave an example of institutional community engagement within the Brockley Assembly in South East London. The general approach of an Assembly involves two stages. An Assembly's Coordinating Committee plans and prepares an agenda, that includes, among others, detailed concept notes of project proposals submitted for funding to the Mayor's or Locality Funds. The discussions involve brief updates on the developments taking place within the localities, the possible local partners to help with project implementation and the collective decisions over whether the proposed projects warrant the proposed budgets. The Assemblies allow project proponents to make an oral presentation on the rationale, objectives, budget lines and community benefits of the initiatives. Members then raise questions before participating in open voting over granting funds to projects. Sometimes, projects being preferred by the community require approval at the cabinet level, bringing up tensions between deliberative and representative democracies. The 'rational' discussions do not necessarily involve everyone—as there are more knowledgeable, confident and outspoken members than the rest.

My participant observations of these Assemblies demonstrate that in most cases, less than 30 per cent of the members make robust contributions to the project proposals, raising questions about informed citizenship and deliberation in Assembly-mediated dialogues. An ongoing ethnographic study into the 'participatoriness' of these Assemblies has revealed two crucial aspects of the politics of public dialogues, especially institutional dialogue. First is that members with higher levels of social capital, community investment and community narratives are active contributors to these dialogues (Taylor, Wilkinson and Cheers, 2008). Such social capital is acquired through charity work, long residence in the Ward and other factors that have allowed them to strengthen their social infrastructure (Taylor, Wilkinson and Cheers, 2008). The second aspect of public dialogue is the need for a priori of equalising power relationships locally, in order to stabilise the levels of social capital among diverse demographic groups in the community. For example, there are very strong ethnic and religious groups who have not yet attended Brockley Assemblies. Though they have larger bonding social capital (Putnam, 2000), the Assembly has not been able to facilitate bridging social capital (Putnam, 2000) with those groups that participate in Assemblies.

THE QUESTION OF POLICY

Policy debates in the field of MCD are very fragmented in two ways. The first fragmentation occurs because of the lack of understanding of how policy debates in the three different approaches (outlined in this book) should be reconsidered differently. This is because the theoretical trajectories that characterise each of these strands are different. The second fragmentation occurs at the juncture of the widespread relevance of the notion of context—and in Mansell's (2012) matrix presented earlier in this chapter, would be described as an obsession with finding a compromise space between producer-led and technologically driven approaches versus the context-centric approaches (that is, finding the balance between the challenges of universalism and contextual specificity). This chapter seeks to examine these two conundrums separately.

The first fragmentation challenges policymakers, scholars and practitioners alike to avoid developing holistic communication for development policies without paying attention to the three approaches. Manyozo (2012) discusses the process and structure of national communication for development (NCD) policy development in West Africa usually funded and mediated by the FAO. The NCD policies were being developed in order to foster the collection and exchange of information among development stakeholders; mobilising communities for development activities, strengthening training skills and communication capacity for development workers; using communication technology in training and education programmes; and alerting development stakeholders to understand grass-roots concerns (Manyozo, 2012). There were some question marks over the policy documents that emerged from the structured workshops: the emphasis on media technology (ICTs, radio, television, press) as reliable pathways for disseminating and exchanging development information, the importance of enabling institutional and juridical frameworks, capacity building and behavioural change communication among others. What is worth noting is that even though UNESCO (1980) had understood and spelt out the three communication for development approaches as part of the ICSCP study by 1980, FAO's processes of developing these policies conflated the three approaches, by not demonstrating that these require completely sets of objectives, needs, indicators, stakeholders and approaches.

It is very obvious that thinking about media development policies that aim to promote good governance and democracy would require engagement with law makers, judiciary, media businesses, media and communication regulatory institutions, civil society, tax departments, mass media institutions and practitioners in order to find a common ground where media can be independent, professional, critical and free. On the contrary, media for development policies seeking to emphasise community-based engagement processes in sustainable livelihoods interventions require engagement with established social enterprises, community development institutions, traditional governance structures, farmers groups (especially in agrarian economies), ministries such as health and agriculture. Likewise, for the media development policies that seek to address community development objectives, the process would require engagement with the latter set of stakeholders than those spelt out under media development-governance strand. For FAO, this was a problem from the start. As it has been observed by Manyozo (2012), the organisation and others (such as UNICEF) have tended to focus on livelihoods interventions and objectives, and, as a consequence, the debates on communication for development policies oftentimes exclude democracy and good governance subjects. Such a divergence in policy approaches by governments and international development organisations consequently influences the way university and non-university training programmes are designed and affected.

Global Policymaking Forums

Central to the expansion of the field of media, communication and development has been the organisation of regional and global forums in which scholars and practitioners have come together to rethink the philosophical foundations of the field. There have been conferences organised to specifically examine one aspect of the field and also clarify the relationship between communication and development.[2] This chapter, however, explores the global forums and initiatives that have attempted to examine the field holistically. After sustainable development became a principal paradigm for organising development thinking within the UN (largely as a response to the increasing poverty and underdevelopment emanating from modernisation approaches) in the 1970s, the UN officially got involved in the field of communication for development when UNDP/UNICEF established the Development Support Communication Service in the Bangkok office, which would be headed by notable individuals like John Woods and Erskine Childers (Quebral, 1988). Alongside this development were efforts by UNESCO (the NWICO debate) and the research centres of Consultative Group for International Agricultural Research (CGIAR).

The UN Inter-agency Roundtable on Communication for Development series have often been facilitated by FAO or other UN organisations whose work focuses on poverty reduction in one way or the other. The discussion themes in these sessions comprise 'sustainable development' topics such as dialogue, learning and participation in natural resource management, communication with isolated and marginal groups, and communication in support of research, extension and education (O'Farrell, 2005). The objective of such roundtables is to demonstrate that "communication for development lies at the heart of the sustainable development" and that it is a powerful instrument for alleviating "poverty and hunger, for learning and empowerment, for advocating and

---

[2.]As observed in Chapter 1, the notable policy forums have included: the Rockefeller Foundation-funded Communication and Social Change Conferences, held in Bellagio, Italy, in 1997 and 2002; the Entertainment Education Conferences for Social Change organised by the Johns Hopkins University Centre for Communication Programs and hosted by different Universities and organisations since 2000; the 2003 Communication for social change conferences organised by the Universidad de Norte, Communication Initiative Latin America (CILA), South Asian Partnership Canada and Canadian International Development Agency (CIDA); the July 2006 Communication, Globalisation and Cultural Identities Conference at Brisbane, Australia; the World Bank–facilitated World Congress on Communication for Development held in Italy in 2006, which brought together practitioners, academicians and policy and decision-makers to map coherent pathways in rethinking and reaffirming the centrality and importance of communication and participation in local, national and international development policies (Communication Initiative, FAO and World Bank, 2007).

stimulating local and international debate on development and social change" (O'Farrell, 2005). To mobilise the UN, governments and other development partners to build communication for development within their work, the roundtable series have proposed and implemented critical strategies such as:

> Compil[ing] evidence to convince policy makers and development planners; Scaling up and better resourcing of communication for development; Building a communication component into development projects from inception; Ensuring that national frameworks support free and pluralistic information systems and community media improving both research and training for communication practitioners; Developing new tools and skills for evaluation and impact assessments; Building alliances, and fostering local, national and regional communication for development processes. (O'Farrell, 2005)

Probably building on these afore-stated strategic objectives, FAO funded and led national initiatives to develop National Communication for Development (NCD) Policies in West Africa between the mid-1990s and the mid-2000 (Manyozo, 2012). An NCD Policy is considered an action plan–based statement that frames the design and implementation of "overall development priorities" (Balit and Ilboudo, 1996: n.p.). This is achieved through establishing the development of a "communication system that encourages people's participation, the sharing of knowledge and skills at all levels and the coordination of efforts among all partners involved in the development process" (Balit and Ilboudo, 1996). With "technical and scientific support" from FAO and UNDP, Mali was the first African country to establish a national communication for development policy in 1993, followed by Guinea-Bissau in 1995, Burkina Faso in 2001 and Niger in 2002 (Manyozo, 2012). These were policy initiatives that never really took off the ground because of poor planning, lack of political will and capital, and as has always been the case with many white elephants, lack of donor funding.

By 2006, the UN was ready to organise the biggest forum that would bring together different stakeholders, from academics to policymakers, from frontline development officers to community development and media organisations. This would see the organisation of the first ever (and as it transpired later, probably the last) World Congress on Communication for Development which would be held in Rome at the FAO headquarters. The actual organisation involved the FAO itself, World Bank and the Communication Initiative. The Congress itself was held between 25 and 27 October 2006, but was supported by prior regional forums and meetings which provided discussion reports and themes for the Rome Congress. At the end of the event, the Rome Consensus (on Communication for Development) was adopted. The most interesting policy development emanating from the Rome Congress was not the reaffirmed commitment to communication for development as a reliable strategy that allows the active involvement of people and other stakeholders in the development process. It was the identification of the four major areas in the field: (*a*) communication and health; (*b*) communication and governance; (*c*) communication and sustainable development; and (*d*) communication labs. These key areas were more or less identical to the others which were identified at other regional roundtables such as the one organised in Nicaragua in 2001—which had emphasised three key paradigms (communication in governance, communication in support of specific development sectors as well as knowledge and information and communication technologies). Importantly, the Congress themes in a way reflect the three approaches presented in this book.

The first thematic area of *communication and health* (reflecting the media for development approach) allowed participants to discuss and make the following recommendations: that there was need to move from behavioural factors towards ecological factors in promoting public and community health; that health education programmes and content be acceptable from the perspective of the targeted audiences; that multimedia approaches should be supported by community engagement processes on the ground; that health communication can only be effective in promoting behaviour and social change if supported by enabling policy; that good communication should enable a shift in power; that communications are effective if they are consistent and carried out over a long period of time; and that representation of multiple voices is an important aspect of empowerment within health communication (Communication Initiative, FAO and World Bank, 2007). The theme of communication and health would be picked up by other development organisations such as the Joint United Nations

Programme on HIV/AIDS (UNAIDS), which would, in August of 2007, organise a 'technical consultation' session on social communication in Geneva.

The second thematic area of *communication and governance* (reflecting the good governance strand of the media development approach) involved examining the role of media in promoting democracy, participation and transparency (Communication Initiative, FAO and World Bank, 2007). The Congress observed that a responsible free media coupled with people's access and participation in the governance processes provided platforms for communication to hold leaders accountable, increasing electoral transparency and other social and financial transparencies, increased people's knowledge of their citizenship rights and their participation in public life (Communication Initiative, FAO and World Bank, 2007). It was also observed that regulatory mechanisms require protection and strengthening to allow for free flow of information, more bottom-up flows of information and communication and move beyond propaganda (Communication Initiative, FAO and World Bank, 2007). Probably emanating from this thematic forum and the resulting recommendations, the work of the GFMD would be consolidated, by bringing together over 500 media development organisations to support the planning, design and evaluation of independent and free media globally.

The third theme of *communication and sustainable development* (reflecting the participatory communication and the media for development approaches, including the community development strand of the media development trajectory) provided the holistic observations regarding the field as a whole compared to other themes. The discussion sessions identified five main problems facing the field of media, communication and development (Communication Initiative, FAO and World Bank, 2007). These challenges comprised the lack of: *(a)* knowledge and capacity by decision makers, *(b)* well-trained trained practitioners, *(c)* political will by governments, *(d)* working partnerships among key stakeholders, and finally, *(e)* the understanding over the role of ICTs and new media. The discussions within this theme gave priority to 'sustainable development' topics such as poverty reduction, food security, natural resource management, and the importance of local and indigenous knowledge. Major recommendations included the proposal to develop national policies in communication for development (something FAO had attempted to do in West Africa), integrating development communication approaches within national development programmes, developing rural communication systems in much of the global south, the need to rethink and revisit the role of ICTs in socio-economic development (especially in relation to regulation, access and costs), the need to strengthen partnerships among academic institutions, donors, governments and NGOs (Communication Initiative, FAO and World Bank, 2007).

The fourth thematic issue, *communication labs*, was more of a discussion strand at the Congress that examined cross-cutting "methodological issues such as impact evaluation and the adoption of participatory communication approaches, as well as the use of media (including community media) and ICTs in development initiatives" (Communication Initiative, FAO and World Bank, 2007: 87). The debates centred on threats (such as media concentration, widening digital and economic divides, digital and social exclusion) and opportunities (improved media access and participation, consolidation of horizontal communications). This fourth strand has allowed for a rethink of the integration of ICTs within communication for development based on four negotiation points: (*a*) that ICT for development policies should not be technologically deterministic by being more participatory (as in collaborative open software development, cf. Berdou, 2011), thus become what Quebral (1988: 45) terms as 'participative communication technology'; (*b*) that policies must focus on enabling the effective use of and impact of ICTs at the grass-roots level; (*c*) that policies should consider people with disabilities and other special needs and rights (such as those of minorities); and (*d*) that ICT policies should aim to improve people's livelihoods (Communication Initiative, FAO and World Bank, 2007).

As a global policymaking forum, the Rome Congress, made some crucial observations about the nature, past and future of the field of communication for development. Critical to the Congress was defining what the field is all about: that it refers to a "social process based on dialogue" that aims to achieve positive change through "listening, building trust, sharing knowledge and skills, building policies, debating and learning" (Communication Initiative, FAO and World Bank, 2007: xxxiii). One factor identified as threatening the field, however, was lack of trained practitioners, as that directly impacts on the generation of thinkers, policymakers, planners as well as practitioners on the ground. Whereas there are still very few relevant training programmes in the field, it is important to examine what these training programmes are offering in relation to the ideals and recommendations of the Congress.

TRAINING IN COMMUNICATION FOR DEVELOPMENT

In a viewpoint article published in *Media Asia*, Manyozo (2007) examines the six schools of thought in the field and establishes the two major perspectives and approaches towards degree-level training in the field. These two approaches should not be conceived as antagonistic or in binary opposition to each other. The work of Freire (1972, 1996) has become a negotiation point that is bringing them together. The two perspectives are: (*a*) the development communication model, which has its roots in agriculture development and can easily be identified with the Congress' third thematic area of *communication and sustainable development*; and (*b*) the social change blueprint, which can be identified with the first and second thematic areas of the Congress—the *communication and health* as well as the *communication and governance* strands.

The Development Communication Model

The intellectual philosophical foundation of the development communication training model can be traced to the College of Agriculture at the University of Philippines-Los Baños from the mid-1960s. The college had just put together an MSc Programme in Agriculture Communication and also introduced a major in development communication. As Librero (2009) observes, all the college was doing was to experiment with creative and theory-informed methodologies for scaling out and scaling up of the knowledge, best-bet practices and TIPOs generated from training and research institutions to those considered the end users of knowledge and technology, the rural farming communities. As a training model, development communication recognises the challenges of underdevelopment as a result of colonialism and postcolonialism (Manyozo, 2007; Quebral, 2011). Historically, the devCom model evolved from within universities but was complemented further by international development organisations (working in the developing world), who saw the need for interactive communication processes that would encourage community participation and ownership of development interventions (Gumucio and Rodriguez, 2006).

There are three fundamentals to this training model. First is that because the devCom training model has origins in agricultural extension and rural and community development, the curriculum and courses have largely been formulated around the sustainable livelihoods thinking (Quebral and Gomez, 1976). Helmore and Singh (2001: 2–3) observe that the sustainable livelihoods paradigm "builds on the building blocks of development", focusing on the wealth of poor people, and this includes issues such as income generation, environmental and natural resources management, the empowerment of women, appropriate technology, good governance and education. The paradigm offers a holistic strategy towards addressing underdevelopment and poverty, focusing on poor people's assets, adaptive strategies, participation and empowerment, finances, indigenous knowledge and their forms of governance (Helmore and Singh, 2001). The resulting devCom programmes and courses, especially from South East Asia, were designed to reflect the aspirations of a people as articulated in national development goals, a reason probably that caused some Western scholars to confuse development communication with government propaganda (Manyozo, 2007; Quebral, 2011).

The second fundamental of this devCom training model is a methodological question, the emphasis on participatory action research. Emerging in the mid-1970s, as an alternative approach to formalist and traditional approaches to research which position(ed) the researcher and the research subjects in binary opposition based on the differences in knowledge capital between the two, PAR is a decentralised approach to research in which professional researchers and local communities work together to improve a specific situation (Bacon, Brown and Mendez, 2005; Chambers, 2005; Kamlongera, 2005). As a methodological strategy, PAR is considered a cyclical process of learning, looking, reflecting, sharing and acting that "involves a wider diversity of stakeholders as active participants in a process of both research activities and efforts to act for positive change" (Bacon, Brown and Mendez, 2005: 2). Participatory Action Research, therefore, goes beyond traditional ethnography, in that focus is no longer on constructing a 'thick description' but using the collaboratively generated thick description to solve local development conundrums. Within PAR, the traditional power relationships that characterise the inequality between researchers and researched are deconstructed, and thus the researched becomes both an active participant and a subject matter specialists in the research process.

The third fundamental of this training model is development economics, especially the knowledge economy debate, in which political economy perspectives (Mansell and Wehn, 1998; Mansell, 2011; Pejout, 2010) are being drafted into the field to explain how ICTs can be harnessed to bridge both the digital and economic divides. Studies and experiments have focused on possibilities of e-banking in rural and regional communities (as in M-Pesa in Kenya), improvement in e-governance and e-democracy (as is being carried out by the Cambridge University's Centre of Governance and Human Rights [CGHR]) or whether ICTs can create and expand employment opportunities in the global south (Pejout, 2010). This third fundamental has been an important trajectory in the model and the field as a whole, largely because development communication scholarship has often suffered from the footnoting of political economy perspectives. The financial and strategic support for the design, implementation and scaling out/up of ICT for development research and interventions has mostly come from international development organisations, especially The World Bank, the United Nations Commission on Science and Technology for Development (UNCSTD), or the International Development Research Centre (IDRC).

As discussed in Chapter 1, the first university to implement the devCom model based on the sustainable livelihoods approach was the University of Philippines, which, in the 1960s, started offering a major in development communication within the MSc Programme in Agriculture Communications. Principal to this offering was the university-based radio station, Radio DZLB, through which agricultural staff members and researchers used as an agricultural extension facility to assist in "conducting rural broadcasting research relating to the effective dissemination of agricultural information" (Librero, 1985: 2–3). Historical developments led to the development communication unit becoming a department, an institute and, today, a full college on its own. Having experimented with using strategically and purposively designed communication tools in agricultural extension, Quebral then proposed and developed a four-year Bachelor of Science degree curriculum in development communication, which was offered from the 1974/1975 school year (Quebral, 1975; Manyozo, 2006, 2012). By offering this full-fledged curriculum, the Department of Development Communication became the first to offer devCom degree training in the world. The bachelor's programme, then as well as today, had four areas of majoring: development broadcasting, educational communication, development journalism and science communication, the principal objective of the university being to help students "grasp" the "issues and problems of development" and "apply the concepts, principles and skills of communication in the solution of problems in a developing society" (Quebral, 1975: 31).

Probably with the influence of the College of Development Communication (CDC), other universities have employed a similar DevCom model in designing their own communication for development programmes within the same region and in other parts of the world; after all, the CDC "does not own the intellectual property rights to development communication" (Quebral, 2002: 16). The CDC has helped institutions to establish postgraduate devCom programmes perceived from local perspectives and contexts, a case in example being CDC's collaboration with the Kasetsart University in Thailand, helping the latter develop a postgraduate programme in devCom (Librero, 2009). Manyozo (2007) observes that Kasetsart's devCom courses such as broadcasting for development, writing for development or communication systems management, reflect the influence of the agricultural origins of the Los Baños development communication. Similar programmes have emerged in India (Govind Ballabh Pant University of Agriculture and Technology), Europe (University of Reading) and Africa (Universities of Malawi, Mozambique and Zambia). It is important to note that some of these programmes do not necessarily offer subjects directly dealing with development, poverty reduction, economics or sociology, but their philosophical orientation leans towards poverty reduction as well as the farming and rural communities since the "sheer number and its central role in the economy give the rural family the edge" when it comes to development communication training (Quebral and Gomez, 1976: 5).

The Social Change Training Model

Manyozo (2007) argues that the social change training model has origins in Western social psychology, political science and Latin American educational communication. The theoretical foundations of this model can therefore be traced to the enlightenment philosophies of Jurgen Habermas (public sphere and deliberative democracy), behavioural change models (such as Health Belief Model, Theory of Reasoned Action), Jan Servaes (information highways), John Keane (media and democracy) and Clemencia Rodriguez (citizens' media). Unlike the development communication model, which emphasises the sustainable livelihoods thinking, the social change training model is largely media-centric—as it attempts to train students who can understand the excellent approaches of using media to advance social change objectives. There are three fundamentals to this training model.

The first is that media is an important instrument of democracy. As discussed in the media development approach (especially in the good governance strand), the organisation of regulation of media systems and structures have a huge impact on the way democracy flourishes within nation states. Apart from holding leaders to account, the media informs and educates the citizenry, mobilises them to perform their citizenship and act as a mediator between citizens and the state. Scholarship emerging from within this model, therefore, builds on the work of Habermas and other political philosophers and centres on the question of deliberative democracy as well as the tensions between and among the three spheres of the state, market and civil society.

The second fundamental of this training model is that the strategic use of media can directly impact on behavioural and social change in society. Key to this thesis is the entertainment–education approach building on the communication theory approach, developed by Miguel Sabido and the Population Communication International, and further elaborated by the John Hopkins University and other public health communication research centres in the Western world. This has seen the development, scaling up and scaling out of mass media-based social communication campaigns in the global north and south, in which attempts have been made to influence positive changes in behaviour. Examples of campaigns include HIV/AIDS, maternal and child health, reproductive health or human rights. In the end, the summative evaluations attempt to demonstrate that a particular change in behaviour or practice can be attributed to a specific communication intervention.

The third attribute of the model rests in the importance of local and community-owned media that advances the tenets of access and participation, otherwise known as citizens' media (Rodriguez, 2001). The concept of citizens' media can be explained and understood as ongoing communication processes, in which communities employ and appropriate media tools to generate and circulate alternative histories, reflective consumption of which enables them to generate power, new identities and social action (Rodriguez, 2001). The emergence of the internet has changed the way access and participation are conceived, as it has allowed those traditionally considered consumers to become producers. Internet has also enabled community media to overcome the strength and limitation of locality and reach global communities, thereby *glocalising* (Hemer and Tufte, 2005) citizens' media themselves. Studies and scholarship have, therefore, focused on re-examining the whole question of democratising communication, empowerment and how such media use these available luminal spaces (Mbembe, 2001) to contest hegemony and ideology.

Building on such theoretical terrains, the social change model can thus be seen as attempting to formulate a communication for development paradigm that is relevant to both developing and developed societies. Since the term "development" is seen as reducing issues of empowerment to livelihoods only, the term "communication for social change" has been promoted by some researchers and practitioners, as it is seen to embrace issues of empowerment, active citizenship and social change (Figueroa et al., 2005; Manyozo, 2007; Quebral, 2002, 2011). The emphasis is, therefore, on training social change communicators who "can apply communication concepts and techniques to promote active participation among citizens in their society's development processes" (Peirano, 2006: n.p.). Though communities will be encouraged to participate in policy dialogues affecting their governance and development, it is the social change communicator who is the "expert in diagnosing communication problems, planning solutions and monitoring and evaluating results" (Peirano, 2006; Gumucio and Rodriguez, 2006). For example, the School of Communication Arts and Sciences of the Catholic University of Peru offers media-centric social change courses such as writing for media, communication theory, photography, persuasion, theoretical perspectives on communication for development, interpersonal communication, advertising production, digital journalism and investigative journalism (Peirano, 2006).

Similarly, the University of Ohio's Centre for International Studies, located in the School of Telecommunication, offers a master's in international affairs, and courses include communication and development, research methods in mass communication, mass communication theory, tropical public health, international journalism, film production and, not least, communication and campaigns. Other institutions offering this social change model include: Malmo University in Sweden (which offers a distance education communication for development master's, which is theoretically located within discourses of social change, globalisation and communication); the University of West Indies' Caribbean Institute of Media and Communication (CARIMAC) offers a Master of Arts in communication for social and behaviour change; Institute of Social Communication at the Tangaza College in Kenya; other offerings are available in the Department of Public Relations at Chulalongkorn University in Thailand, the Department of Community and Performing Arts at King Alfred's College in Winchester as well as journalism and communication departments of American, Australian, African and European universities (Manyozo, 2007).

It should be mentioned that the development communication and social change models should not be entirely seen as too exclusive—there have been consistent attempts to bridge the gap. Apart from the efforts of the Communication for Social Change Consortium, funded by the Rockefeller Foundation, the work of Freire (1972, 1996) is another connecting point, and his theories on critical pedagogy have become useful to scholars and students working within the two training paradigms. Freire's thinking on critical pedagogy, consciousness building, adult education, and the participatory nature of the education and communication process has contributed a lot to a rethink of how both training models and approaches conceive notions of participation, power and policy.

CONCLUDING THOUGHTS: MCD POST-QUEBRAL

This chapter has attempted to crystallise how Mansell's (2011) knowledge for development typology enables a huge rethink in the way the field of media, communication and development is imagined at the level of power, policy and participation. It is no longer a question of relevant technology or local contexts, nor is it a question of top-down or bottom-up approaches. It is a question of how power (as in delegated authority, à la Arnstein, 1969; Graham, 2005; Mansell, 2004) figures in the political economy of both development and communication. A key indicator of whether MCD interventions have played a critical role in society then should revolve around a careful and systematic understanding of how power has been negotiated and contested in favour of people (Melkote and Steeves, 2001; Servaes, 2008). For those that did not have power in the first place, indicators should challenge practitioners, policymakers and scholars to gauge whether power (and how much of it) has been passed into the hands of communities. For those that had power but could not exercise it, indicators and interventions should explain how the constraints that prevented them from exercising it have been removed or alleviated. Empowerment requires tipping the balance of power in favour of those who did not have it—a question that is the objective of all media, communication and development interventions, not just behavioural and social change. In fact, social change that does not address the root causes of inequality serves temporary objectives and, over time, people find themselves in the same situation that caused them problems in the first place.

The book in general has attempted to posit a three-tiered theoretical framework for examining the field of applied communication as well as the intellectual tradition known as media, communication and development. Whereas Quebral's two seminal publications on development communication (1975, 1988) provided the pioneering Magna Carta of this field; whereas Melkote and Steeves (2001) provided a coherent and detailed (but Western-centric) theoretical overview of the field; whereas Servaes (2003, 2008) explored the different strands and approaches that have evolved from both the global north and the global south, this book has gone a step further. Its frame has been informed by years of designing and teaching modules in Africa and Europe and has been located within postcolonial thinking (deliberately to unsettle the post-Rogers revisionism that attempts to locate the origin and nature of the field within Western and neo-liberal concepts of de-velopment and social change), and has importantly propounded a three-tiered theoretical framework for examining the questions of media and communication as applied within the attempts to transform the political economy of development.

As such, this book pushes the boundary of the field even further. It moves the debate from emphasis on information and communi-cation, from participatory communication, from the development of media systems and structures, from the empowerment of peo-ple just to improve their lives. Rather, it employs Mansell's (1982, 2011) argument that no matter how much participatory media and communication interventions can be designed and implemented, as long as they do not unsettle, destabilise and transform domi-nant paradigm of development (that has contributed to so much poverty, underdevelopment, degradation of the environment, unemployment and other forms of misery and social evils), then nothing will have been achieved. Mansell (1982, 2011) contends that the debate should be about how media and communication (including new media and ICTs) can be harnessed to *transform* the political economy of development itself in order to establish sus-tainable socio-economic orders that enable the efforts of people to bear fruits and improve their lives. So, for Mansell (1982, 2011), it does not matter how many condoms are distributed and used as a result of HIV/AIDS communication campaigns, but whether the socio-economic conditions that place people in unequal relation-ships (with other people, institutions and ideologies) have been transformed, to ensure that their lives are no longer exposed to conditions that contribute to the spread of the epidemic. Thus, it is not just a question of teaching farmers new farming methods or giving them fertiliser to increase their yield, when the farm-ers themselves have no ownership rights over the land they are working on, when unscrupulous businessmen exploit the market practices to rob the farmers of their hard-earned yields, when policies leave the same farmers vulnerable to exploitative landlords. The important lesson emerging from this book is that there should be a well-organised synergy between international and local efforts at transforming the political economy of development.

This book has attempted and successfully demonstrated that the three approaches (that are in themselves, theoretical trajectories) make amenable the examination of the heterogeneous strands that contributed to the development of the field we call development communication or communication for development, or, as has been the case in this book, media, communication and development. The field did not emerge as a homogenous intellectual tradition, nor did it originate in the West as has been popularly contended (Gumucio, 2001; McPhail, 2009; Melkote and Steeves, 2001; Quarry and Ramirez, 2009; Rogers, 1976, 1993; Servaes, 2003, 2008). As demonstrated in Chapter 1, the field originated in the activities of practitioners in Asia, Latin America, Africa and much of the global south, as they grappled with making sense of growing poverty and inequality. Much as the north provided the theoretical illumination that enabled a rethink of the theoretical framework that would enable development communication to grow, it was the efforts of the development broadcasters of Radio DZLB in Philippines and Radio Sutatenza in Colombia, it was the efforts of the development journalists in Philippines and India, it was the efforts of the members of theatre for development troupes in Africa and Asia that finally provided an intellectual and philosophical springboard to Nora Quebral and the UPLB's College of Development Communication to invent the term 'development communication' to describe theory-based and method-driven employment of media and communication as tools and processes in making development work for subaltern constituents. The three approaches presented in this book allow us to acquire a holistic history-from-below perspective of how the field emerged, where it is now and the prospects facing practitioners, students, scholars and policymakers in the future.

Postscript
The Day Development Dies
(and the Expert Survives)[1]

There is a certain kind of assumption that permits the Western thinking that sacrifices rich narratives for theory. Theory becomes a prison, limiting knowledge production to references to (largely Western) scholarship. However, theory is not inaccessible: theory is coherent, theory is liberating, theory is narrative, and it is every day. This postcolonist auto-ethnographic orality uses personal experiences as a theoretical tool for explaining that in development thinking, the 'experts' are morally and ideologically distant from local people, knowledge, and places, and hence they are illegitimate representatives who should never be consulted in the first place.

Even during the emergence of the modernisation paradigm in the 1940s, postcolonist development thinkers were already questioning the role of the 'expert'. There are two kinds of experts: the external and the internal. The external expert is always an outsider but relies on the internal expert, mostly an educated local professing an objective understanding of people, places and development issues. The following discussion demonstrates that the internal expert is an obstruction to people-centred development processes.

Growing up in poverty in Malawi was somehow a blessing. Apart from the many material things we did not have, we were privileged to grow up in a dysfunctional community and family.

---

[1]This postscript was originally published as 'The Day Development Dies' in Manyozo (2010).

One advantage of being raised in a dysfunctional family is that one grows up rough and tough. No matter what comes your way, life does not scare you. Families in our clan used to brew illegal traditional gin, and there were always drunken people in the compound. I grew up surrounded by noise and by lots of children. It was as if the parents were not around. Not that this bothered me, since my father, too, used to disappear once in a while, leaving my unemployed mother with two children, myself and a sister. Absent fathers have been an infectious disease in our clan.

I resented my mother's selling traditional gin, because there were so many men in our yard, and worse, because of the noise. Nevertheless, I admired my mother for her ability to manage the shebeen business and still raise her kids in a religious way. She has always been a wise woman, but determined. When the rains washed away the only wooden bridge between our village and the primary school, almost every kid in the village dropped out from school. She would, despite my protests, wrap up my uniform in a plastic satchel, escort me through the muddy waters and dress me in my uniform. For her, this was the only way I could 'complete the white man's education'.

Apart from the dramas in the shebeen, the thing I loved most was spending time with fellow goat herders. After school, every boy (for this was considered a boy's job) would take his family goats to the village forests, where there was green grass. We would learn to play games, hunt mice, rabbits and grasshoppers and of course, do what boys always do when they just want to be boys—fight. We watched traditional dances in the moonlight together, as the ladies in the village performed those nice dances that involve shaking the waists and the beads, consequently shaking the manhood out of every living boy and man who happened to be watching.

Football also preoccupied our minds. We played football when we went to school. We played football during break. We played on the road when we came back from school. We played football all the time. The village had about three teams. The big boys played in the A team, and they used the leather ball. The B team, like us the C team, used the plastic paper balls, which we rolled into a spherical shape and tightened with strings. My team mates were those that I used to herd goats with. They were the same buddies I used to swim with at the village river. They were the same friends who taught me to eat stolen chicken. We were together when we received the Eucharist sacrament. Our being together all the time made up for the absent fathers, I guess.

Football was everything, because it had the ability to bring the whole village together, even though our senior team usually lost. All I remember is that when they won, there were evening 'reward sessions', when they would allocate the nice girls to each other and pair by pair they would disappear into the night. It was as if even the girls themselves always looked forward to our village's victory, because of such 'rewards'. As C team players, we grew up expecting to be rewarded one day, if we were to bring glory to our village.

Time seemed to move slowly. Wedding after wedding, traditional dances after traditional dances, football games after football games, funerals after funerals, we were growing up, but perhaps we were too preoccupied to notice.

Most of the A and B team players must have grown older, married or moved from the village for reasons one never knows. I just know that one day we were on the pitch representing the village, using the leather ball now. We were beaten 10–0 and were even jeered by our own village. Then the team went on a long losing streak. Until one day, two refugee boys came to live in the village, after their families had fled from the war in Mozambique. These boys joined us in herding the goats, swimming and playing football. One of them was a very good striker, and the older one joined me in defence. They encouraged us to be much rougher with our opponents, to instil fear in them. While waiting for a corner, for instance, we could slap our opponents, irritate them and if they retaliated, we would fight them, because we were good at that.

Over time, we started experiencing draws and then unconvincing victories followed. There was once again growing interest in football in the village. The key was to play rough: after all, games in those days had no referees. A corner could be contested verbally or through a fist fight between the striker who was claiming it and the defender who was arguing for a goal kick. Teams would come together, find a solution and the game would continue. Our football team grew up together, and within a short time the Mozambican boys began to speak our language fluently. We would sit and listen to their stories about war, about how soldiers would force women to cook and eat their own children. In the meantime, we were becoming a feared team in the traditional authority.

Two rivers away from our village, there was another football team, which was well known and had beaten our village a couple of times in the past. Whoever introduced the idea is not important, but we discussed it at length, especially knowing that it would involve money. We collected money from every willing adult in the village, as did the other team in their village. Added together, the money would be awarded to the winners.

The build-up was rife with rumours of members of both teams sleeping at graveyards to boost their athleticism. We might have slept at the village graveyard, I am not sure, but even if we did, it would not have been the first time. As a boost to our morale, a distant relative of mine, who had been living in the city, came for a short visit. He had been a good goalkeeper when he left many rain seasons before. We used to call him 'The Cat', because of the way he jumped to save shots that were almost going into the net. He had come back in time, but we suspected that the village store owner had brought him back for the match.

All over the place, there was talk of this match. The women and men in the fields, the girls at the river, all talked about the game. We were pumped up because we had not lost on home ground in a long period of time. When he joined us, 'The Cat' started to act like our coach. It was the first time we noticed that we did not have a coach—it was something our group had never discussed. Our strategies had always resulted from collective negotiations during the game or at half time, when village elders would come and swear at us for missing this or that ball. Sometimes five of them would be talking at the same time, and even though we could not remember what they actually said, we always got the point: that the second half had to be better than the first.

'The Cat' talked about a 4–3–3 'system', because we needed the third striker to drop and strengthen the midfield. He expressed reservations about our team being full of attacking players, and he did not think I was tall enough to be a defender. A taller and stronger boy in midfield was brought back into defence, and because of my short height, I was asked to play on the right midfield berth and supply the crosses. To be sure, we had a strength-testing match against another village team that had caused us problems. With 'The Cat' in goal, we had plenty of confidence and we smashed them 4–0. The new system that he introduced seemed to be working miracles. He organised our attacks and our defence, and with him in goal, we were ready to win the eagerly awaited game.

Days passed by quickly, and soon it was this big Saturday. The whole village stopped, except for the shebeens. It was not only money that was at stake here. Bragging rights were also at stake. Someone may also have said that there could likely be 'rewards' afterwards!

The first half was a dull affair, and it ended goal-less. The visitors were also too defensive. The second half started the same way, until half-way through it 'The Cat' decided to take out one of the Mozambican boys playing in defence and bring in another boy, a very good striker, but who had not played with us on a regular basis. Although most of us were unhappy with the substitution, we did not protest openly — after all, 'The Cat' was the oldest, and the only one who understood 'the system'. But we also knew that he was the only one who could shout back at the elders if they shouted at us during the half-time break.

A few minutes after the substitution, we scored. The women started singing praises to 'The Cat'. That goal, however, seemed to have made the visitors grow extra legs, and they equalised. 'The Cat' started shouting at everyone. For the first time, we started blaming each other in the middle of a game. To strengthen our defence, we tried to revert to our traditional pre-system system: pack the backline with bodies, and then deliberately hurt their effective players, which would eventually slow them down. 'The Cat' insisted that we remain faithful to the 'system', and that meant going back into 'our positions'. They scored. 'The Cat' made a couple of changes. They scored two more. We lost everything.

The village blamed the whole team except 'The Cat'. If it was not for him, the score could have been worse, it was being said. He openly criticised us after the match. We never talked about that match again, even when we went back to swim or herd goats together. Deep down in our hearts, we knew that we lost the game on the day when 'The Cat' walked into our midst as the football expert. We could not comprehend 'the system', but the village blamed us for not understanding it. More painfully, 'The Cat' seemed to have walked off the defeat as a victor. We saw him before he left for the city, drinking and laughing with village elders.

I was about to leave for high school, still a virgin. We believed that it was The Cat's expertise and the system that were the actual source of the defeat, as we could not play to our strengths. If we had lost when playing our traditional system, we might not have won, but it would not have hurt so much, and maybe it would have propelled us to prepare effectively for another game.

Like that lost game of football, the developing world is littered with bodies of abandoned or dead development initiatives. The modernisation paradigm has re-emerged within numerous participation-resistant models, which depoliticise questions of power, decision-making, engagement and local knowledge. Development dies on the very day that external and internal experts, without an understanding of the local setting, come in with their fancy ideas about implementing strategies and initiatives that do not build on local knowledge and strengths.

When Western development industries urge the developing world to build their project initiatives upon recommendations from experts who do not understand local development contexts, when these experts enter the communities and begin to propose strange systems and strategies, you should get a pen and paper and immediately start writing an obituary for that development intervention.

Bibliography

Adhikarya, R. 2004. 'A Personal Tribute to Everett Rogers', *Media Asia: An Asian Communication Quarterly*, 31 (3): 123–26.

Adjaye, J. 2008. 'The Technology of the Human Voice: Oral Systems of Information Dissemination and Retrieval among the Akan of Ghana', *The International Information and Library Review*, 40 (4/December): 236–42.

Adorno, T. 1959/2001. *Kant's Critique of Pure Reason*. Cambridge: Polity.

Adorno, T. and M. Horkheimer. 1944/1972. *The Culture Industry: Enlightenment as Mass Deception in Dialectic of Enlightenment*. New York: Seabury Press.

Agrawal, B. 1981. *SITE Social Evaluation: Results, Experiences and Implications*. Ahmedabad, India: Space Applications Centre, ISRO.

Airhihenbuwa, C. and R. Obregon. 2000. 'A Critical Assessment of Theories/Models Used in Health Communication for HIV/AIDS', *Journal of Health Communication*, 5 (Supplement): 5–15.

Allen, T. and N. Stremlau. 2005. 'Media Policy, Peace and State Reconstruction', in O. Hemer and T. Tufte (eds), *Media and Glocal Change: Rethinking Communication for Development*, pp. 215–32. Buenos Aires: Clacso and NORDICOM. Available online at http://bibliotecavirtual.clacso.org.ar/ar/libros/edicion/media/18Chapter12.pdf (accessed on 12 April 2012).

Amin, S. 1984. 'Self-reliance and the New International Economic Order', in H. Addo (ed.), *Transforming the World Economy? Critical Essays on the New International Economic Order*, pp. 204–19. London, Sydney, Auckland and Toronto: Hodder and Stoughton.

———. 1989. *Eurocentrism*. Translated by Russell Moore. New York: Monthly Review.

Ansu-Kyeremeh, K. 1994. *Communication, Education and Development: Exploring an African Cultural Setting*. Alberta: EISA Publishers.

Anyaegbunam, C., P. Mefalopulos and T. Moetsabi. 1998. *Participatory Rural Communication Appraisal: Starting with the People*. Harare and Rome: SADC Centre of Communication for Development and FAO.

Arnold, A. K. 2010. 'Media Development vs. Communication for Development: Structure vs. Process'. Available online at http://blogs.worldbank.org/publicsphere/media-development-vs-communication-development-structure-vs-process (accessed on 12 April 2012).

Arnstein, S. 1969. 'A Ladder of Citizen Participation', *Journal of the American Planning Association*, 35 (4): 216–24. Available online at http://lithgow-schmidt.dk/sherry-arnstein/ladder-of-citizen-participation.html (accessed on 12 April 2012).

Ascroft, J. 1974. 'A Conspiracy of Courtesy', in *Ceres, The FAO Review*. Reprinted in 1978, *International Development Review*, 3. Reprinted in A. Gumucio and T. Tufte (eds) (2006), *Communication for Social Change Anthology: Historical and Contemporary Readings* (pp. 71–75). New Jersey: CFSC Consortium.

Ascroft, J. and S. Masilela. 1994. 'Participatory Decision Making in Third World Development', in S. White, K. Sadanandan Nair and J. Ascroft (eds), *Participatory Communication: Working for Change and Development*, pp. 259–94. New Delhi: SAGE Publications.

Aubel, J. and the Grandmother Project. 2006. 'Grandmothers Promote Maternal and Child Health: The Role of Indigenous Knowledge Systems' Managers', *IK Notes*, 89 (February). Available online at http://siteresources.worldbank.org/EXTINDKNOWLEDGE/Resources/iknt89.pdf (accessed on 12 April 2012).

Bacon, C., M. Brown and E. Mendez. 2005. 'Participatory Action Research and Support for Community Development and Conservation: Examples from Shade Coffee Landscapes in Nicaragua and El Salvador'. University of California, Santa Cruz, Center for Agroecology and Sustainable Food Systems. Research Briefs, Paper Number 6: 1–12. Available online at http://repositories.cdlib.org/cgi/viewcontent.cgi?article=1021&context=casfs (accessed on 12 April 2012).

Bailey, O., B. Cammaerts and N. Carpentier. 2007. *Understanding Alternative Media*. Maidenhead: Open University Press.

Balit, S. and J. P. Ilboudo. 1996. 'Towards National Communication for Development Policies in Africa'. Rome: FAO, Communication for Development Branch. Available online at http://www.fao.org/sd/cddirect/cdan0001.htm (accessed on 12 April 2012).

Beckett, C. 2008. *Supermedia: Saving Journalism So It Can Save the World*. Oxford: Blackwell.

Beltrán, L. R. 2004. 'I Have Lived My Life As a Communication Artist, Not a Scientist: Transcript of a Conversation with Alfonso Gumucio', *Mazi: The Communication for Social Change Report*, 1 (November). Available online at http://www.communicationforsocialchange.org/dialogues.php?id=233 (accessed on 12 April 2012).

Berdou, E. 2011. 'Participatory Methodologies and Participatory Technologies: Resonances, Opportunities and Misunderstandings', *Global*

Purse. Available online at http://www.unglobalpulse.org/blog/partic-ipatory-methodologies-and-participatory-technologies-resonances-opportunities-and-misunde (accessed on 12 April 2012).

Bessette, G. and C. V. Rajasunderam (eds). 1996. *Participatory Development Communication: A West African Agenda.* Ottawa, Canada: IDRC.

Bessette, G. 2004. *Involving the Community: A Guide to Participatory Development Communication.* Ottawa, Ontario, Dakar, Montevideo, Nairobi, New Delhi and Singapore: IDRC and Southbound.

Bjorkman, I. 1989. *Mother Sing for Me: People's Theatre in Kenya.* London: ZED Books.

Boal, A. 1979. *Theatre of the Oppressed.* London: Pluto Press.

Brockley Local Assembly. 2009. *Brockley Local Assembly Mayor's Fund: Summary of Bids.* Lewisham, London: Lewisham Council, unpublished discussion document.

Brokensha, D., D. M. Warren and O. Werner (eds). 1980. *Indigenous Knowledge Systems and Development.* Lanham, MD: University Press of America.

Cadiz, M. C. 1991. *Educational Communication for Development: Basic Concepts, Theories and Know-how.* Laguna: UPLB College of Agriculture.

———. 1994. *Communication and Participatory Development: A Review of Concepts, Approaches and Lessons.* Laguna: University of the Philippines.

Calhoun, C. (ed.). 1992. *Habermas and the Public Sphere.* Cambridge, MA: MIT Press.

Cammaerts, B. 2008. *Internet-mediated Participation Beyond the Nation State.* Manchester: Manchester University Press.

Carpentier, N., R. Lie and J. Servaes. 2003. 'Community Media: Muting the Democratic Media Discourse', *Continuum: Journal of Media and Cultural Studies,* 17 (1): 51–68.

Castells, M. 2009. *Communication Power.* Oxford: Oxford University Press.

Chalkley, A. 1972. *A Manual of Development Journalism.* Manila: Philippine Press Institute.

Chambers, R. 1981. 'Poor Visibility: How Poor Policy Makers Overlook The Poor', *The New Internationalist,* 96 (February). Available online at http://www.newint.org/features/1981/02/01/poor-visibility/(accessed on 12 April 2012).

———. 2005. *Ideas for Development.* London and Sterling: Earthscan.

Childers, E. and M. Vajrathon. 1975. 'Social Communication Components in Development Programs', in J. Jamias (ed.), *Readings in Development Communication,* pp. 37–46. Laguna: UPLB College of Agriculture.

Childers, E. 1976. 'Development Support Communication: Thread for Development Planning', *Information Centre on Instructional Technology (ICIT) Report,* 16 (October): 1, 5–6.

Chinsinga, B. 2005. 'District Assemblies in a Fix: The Perils of the Politics of Capacity in the Political and Administrative Reforms in Malawi', *Development Southern Africa,* 22 (4): 529–48.

Chouliaraki, L. 2006. *The Spectatorship of Suffering*. London, Thousand Oaks and New Delhi: SAGE Publications.

———. 2010. 'Post-Humanitarianism: Humanitarian Communication beyond a Politics of Pity', *International Journal of Cultural Studies*, 13 (2): 107–126.

Christians, C. 2004. '*Ubuntu* and Communitarianism in Media Ethics', *Ecquid Novi*, 25 (2): 235–56.

CIFOR. 2005. *Contributing to Africa's Development Through Forests; Strategy for Engagement in Sub-Saharan Africa*. Bogor Barat, Indonesia: Centre for International Forestry Research.

Cohen, J. 1997. 'Deliberation and Democratic Legitimacy', in J. Bohman and W. Regh (eds), *Deliberative Democracy: Essays on Reason and Politics*, pp. 67–92. Massachusetts, London and Cambridge: MIT Press.

Colle, R. 2003. 'Threads of Development Communication', in J. Servaes (ed.), *Approaches to Development: Studies on Communication for Development*, Chapter 6, pp. 1–77. Paris: UNESCO Communication and Information Sector.

Communication Initiative, FAO and World Bank. 2007. *World Congress on Communication for Development: Lessons, Challenges and the Way Forward*. Washington DC: The World Bank. Available online at ftp://ftp.fao.org/docrep/fao/010/ai143e/ai143e00.pdf (accessed on 12 April 2012).

Communities Scotland. 2007. 'National Standards for Community Engagement'. Glasgow: Ministry of Communities. Available online at http://www.scotland.gov.uk/Resource/Doc/94257/0084550.pdf (accessed on 12 April 2012).

Cruickshank, M. and A. Darbyshire. 2005. 'Who Changed Tara? A Case Study of Community Participation and Engagement', International Conference on Engaging Communities, 14–17 August 2005, Brisbane Convention Exhibition Centre. Available online at http://www.engagingcommunities2005.org/abstracts/Darbyshire-Andrew-final.pdf (accessed on 12 April 2012).

Davenport Sypher, B., M. McKinley, S. Ventsam and E. E. Valdeavellano. 2002. 'Fostering Reproductive Health Through Entertainment-Education in the Peruvian Amazon: The Social Construction of Bienvenida Salud!', *Communication Theory*, 12 (2/May): 192–205.

Davidson, J. 2009. 'Media and Development: Where's the Gap?'. Available online at http://www.charliebeckett.org/?p=1393 (accessed on 12 April 2012).

Deane, J. 2008. 'Media Development or Media for Development? Wrong question—But what's The Right One?'. Available online at http://www.comminit.com/en/node/277011/bbc (accessed on 12 April 2012).

Diaz Bordenave, J. E. 1977. *Communication and Rural Development*. Paris: UNESCO.

Dowa District Executive Committee. 2006. *Report on Dowa DEC Meeting*. Unpublished, 20 February.

Dura, L., A. Singhal and E. Elias. 2008. 'Listener as Producer: Minga Perú's Intercultural Radio Educative Project in the Peruvian Amazon', in M. B. Hinner (ed.), *A Forum for General and Intercultural Business Communication* (Freiberger Beitrage Zur Interkulturellen Und Wirtschaftskommunikation). Frankfurt am Main, Germany: Peter Lang GmbH. Available online at http://utminers.utep.edu/asinghal/Book%20Chapters/BC_Dura-Singhal-Elias-2008-Intercultural%20Radio%20Educative%20Project.pdf (accessed on 12 April 2012).

ECA. 2007. *Harnessing Traditional Governance in Southern Africa*. Lusaka: Economic Commission for Africa, Southern Africa Office. Available online at http://www.uneca.org/srdc/sa/publications/HarnessingTradGovrSA.pdf (accessed on 12 April 2012).

Escobar, A. 1995. *Encountering Development: The Making and Unmaking of the Third World*. New Jersey: Princeton University Press.

FAO. 2005. *Communication for Development Roundtable Report: Focus on Sustainable Development*. 9th United Nations Communication for Development Roundtable. Rome: Government of Italy, UNESCO, World Bank, IDRC, CTA. Available online at http://www.fao.org/docrep/008/y5983e/y5983e00.htm (accessed on 12 April 2012).

Fanon, F. 1960. *The Wretched of the Earth*. New York: Grove Press.

———. 1965. *A Dying Colonialism*. New York: Grove Press.

Figueroa, M. E., D. L. Kincaid, M. Rani and G. Lewis. 2005. *Communication for Social Change: An Integrated Model for Measuring the Process and Its Outcomes*. Communication for Social Change Working Paper Series. New York: Rockefeller Foundation.

Finnegan, R. 1970. *Oral Literature in Africa*. Oxford: Oxford University Press.

Flor, A. 1995. *Broadcast-based Distance Learning Systems*. Quezon City: University of the Philippines Press.

———. 2004. *Environmental Communication: Principles, Approaches, and Strategies of Communication Applied to Environmental Management*. Diliman, Quezon City: Open University of the Philippines.

Ford, L. 2007. 'Katine Project'. Available online at www.guaardian.co.uk/katine (accessed on 12 April 2012).

Frankfurt, H. 1988. *The Importance of What We Care About: Philosophical Essays*. Cambridge and New York: Cambridge University Press.

Freire, P. and M. Horton. 1990. *We Make the Road by Walking: Conversations on Education and Social Change Between Myles Horton and Paulo Freire*. Edited by Brenda Bell, John Gaventa and John Peters. Philadelphia: Temple University Press.

Freire, P. 1972. *Pedagogy of the Oppressed*. New York: Continuum.

———. 1978. *Pedagogy in Process: The Letters to Guinea Bissau*. London: Writers and Readers Publishing Cooperative.

Freire, P. 1996. *Letters to Cristina. Reflections on my Life and Work.* New York and London: Routledge.

FRIM. n.d. 'Forestry Research Institute of Malawi'. Available online at http://www.frim.org.mw/contents_frim.html (accessed on 12 April 2012).

Fulcher, J. and J. Scott. 2007. *Sociology.* Oxford and New York: Oxford University Press.

Galeano, E. 1973. *Open Veins of Latin America: Five Centuries of the Pillage of a Continent.* New York and London: Monthly Review Press.

Gibson, C. and M. Woolcock. 2007. 'Empowerment, Deliberative Development and Local Level Politics in Indonesia: Participatory Projects as a Source of Countervailing Power'. Brooks World Poverty Institute (BWPI), Manchester. Available online at http://www.bwpi.manchester.ac.uk/resources/Working-Papers/bwpi-wp-0807.pdf (accessed on 12 April 2012).

Graham, P. 2005. 'Political Economy of Communication: A Critique'. Canada Research Chair in Communication and Technology, University of Waterloo. Available online at http://www.philgraham.net/MME%20Chapter_Final.pdf (accessed on 12 April 2012).

Gumucio, A. 2001. *Making Waves: Stories of Participatory Communication and Social Change.* New York: Rockefeller Foundation.

———. 2004. 'Open Conclusion', in A. O'Connor (ed.), *Community Radio in Bolivia: The Miners' Radio Stations,* pp. 129–32. Lewiston, New York: Edwin Mellen.

Gumucio, A. and C. Rodriguez. 2006. 'Time to Call Things by Their Name: The Field of Communication and Social Change', *Media Development,* 3. Available online at http://www.waccglobal.org/en/20063-communication-for-development-and-social-justice/586-Time-to-Call-Things-by-Their-Name-The-Field-of-Communication—Social-Change.html (accessed on 12 April 2012).

Gunaratne, S. 1996. 'Old Wine in a New Bottle: Public Journalism Movement in the United States and the Erstwhile NWICO Debate', paper presented at the 20th General Assembly, Scientific Conference of the International Association for Media and Communication Research, Sydney, 18–22 August.

Habermas, J. 1962/1989. *The Structural Transformation of the Public Sphere.* Cambridge: Polity.

Hallin, D. C. and P. Mancini. 2004. *Comparing Media Systems: Three Models of Media and Politics.* Cambridge: Cambridge University Press.

Hashagen, S. 2002. 'Models of Community Engagement'. Glasgow: Scottish Community Development Centre. Available online at http://leap.scdc.org.uk/uploads/modelsofcommunityengagement.pdf (accessed on 12 April 2012).

Health Communication Partnership. 2003. 'The New P-Process: Steps in Strategic Communication'. Available online at http://www.hcpartnership.org/Publications/P-Process.pdf (accessed on 12 April 2012).

Hedebro, G. 1982. *Communication and Social Change in Developing Nations: A Critical View*. Ames: Iowa State University Press.

Helmore, K. and N. Singh. 2001. *Sustainable Livelihoods: Building on the Wealth of the Poor*. Bloomfield, CT: Kumarian Press.

Hemer, O. and T. Tufte (eds). 2005. *Media and Glocal Change: Rethinking Communication for Development*. Göteborg and Buenos Aires: NORDICOM and CLACSO Books.

Hickey, S. and G. Mohan. 2004. 'Towards Participation as Transformation: Critical Themes and Challenges', in S. Hickey and G. Mohan (eds), *Participation: From Tyranny to Transformation? Exploring New Approaches to Participation in Development*, pp. 3–24. London and New York: ZED Books.

Hilliard, R. and M. Keith. 2001. *The Broadcast Century and Beyond: A Biography of American Broadcasting*. Boston, Oxford, Auckland, Johannesburg, Melbourne and New Delhi: Focal Press.

Hilliard, R. 2003. 'Farm and Rural Radio in the United States: Some Beginnings and Models', in B. Girard (ed.), *The One to Watch: Radio, New ICTs and Interactivity*, pp. 201–08. Rome: FAO and Friedrich Ebert Foundation.

Huesca, R. 2003. 'Tracing the History of Participatory Communication Approaches to Development: A Critical Appraisal', in J. Servaes (ed.), *Approaches to Development: Studies on Communication for Development*, Chapter 8, pp. 1–36. Paris: UNESCO Communication and Information Sector.

ICARDA. n.d. 'Mega Project 6: Knowledge Management and Dissemination for Sustainable Development in Dry Areas'. Available online at http://www.icarda.org/Megaproject6.htm (accessed on 12 April 2012).

Ilboudo, J. 2003. 'After 50 Years: The Role and Use of Rural Radio in Africa', in G. Girard (ed.), *The One to Watch: Radio, New ICTs and Interactivity*, pp. 209–20. Rome: FAO and Friedrich Ebert Stiftung.

Jallov, B. 2005. 'Assessing Community Change: Development of a "Barefoot" Impact Assessment Methodology', *The Radio Journal: International Studies in Broadcast and Audio Media*, 3 (1): 21–34.

Jamias, J. 1975. 'The Philosophy of Development Communication', in J. Jamias (ed.), *Readings in Development Communication*, pp. 13–24. Laguna: UPLB College of Agriculture.

———. 1991. *Writing for Development: Focus on Specialised Reporting Areas*. Laguna: UPLB College of Development Communication and the Foundation for Development and Communication.

Jayaweera, N. 1987. 'Rethinking Development Communication: A Holistic View', in N. Jayaweera and S. Amunugama (eds), *Rethinking Development Communication*, pp. 76–94. Singapore: The Asian Mass Communication Research and Information Centre.

Jonasi, S. 2007. 'What is the Role of a Grandmother in a Malawian Society and How Can We as Health Care Workers Support Her?', *Malawi Medical Journal*, 19 (3): 126–27.

Kaaria, S., J. Njuki, A. Abenakyo, R. Delve and P. Sanginga. 2008. 'Assessment of the Enabling Rural Innovation (ERI) Approach: Case Studies from Malawi and Uganda', *Natural Resources Forum*, 32 (1): 53–63, February.

Kahssay, H. M. and P. Oakley. 1999. *Community Involvement in Health Development: A Review of the Concept and Practice*. World Health Organisation: Geneva.

Kamlongera, C. 1988. *Theatre for Development in Africa with Case Studies from Malawi and Zambia*. Bonn and Zomba: University of Malawi Fine and Performing Arts Department and German Foundation for International Development.

———. 2005. 'Theatre for Development in Africa', in O. Hemer and T. Tufte (eds), *Media and Glocal Change: Rethinking Communication for Development*, pp. 435–52. Göteborg and Buenos Aires: NORDICOM and CLACSO Books.

Kamlongera, C., M. Nambote, B. Soko and E. Timpunza-Mvula. 1992. *Kubvina: An Introduction to Malawian Dance and Theatre*. Zomba: University of Malawi.

Karppinen, K. 2007. 'Making a Difference to Media Pluralism: A Critique of the Pluralistic Consensus in European Media Policy', in B. Cammaerts and N. Carpentier (eds), *Reclaiming the Media: Communication Rights and Democratic Media Roles*, pp. 9–30. Bristol: Intellect Books.

Keane, J. 1991. *The Media and Democracy*. Cambridge: Polity Press.

Khan, M. A. 1995. *The History of Urdu Press: A Case Study of Hyderabad*. New Delhi: Classical Publishing Company.

Kilpatrick, S. 2009. 'Multi-level Rural Community Engagement in Health', *Australian Journal of Rural Health*, 17 (1): 39–44.

Kivikuru, U. 1994. 'Going Grassroots', *Changing Mediascapes? A Case Study in Nine Tanzanian Villages*. Helsinki: University of Helsinki Institute of Development Studies. Reprinted in A. Gumucio and T. Tufte (eds). 2006. *Communication for Social Change Anthology: Historical and Contemporary Readings*, pp. 407–18. South Orange, NJ: CFSC Consortium.

———. 2005. 'The Citizen, Media and Social Change in Namibia', in O. Hemer and T. Tufte (eds), *Media and Glocal Change: Rethinking Communication for Development*, pp. 325–33. Göteborg and Buenos Aires: CLACSO and NORDICOM. Available online at http://bibliotecavirtual.

clacso.org.ar/ar/libros/edicion/media/27Chapter20.pdf (accessed on 12 April 2012).

Krohling Peruzzo, C. 2004. 'Right to Community Communication, Popular Participation and Citizenship', in M. J. Da Costa Oliviera (ed.), *Public Communication*. Alinea: Campinas, Brazil. Reprinted in A. Gumucio and T. Tufte (eds). 2006. *Communication for Social Change Anthology: Historical and Contemporary Readings*, pp. 801–05. South Orange, NJ: CFSC Consortium.

Kruger, L. 1999. *The Drama of South Africa: Plays, Pageants and Public Since 1910*. London: Routledge.

Kumar, K. 1981. *Mass Communication in India*. Bombay, Hyderabad, Calcutta, Madrass, Delhi and Bangalore: Jaico Publishing.

———. 1994. 'Communication Approaches towards Participation and Development: Challenging Assumptions and Perspectives', in S. White, K. Sadanandan Nair and J. Ascroft (eds), *Participatory Communication: Working for Change and Development*, pp. 76–92. New Delhi: SAGE Publications.

Lennie, J. and J. Tacchi. 2011. *Researching, Monitoring and Evaluating Communication for Development: Trends, Challenges and Approaches*. Report on a literature review and consultations with Expert Reference Group and UN Focal Points on C4D Prepared for the United Nations Inter-agency Group on Communication for Development. Available online at http://www.unicef.org/cbsc/files/RME-RP-Evaluating_C4D_Trends_Challenges__Approaches_Final-2011.pdf (accessed on 12 April 2012).

Lerner, D. 1958. *The Passing of Traditional Society: Modernising the Middle East*. New York and London: Free Press and Collier-Macmillan.

———. 1971. 'Toward a Communication Theory of Modernization: A Set of Considerations', in W. Schramm and D. Roberts (eds), *The Process and Effects of Mass Communication*, pp. 861–89. Urbana, Illinois and London: University of Illinios, Urbana.

Lewisham Council. 2007. *Communication, Consultation and Engagement: Strategic Guidance, 2007–2008*. Lewisham, London: Lewisham Council, unpublished document.

Librero, F. 1985. *Rural Educational Broadcasting: A Philippine Experience*. Laguna: UPLB College of Agriculture.

———. 2004. *Community Broadcasting: Concept and Practice in the Philippines*. Singapore: Marshal Cavendish International.

———. 2005. 'The Contribution of the University of Philippines at Los Baños to Communication for Development'. Telephonic interview conducted by Linje Manyozo. 19 August.

———. 2009. 'Development Communication Los Banos Style: The Story behind the Story'. Presented in the symposium with the theme— *Development Communication: Looking Back, Moving Forward*, sponsored by the UP Alliance of Development Communication Students, UPLB College of Development Communication, 8 December 2008. Available online at http://www.upou.edu.ph/papers/flibrero_2009/ DevcomLB_history.pdf (accessed on 12 April 2012).

Loo, E. 2009. *Best Practices of Journalism in Asia*. Singapore: Konrad-Adenauer-Stiftung. Available online at http://www.kas.de/wf/doc/ kas_18665-544-2-30.pdf (accessed on 12 April 2012).

Lukes, S. 2005. *Power: A Radical View*, 2nd Edition. London: Macmillan.

Malawi Government. 2001. *Development Planning System Handbook for District Assemblies*. Lilongwe: Ministry of Local Government and Rural Development.

Malinowski, B. 1926. *Crime and Custom in Savage Society*. London: Routledge & Kegan Paul.

Mamdani, M. 2007. 'The Politics of Naming: Genocide, Civil War, Insurgency', *London Review of Books*, 29 (5/8 March): 5–8. Available online at http://www.lrb.co.uk/v29/n05/mahmood-mamdani/the-politics-of-naming-genocide-civil-war-insurgency (accessed on 12 April 2012).

Mansell, R. E. and U. Wehn. 1998. *Knowledge Societies: Information Technology for Sustainable Development*. Oxford: Published for the United Nations Commission on Science and Technology for Development by Oxford University Press.

Mansell, R. E. 1982. 'The "New Dominant Paradigm" In Communication: Transformation versus Adaptation', *Canadian Journal of Communication*, 8 (3): 42–60. Available online at http://www.cjc-online.ca/index. php/journal/article/view/278/184 (accessed on 12 April 2012).

———. 2004. 'Political Economy, Power and New Media', *New Media and Society*, 6 (1): 96–105.

———. 2011. 'Whose Knowledge Counts? A Political Economy of the Knowledge-Based Society/Economy'. Unpublished presentation given to an IDS Seminar, University of Sussex, Brighton, United Kingdom, 26 January.

Manyozo, L. 2002. 'Community Theatre without Community Participation? Reflections on Development Support Communication Programs in Malawi', *Convergence*, 35 (4): 55–69.

———. 2006. 'Manifesto for Development Communication: Nora Quebral and the Los Baños School of Development Communication', *The Asian Journal of Communication*, 16 (1): 79–99.

———. 2007. 'University Training in Communication for Development: Trends and Approaches', *Media Asia: An Asian Communication Quarterly*, 34 (1): 51–60.

———. 2010. 'The Day Development Dies', *Development in Practice*, 20 (2/ April): 265–69.

———. 2012. *People's Radio: Communicating Change Across Africa*. Penang, Malaysia: Southbound.

Marglin, S. 1990. 'Towards the Decolonization of the Mind', in F. Marglin and S. Marglin (eds), *Dominating Knowledge: Development, Culture, and Resistance*, pp. 1–28. Oxford: Clarendon.

Marx, K. 1852/1937. 'The Eighteenth Brumaire of Louis Bonaparte', in *Die Revolution*. New York. Available online at http://www.marxists.org/archive/marx/works/download/pdf/18th-Brumaire.pdf (accessed on 12 April 2012).

Masani, M. 1976. *Broadcasting and the People*. New Delhi: National Book Trust.

Maslog, C. 1999. *Heroes of Asian Journalism*. Manila: Ramon Magsaysay Award Foundation.

Mbembe, A. 2001. *On the Postcolony*. Berkeley, CA: University of California Press.

McLuhan, M. 1964. *Understanding Media*. London and New York: Routledge.

McPhail, T. (ed.). 2009. *Development Communication: Reframing the Role of the Media*. Malden and Oxford: Wiley-Blackwell.

Mda, Z. 1993. *When People Play People: Development Communication through Theatre*. Johannesburg, London and New Jersey: Witwatersrand University Press and Zed Books.

MDDA. 2007. Media Development and Development Agency. Available online at http://www.mdda.org.za/ (accessed on 12 April 2012).

Melkote, S. and H. L. Steeves. 2001. *Communication for Development in the Third World: Theory and Practice for Empowerment*. New Delhi and Thousand Oaks: SAGE Publications.

Menbere, G. and T. Skjerdal. 2008. 'The Potential of *Dagu* Communication in North-eastern Ethiopia', *Media Development*, 1: 19–21. Available online at http://www.waccglobal.org/images/stories/media_development/2008-1/the-potential-of-dagu-communication.pdf (accessed on 12 April 2012).

Mill, J. S. 1859/2003. *On Liberty*. Edited by David Bromwich and George Kateb. New Haven: Yale University Press.

Ministry of Local Government and Rural Development. 2008. *Rural Growth Centres Development Programme: Promoting Participatory Local Governance and Local Development in Malawi*. Lilongwe: Malawi Government, unpublished.

Mlama, P. 1971. *Culture and Development: The Popular Theatre Approach in Africa*. Uppsala: The Scandinavian Institute of African Studies.

Mohanty, C. T. 1991. 'Under Western Eyes: Feminist Scholarship and Colonial Discourses', in C. Mohanty, A. Russo and L. Torres (eds), *Third World Women and the Politics of Feminism*, pp. 51–80. Bloomington, IN: Indiana University Press.

Morris, N. 2005. 'The Diffusion and Participatory Models: A Comparative Analysis', in O. Hemer and T. Tufte (eds), *Media and Glocal Change: Rethinking Communication for Development*, Göteborg and Buenos Aires, pp. 123–44: CLACSO and NORDICOM. Available online at http://bibliotecavirtual.clacso.org.ar/ar/libros/edicion/media/12Chapter7.pdf (accessed on 12 April 2012).

Mouffe, C. 1999. 'Deliberative Democracy or Agonistic Pluralism', *Social Research*, 66 (3): 746–58.

Mundy, P. and L. Compton. 1995. 'Indigenous Communication and Indigenous Knowledge', in O. Warren, L. J. Slikkerveer and D. Brokensha (eds), *The Cultural Dimension of Development: Indigenous Knowledge Systems*, pp. 113–23. London: Intermediate Technology Publications.

Myers, M. 2002. *Institutional Review of Educational Radio Dramas*. Atlanta, Georgia: Centre for Disease Control and Prevention. Available online at http://www.comminit.com/pdf/InstitutionalReviewofRadio-Dramas.pdf (accessed on 12 April 2012).

NHS-NICE. 2008. *Community Engagement to Improve Health*. London: National Institute for Health and Clinical Excellence. Available online at http://www.nice.org.uk/nicemedia/pdf/PH009Guidance.pdf (accessed on 12 April 2012).

Ochieng'-Odhiambo, F. 2010. *Trends and Issues in African Philosophy*. New York: Peter Lang.

O'Farrell, C. 2005. 'Communication for Sustainable Development', paper presented at the 9th United Nations Communication for Development Roundtable, Food and Agriculture Organisation, Rome. Available online at http://www.communicationforsocialchange.org/pdf/ofarrellmdgmeetingnov04.pdf (accessed on 12 April 2012)

Peirano, L. 2006. 'Communication for Social Change Analysis and Opinion: Developing a Unique Proposal for Communication for Development in Latin America', *Mazi: The Communication for Social Change Report*, 6 (February). Available online at http://www.communicationforsocialchange.org/mazi-articles.php?id=298 (accessed on 12 April 2012).

Pejout, N. 2010. 'Africa and the "Second New Economy": How Can Africa Benefit from ICTs for Sustainable Socio-Economic Development?', in V. Padayachee (ed.), *Political Economy of Africa*, pp. 231–44. London and New York: Routledge.

Piotrow, P. T., D. L. Kincaid, J. G. Rimon and W. Rinehart. 1997. *Health Communication: Lessons from Family Planning and Reproductive Health*. Westport, CT: Praeger.

Pottier, J. 2003. 'Negotiating Local Knowledge: An Introduction', in J. Pottier, A. Bicker and P. Sillitoe (eds), *Negotiating Local Knowledge: Identity and Power in Pevelopment*, pp. 1–29. London: Pluto.

Putnam, R. D. 2000. *Bowling Alone: The Collapse and Revival of American Community*. New York: Simon & Schuster.

Quarry, W. and R. Ramirez. 2009. *Communication for Another Development: Listening by Telling*. London and New York: ZED Books.

Quebral, N. 1975. 'Development Communication in the Agricultural Context', in J. Jamias (ed.), *Readings in Development* Communication, pp. 1–11. Laguna: UPLB College of Agriculture.

———. 1988. *Development Communication*. Laguna: UPLB College of Agriculture.

———. 2002. *Reflections on Development Communication, 25 Years After*. Los Baños: UPLB College of Development Communication.

———. 2011. 'Development Communication, Los Banos Style', paper presented at the London School of Economics and Political Science in celebration of her award of Honoraɪy Doctorate in Social Science, London, 14 December.

Quebral, N. and E. Gomez. 1976. *Development Communication Primer*. Laguna: UPLB College of Agriculture.

Queensland Government. 2005. *Engaging Queenslanders: An Introduction to Community Engagement*. Brisbane, Queensland: Department of Communities. Available online at http://www.getinvolved.qld.gov.au/assets/pdfs/Intro_CE.pdf (accessed on 12 April 2012).

Raghawan, G. N. S. and V. S. Gopalakrishnan. 1979. *Towards a National Policy on Communication in Support of Development, The Indian Case: Report Number 43 Prepared for the International Commission for the Study of Communication Problems*. Paris: UNESCO.

Randall, V. 1993. 'The Media and Democratisation in the Third World', *Third World Quarterly*, 14 (3): 625–46.

Rawls, J. 1997. 'The Idea of Public Reason', in J. Bohman and W. Regh (eds), *Deliberative Democracy: Essays on Reason and Politics*, pp. 93–141. Massachusetts, London and Cambridge: MIT Press.

Rodney, W. 1972. *How Europe Underdeveloped Africa*. London and Dar es Salaam: Tanzania Publishing House and Bogle-L'Ouverlure Publications.

Rodriguez, C. 2001. *Fissures in the Mediascape: An International Study of Citizens' Media*. Cresskill, NJ: Hampton Press.

———. 2003. 'The Bishop and His Star: Citizens' Communication in Southern Chile', in N. Couldry and J. Curran (eds), *Contesting Media Power: Alternative Media in a Networked World*, pp. 177–94. Lanham and Oxford: Rowman & Littlefield.

Rogers, E. 1962. *Diffusion of Innovations*. New York: Free Press.

———. 1976. 'Communication and Development: The Passing of the Dominant Paradigm', *Communication Research*, 3 (2): 213–40.

———. 1977. 'Network Analysis of the Diffusion of Innovations: Family Planning in Korean Villages', in D. Lerner and L. Nelson (eds), *Communication Research: A Half-Century Appraisal*, pp. 117–47. Honolulu: East–West Centre, University Press of Hawaii.

———. 1993. 'Perspectives on Development Communication', in K. Sadanandan Nair and S. White (eds), *Perspectives on Development*

     Communication, pp. 35–45. New Delhi, Thousand Oaks and London: SAGE Publications.

Rogers, E., J. R. Braun and M. A. Vermilion. 1977. 'Radio Forums: A Strategy for Rural Development', in P. Spain (et al.), *Radio for Education and Development: Case Studies*, pp. 361–81. World Bank Staff Working Paper 266. Washington DC: The World Bank.

Rostow, W. W. 1950. *The Process of Economic Growth*. Oxford: Clarendon Press.

Rusbridger, A. 2007. 'Introduction on Katine'. Available online at www.guardian.co.uk/katine (accessed on 12 April 2012).

Sachs, W. 1992. 'A Guide to the Ruins', *The New Internationalist*, 232 (June). Available online at http://www.newint.org/features/1992/06/05/keynote/ (accessed on 12 April 2012).

SADC-CCD. 2006. Report of the CTA-FAO-SADC-CCD, *Report of the Sensitisation Workshop on Rural Radio for Policy and Decision Makers in East and Southern Africa*, 26–29 April 2005. Rome: FAO.

SAHRC. 2000. 'Faultlines: Inquiry into Racism in the Media'. Available online at http://www.sahrc.org.za/home/21/files/Reports/Racismin%20the%20media.pdf2000.pdf (accessed on 12 April 2012).

Said, E. 1978/2003. *Orientalism*. New York: Vintage.

Sainath, P. 2009. 'Journalism is For People Not Shareholders: Transcript of an Interview, in E. Loo (ed.), *Best Practices of Journalism in Asia*, pp. 36–44. Singapore: Konrad-Adenauer-Stiftung. Available online at http://www.kas.de/wf/doc/kas_18665-544-2-30.pdf (accessed on 12 April 2012).

Schramm, W. 1964. *Mass Media and National Development: The Role of Information in the Developing Countries*. Stanford, CA: UNESCO and Stanford University.

Scott, J. 2001. *Power*. Cambridge: Polity Press.

Second Vatican Council. 1963. 'Decree on the Media of Social Communications, *Inter Mirifica*, Solemnly Promulgated by His Holiness Pope VI on December 4'. Available online at http://www.vatican.va/archive/hist_councils/ii_vatican_council/documents/vat-ii_decree_19631204_inter-mirifica_en.html (accessed on 12 April 2012).

———. 1965a. 'Declaration on Christian Education, *Gravissimum Educationis*, Proclaimed by His Holiness Pope VI on October 28'. Available online at http://www.vatican.va/archive/hist_councils/ii_vatican_council/documents/vat-ii_decl_19651028_gravissimum-educationis_en.html (accessed on 12 April 2012).

———. 1965b. '*Gaudium et Spes*: Pastoral Constitution on the Church in the Modern World (Parts 1 & 2)'. Available online at http://www.osjspm.org/majordoc_gaudium_et_spes_part_one.aspx (accessed on 12 April 2012).

Second Vatican Council. 1971. 'Pastoral Instruction, *Communio et Progressio*: On the Means of Social Communication, Written by Order of the Second Vatican Council'. Available online at http://www.vatican.va/roman_curia/pontifical_councils/pccs/documents/rc_pc_pccs_doc_23051971_communio_en.html (accessed on 12 April 2012).

Sen, A. 1999. *Development as Freedom*. Oxford: Oxford University Press.

Servaes, J. 1996. 'Participatory Communication Research from a Freirean Perspective', *Africa Media Review*, 10 (1): 73–91.

———. (ed.). 2003. *Approaches to Development: Studies on Communication for Development*. Paris: UNESCO.

———. (ed.). 2008. *Communication for Development and Social Change*. New Delhi, Thousand Oaks, London and Singapore: SAGE Publications.

Shafer, R. 1996. 'Journalists as Reluctant Interventionists: Comparing Development and Civic Journalism', paper presented at the Conference of the Association for Education in Journalism and Mass Communication (AEJMC), Anaheim, California, August. Available online at http://list.msu.edu/cgi-bin/wa?A2=ind9612aandL=aejmcandP=4533 (accessed on 12 April 2012).

Shome, R. and R. Hedge. 2002. 'Postcolonial Approaches to Communication: Charting the Terrain, Engaging the Intersections'. *Communication Theory*, 12 (3/August): 249–70.

SIDA and B. Jallov. 2007. 'Community Radio in East Africa: An Impact and Sustainability Assessment of Three Community Radios within EACMP'. Stockholm: SIDA. Available online at http://webzone.k3.mah.se/projects/comdev/_comdev_PDF_doc/scp08_sem2_Impact_Assessment_EACMP.pdf (accessed on 12 April 2012).

Sillitoe, P. 2002. 'Globalizing Indigenous Knowledge', in P. Sillitoe, A. Bicker and J. Pottier (eds), *Participating in Development: Approaches to Indigenous Knowledge*, pp. 108–38. London and New York: Routledge.

Singhal, A. and E. Rogers. 1999. *Entertainment-Education: A Communication Strategy for Social Change*. New Jersey and London: Lawrence Erlbaum Associates.

Smith, D. 2011. 'Winnie Madikizela-Mandela 'insulted' by movie about her life', *The Guardian Online*, 14 June. Available online at http://www.guardian.co.uk/world/2011/jun/14/winnie-movie-insult-madikizela-mandela (accessed on 12 April 2012).

Sood, S. 2002. 'Audience Involvement and Entertainment-Education', *Communication Theory*, 12 (2): 153–72.

South Australia Government. 2008. *Community Engagement Handbook: A Model Framework for Leading Practice in Local Government in South Australia*. Adelaide: Community Engagement Program, Office of the Executive Committee of Cabinet and the Local Government

Association of South Australia. Available online at: http://www.lga.
sa.gov.au/webdata/resources/files/Community_Engagement_Hand-
book_March_2008_-_PDF.pdf (accessed on 12 April 2012).

Spivak, G. 1988. 'Can the Subaltern Speak?', in L. Grossberg and C. Nelson
(eds), *Marxism and the Interpretation of Culture*, pp. 271–313. Urbana-
Champaign, IL: University of Illinois Press.

Stehlik, D. and L. Chenoweth. 2005. 'Innovation and Transformation in
Community Practice: Lessons from Ten years of Regional and Rural
Community Research'. International Conference on Engaging Com-
munities, 14–17 August 2005, Brisbane Convention Exhibition Centre
[Online]. Available online at http://www.engagingcommunities2005.
org/abstracts/Stehlik-Daniela-final.pdf (accessed on 12 April 2012).

Suzman, J. 2002/2003. 'Kalahari Conundrums: Relocation, Resistance
and International Support in the Central Kalahari Botswana', *Before
Farming*, 2002/3–4 (12): 1–10. Available online at http://www.unl.edu/
rhames/courses/current/readings/suzman-corry.pdf (accessed on 12
April 2012).

Taylor, J., D. Wilkinson and B. Cheers. 2008. *Working with Communities in
Health and Human Services*. Oxford: Oxford University Press.

Thomas, P. 2001. 'The Political Economy of Communications in India', in
S. Melkote and S. Rao (eds), *Critical Issues in Communication: Looking
Inwards for Answers*, pp. 78–99. New Delhi, Thousand Oaks and Lon-
don: SAGE Publications.

———. 2010. *The Political Economy of Communications in India: The Good, The
Bad and The Ugly*. New Delhi: SAGE Publications.

Thompson, E. P. 1963. *The Making of the English Working Class*. London:
Penguin.

Thompson, J. B. 1995. *The Media and Modernity: A Social Theory of the Media*. Cambridge: Polity Press.

Tomaselli, K. (ed.). 2006. *Writing in the Sand: Autoethnography among Indigenous South Africans*. Lanham, New York, Toronto and Plymouth:
Altamira Press.

Tufte, T. and P. Mefalopulous. 2009. *Participatory Communication: A Practical Guide*. The World Bank Working Paper Number 170. Washington DC: The World Bank. Available online at http://orecomm.net/
wp-content/uploads/2009/10/Participatory_Communication.pdf (accessed on 12 April 2012).

Ugboajah, F. (ed.). 1985. *Mass Communication, Culture and Society in West
Africa*. New York: Saur Publishers.

UK Government. 2008. *Communities in Control: Real People, Real Power*.
London: Ministry of Communities and Local Government.

United Nations Development Programme (UNDP). 2006. *The Guide to
Measuring the Impact of the Right to Information Programmes: Practical Guidance Note*. Oslo: UNDP Democratic Governance Bureau.

Available online at http://www.undp.org/oslocentre/docs06/A%20
Guide%20to%20Measuring%20the%20Impact%20of%20Right%20
to%20Information%20Programmes%20-%20final%20(11%2004%20
06).pdf (accessed on 12 April 2012).

United Nations Educational, Scientific and Cultural Organisation
(UNESCO). 1980. *Many Voices One World: Communication and Society,
Today and Tomorrow; Towards a New More Just and More Efficient World
Information and Communication Order*. London, New York and Paris:
Kogan Page and UNESCO.

———. 2008. *Media Development Indicators: A Framework for Assessing Media
Development*. Paris: UNESCO.

Valbuena, V. 1986. *Philippine Folk Media in Development Communication*.
Singapore: The Asian Mass Communication Research and Information Centre.

Vargas, L. 1995. *Social Uses and Radio Practices: The Use of Participatory
Radio by Ethnic Minorities in Mexico*. Boulder, San Francisco and
Oxford: Westview.

Vaughan, P. W. and E. M. Rogers. 2000. 'A Staged Model of Communication Effects: Evidence from an Entertainment-Education Radio
Soap Opera in Tanzania', *Journal of Health Communication*, 5 (3):
203–27.

Velacherry, J. 1993. *Social Impact of Mass Media in Kerala*. Delhi and Bangalore: Indian Society for Promoting Christian Knowledge.

Verghese, G. 1976. *Project Chhatera: An Experiment in Development Journalism*. Occasional Paper Number 4. Singapore: Asian Mass Communication Research and Information Centre.

———. 2009. 'Reclaim Public Service Values of Journalism: Transcript of
an Interview', in E. Loo (ed.), *Best Practices of Journalism in Asia*, pp.
48–52. Singapore: Konrad-Adenauer-Stiftung. Available online at
http://www.kas.de/wf/doc/kas_18665-544-2-30.pdf (accessed on 12
April 2012).

Wa Thiong'o, N. 1993. *Moving the Centre: The Struggle for Cultural Freedoms*.
London: Nairobi and Portsmouth: James Currey, Heinemann and
East African Educational Publishers.

Wall, M. 1997. 'An Analysis of News Magazine Coverage of the Rwanda
Crisis in the United States', *International Communication Gazette*, 59
(2): 121–34.

Wang, G. 1982. 'Indigenous Communication in Research and Develop-
ment', paper presented at the Convergence of Knowledge Utilisation:
Theory and Methodology Conference, Honolulu, Hawaii, East–West
Centre, 25–30 April.

Warren, D. M. 1991. 'Using Indigenous Knowledge in Agricultural Development'. World Bank Discussion Paper Number 127. Washington
DC: World Bank.

Watt, N. 2010. 'Cameron Promises Power for the Man and Woman on the Street', *The Guardian Online*, 19 July. Available online at http://www.guardian.co.uk/politics/2010/jul/19/david-cameron-big-society-cuts?intcmp=239 (accessed on 12 April 2012).

Wilkins, K. G. and B. Mody. 2001. 'Reshaping Development Communication: Developing Communication and Communicating Development', *Communication Theory*, 11 (4): 385–96.

Williamson, H. A. 1991. 'The Fogo Process: Development Support Communication in Canada and the Developing World', in F. Casmir (ed.), *Communication in Development*, pp. 270–87. Norwood, New Jersey: Ablex.

Willis, K. 2005. *Theories and Practices of Development*. London and New York: Routledge.

World Bank. 1990. *Agricultural Extension: The Next Step*. Washington DC: The World Bank, Agriculture and Rural Development Department.

World Health Organisation (WHO). 1994. *Health Promotion and Community Action for Health in Developing Countries*. WHO: Geneva.

Wright, C. 1959. *Mass Communication: A Sociological Perspective*. New York: Random House.

Yunus, M. 2007. *Creating a World without Poverty: Social Business and the Future of Capitalism*. New York: Public Affairs.

Zuma, J. 2010. 'Let the Real Media Debate Begin', *ANC Today*, 13–19 August. Available online at http://www.anc.org.za/docs/anctoday/2010/at30.htm#art1 (accessed on 12 April 2012).

Index

About the Author

Linje Manyozo is a Lecturer and Director of the MSc Programme in Media, Communications and Development in the Department of Media and Communications, London School of Economics and Political Science. He has taught development communication in South Africa and Malawi, where in 2005, he successfully proposed and introduced Africa's first ever undergraduate degree programme in development communication at the University of Malawi. He continues to guest-lecture in Europe, as he strongly believes that development communication is even more relevant to the global north. Linje's teaching and research are informed by his upbringing in postcolonial Malawi as well as his work as a development journalist, creating educational communications with marginalized communities. His past and current research examines questions of subaltern representation, voice and authority in development policy formulation and implementation.